ID0641883

ENVIRONMENTAL
SCIENCE AND
THEOLOGY
IN DIALOGUE

THEOLOGY IN DIALOGUE SERIES

Russell A. Butkus, Anne Clifford, Carol J. Dempsey, Series Editors

The Theology in Dialogue Series expresses a vision for the possibilities of theology in conversation with other academic disciplines. The series stems from two primary sources. The first is historical. To some degree Christian theology has always been in dialogue with the major elements of its social context, drawing on insights and methods from diverse knowledge traditions in order to address pressing and timely issues. The second source is the contemporary world. Given the complexity of contemporary life, its questions and struggles, books in the Theology in Dialogue Series reflect the perspective that creative dialogue and strategic collaboration between theology and other disciplines are necessary in seeking effective solutions to contemporary problems.

Yes, resolving problems is important, but our hope is that creative dialogue will result in more than problem solving, that it will make the positive contributions needed in an increasingly complex world. The overarching aim of the series is to demonstrate the creativity of theology in dialogue with various academic disciplines and, in doing so, to broaden the appeal of theology while enriching the pursuit of intellectual inquiry.

Previously published in the series

Reading the Bible, Transforming Conflict
Carol J. Dempsey and Elayne J. Shapiro

ENVIRONMENTAL SCIENCE AND THEOLOGY IN DIALOGUE

RUSSELL A. BUTKUS
AND STEVEN A. KOLMES

ORBIS BOOKS
Maryknoll, New York 10545

Founded in 1970, Orbis Books endeavors to publish works that enlighten the mind, nourish the spirit, and challenge the conscience. The publishing arm of the Maryknoll Fathers and Brothers, Orbis seeks to explore the global dimensions of the Christian faith and mission, to invite dialogue with diverse cultures and religious traditions, and to serve the cause of reconciliation and peace. The books published reflect the views of their authors and do not represent the official position of the Maryknoll Society. To learn more about Maryknoll and Orbis Books, please visit our website at www.maryknollsociety.org.

Copyright © 2011 Russell A. Butkus and Steven A. Kolmes

Published by Orbis Books, Maryknoll, NY 10545-0302.

All rights reserved.

No part of this publication may be reproduced or transmitted in any form or by any means, electronic or mechanical, including photocopying, recording, or any information storage or retrieval system, without prior permission in writing from the publisher.

Queries regarding rights and permissions should be addressed to
Orbis Books, P.O. Box 302, Maryknoll, NY 10545-0302.

Manufactured in the United States of America.

Library of Congress Cataloging-in-Publication Data

Butkus, Russell A.
    Environmental science and theology in dialogue / Russell A. Butkus and Steven
  A. Kolmes.
      p. cm. – (Theology in dialogue series)
    Includes bibliographical references and index.
    ISBN 978-1-57075-912-3 (pbk.)
    1. Human ecology – Religious aspects. I. Kolmes, Steven A. II. Title.
  GF80.B87 2011
  261.8'8 – dc22   2011004448

To all of those who labor, in whatever capacity,
for environmental sustainability,
ecological and social justice,
and the future that all creatures will inherit

Contents

Acknowledgments

The authors want to acknowledge the generosity of Maude Barlow, Karl-Henrik Robèrt, and Bishop William Skylstad of Spokane, who took the time to write contributions to this book. We also want to thank John Haught, Sallie McFague, and Denis Edwards for allowing us to use their photographs.

We thank Anne Clifford for her review of the manuscript and Carol Dempsey in her role as consulting editor for the Theology in Dialogue Series. We thank Janelle Stone, an undergraduate student at the University of Portland, for assisting us in preparing the manuscript and Sara Kolmes for proofreading the entire manuscript. We especially thank our spouses, Linda Fergusson-Kolmes and Lynn Butkus, for all their support, and we thank all the members of our families for bearing with our distraction through this process. We thank our faculty and staff colleagues at the University of Portland, who helped us in ways too varied to describe. We thank Susan Perry, senior editor of Orbis Books, for agreeing to publish the Theology in Dialogue Series and for helping us complete a better book than we originally sent her.

A website available in July 2011 provides access to expanded and updated URLs for web-based resources; active learning exercises; access to denominational documents that pertain to environmental issues; classroom resources; and other features. The website will be updated regularly with contributions by the authors and others who are using the book in their teaching or studies. Please see *published.up.edu/envscitheobook*.

Introduction

April 20, 2010, will, for years to come, mark the date and beginning of what many people will consider one of the worst environmental disasters to unfold in the United States. On that date Deepwater Horizon, a deepwater oil drilling platform, exploded in flames, killing eleven workers and unleashing the worst oil spill in U.S. history. People in this country have been very focused on the oil platform leak in the Gulf of Mexico, a debacle that has captured public attention and has left many questions unanswered. How many engineering and safety shortcuts were taken in the name of cost savings?

A review of the catastrophe carried out by the National Commission on the BP Deepwater Horizon Oil Spill and Offshore Drilling identified regulatory failures in which the federal Minerals Management Service (MMS) allowed industry to make key safety determinations, as well as numerous operations failures by the corporations involved, including BP (the leaseholder of the Macondo well site and the Deepwater Horizon drilling rig), Halliburton (which was in charge of sealing the well with cement), and Transocean (which owned the Deepwater Horizon drilling rig and was in charge of many aspects of the operation).[1]

Among other steps taken that contributed to a risky operation of the Deepwater Horizon, BP used fewer centralizers in the well than its original design called for,[2] it used leftover material from an earlier stage in the operations as a spacer fluid (which saved it disposal costs),[3] and it neglected to install additional physical barriers during the temporary well abandonment procedure that went awry and led to the blowout. Transocean and BP probably share responsibility for never carrying out sufficient diagnostic procedures to explain the anomalous negative pressure test results that actually pointed in advance to the potential for a blowout. Halliburton employed cement foam that had failed its own company analyses for stability, but it never took time to integrate this information into its activities on the well.[4]

A pervasive culture of speed over professional caution seems to have pervaded all three companies' activities at Deepwater Horizon, and the President's Commission stated that although it could not discern if decisions were made consciously to increase risk in favor of less expensive operations,

Decisionmaking processes at Macondo did not adequately ensure that personnel fully considered the risks created by time- and money-saving decisions. Whether purposeful or not, many of the decisions that BP, Halliburton, and Transocean made that increased the risk of the

1

Macondo blowout clearly saved those companies significant time (and money).[5]

The immediate causes of the Macondo well blowout can be traced to a series of identifiable mistakes made by BP, Halliburton, and Transocean that reveal such systematic failures in risk management that they place in doubt the safety culture of the entire industry.[6]

However the question of conscious intention is eventually answered, probably in a court of law if at all, the consequences of the well explosion and blowout are apparent. Various estimates of the oil flow exist, but certainly at least 50 million gallons and perhaps as many as 200 million gallons of oil leaked by July 15, 2010, when the first really effective cap was placed on the well. Nearly six hundred miles of Gulf Coast shoreline were fouled by then, including highly sensitive ecological zones and habitats.

The oil leak initiated huge cleanup efforts involving boats, ships, shore workers, and the use of contentious chemical dispersants (which some people believe to be designed more for a cover-up than a cleanup). But how many people reading or watching news about the enormous spill connected this catastrophe to their personal use of fossil fuels as they drive about in vehicles powered by internal combustion engines? Other than local residents who lost their livelihoods in the seafood and tourism industries, how many people will still remember this catastrophe a year, or two, or three later?

Prior to the destruction of Deepwater Horizon, how many people remembered or even knew about the blowout of the Ixtoc oil platform in the Gulf of Mexico in 1979 and 1980? That earlier accident, which occurred under the watch of the Mexican state-run oil company PEMEX, dumped about 140 million gallons of oil into the Gulf. While much of the damage to the Gulf shoreline repaired itself through the actions of what is a very resilient ecosystem, even today the shoreline mangrove swamps in Mexico are sparser than they should be and oil can be seen and smelled in shallow sediments. Did anyone learn from the Ixtoc event?

Scientists studying the aftermaths of major oil spills in the past tell us that a dozen years after the *Exxon Valdez* spill in Prince William Sound, Alaska, one needed only to dig a hole in the apparently clean shoreline to strike a puddle of oil. Roughly one in ten holes dug in the oil-fouled area still hit oil over two decades later, and sea otters (whose populations have not yet fully recovered) dig for food in areas made toxic by these residues.

In 1974 the oil barge *Bouchard 65* dumped tens of thousands of gallons into Buzzards Bay, Massachusetts, causing extensive beach erosion by killing off the *Spartina* grass whose roots held the shore together. Shoreline recovery three and a half decades later is only now beginning to occur, as the grasses struggle to regain their foothold. Hydrocarbons can still be detected in nearby salt marshes.

If it is hard to recall our own shorelines and those of our immediate neighbors, what about the devastation of the Lusi Mud Volcano in Indonesia, produced by an accident in 2006 that took place at a site drilling for natural gas? Does anyone in the United States know that it vomits a hundred thousand tons of stinking mud a day and has done so for five years, or that sixty thousand people have been evacuated and a dozen villages so far covered in an ever-increasing lake of mud that in places reaches sixty-five feet in depth? Were the two thousand acres now engulfed worth the energy hunger of our society? Was the profit motive of the drillers any comfort to the local residents who still see the mud approaching, as heroic efforts to stop it with dikes and pumps and heavy equipment slowly fail?

We remind readers of these events because, like the current catastrophe in the Gulf of Mexico, they serve to highlight the major reason for this book: ecologically unsustainable human conduct threatens future human and non-human generations. These oil spills also underscore broader issues that have accompanied our seemingly unquenchable quest for energy resources and other raw materials. Are there cleaner alternative energy resources that would be more practical and benign to utilize? How can the oceans be saved from pollution of various sorts, oceanic dead zones, ocean acidification, and overfishing?

What can be done to balance economic and ecological needs so that we can correct biogeochemical cycle deformations, like the carbon cycle imbalance that is the major contributor to climatic instability? What are the impacts of toxic pollutants, such as chemical oil dispersants, released into the environment on the development and growth of infants and children; could they prevent children from achieving their full potential for a fulfilling and productive life? Do commonly used chemicals cross the placenta to diminish IQ and increase cancer rates?

How can deforestation and desertification be halted or reversed? Does it make any real difference when people rely on local or regional food resources or eat a diet with less meat in it? What is "sustainability" and how can it be more than a term favored for advertising campaigns? Are there actually disinformation campaigns being run by identifiable corporations in order to confuse the public about environmental issues?

What is the future of our planet's biodiversity, and what do people mean by the Anthropocene Era? And what about water? How can there be such concern about freshwater supplies for agriculture and drinking when every supermarket has stacks of water bottles for sale and the oceans cover most of the planet? Are our national and international leaders, and indeed our electorate, well enough informed about these issues for us to be making wise decisions?

If the ecology of historical amnesia and arrogance deserves to be examined in these and other dimensions, what about theological and ethical implications of poor human conduct toward the Earth? Are there ethical norms for what we can and cannot forget? Does a shoreline covered in oil still count in prayers for the care of creation, or has it become something we would rather not remember?

Does promoting a social vision in which the ever-increasing consumption of resources is considered a personal good, and indeed a social good, incur any shared responsibility for unintended consequences of resource development that rushes to keep up with economic demand? What do these questions and ecological issues mean for the Christian theological tradition? From a posture of interdisciplinary dialogue, both ecology and theology interpret past and recent environmental disasters as hallmarks of broken relationships — between human and human, human and earth, and human and God.

The timeline of the Deepwater Horizon debacle reminds us of the declaration of the Ecumenical Patriarch Bartholomew I, known as the "Green Patriarch":

> To commit a crime against the natural world is a sin. For humans to cause species to become extinct and to destroy the biological diversity of God's creation,...to degrade the integrity of Earth by causing changes in its climate, by stripping the Earth of its natural forests, or destroying its wetlands...to contaminate the Earth's waters, its land, its air, and its life, with poisonous substances...these are sins.[7]

He strongly suggests that the root cause of our global environmental crisis is broken relationships. And while this book will examine the numerous scientific consequences of our broken relationship with the Earth, in the spirit of interdisciplinary dialogue and collaboration it will propose a practical vision of hope that broken relationships can be healed and restored and that a sustainable future is achievable, *if* we are willing to engage in the practice of right relationships required for the planet and all its inhabitants to flourish. We invite the reader, therefore, to move beyond the confines of disciplinary boundaries and engage in a conversation across the borders of science and theology on one of the most pressing issues of the twenty-first century.

1

Environmental Science
and Theology in Dialogue
The Need for Interdisciplinarity

Environmental science is uncommon among the sciences because it is within itself a *transdisciplinary* undertaking. Environmental scientists are in constant dialogue with a range of scientific disciplines necessary for this undertaking. For example, the challenges that we face in the environmental arena have aspects that are comprehensible only from the perspective of chemistry, or biology, or physics, or geoscience, or toxicology, or climatology, or, most often, some combination of these and other traditional scientific disciplines. Utilizing the tools of analysis from these various scientific disciplines, environmental science examines our biophysical environment with the aim of providing solutions to environmental problems.

Going a step further, the implications of environmental issues and the pathway to policy formation broaden out to the social sciences and humanities. Policies that meet the needs of varied human stakeholders and also preserve ecosystems can be framed only with consideration for and in conversation with political science, sociology, economics, history, anthropology, and other fields of study. Environmental scientists must enter into dialogue with scholars and practitioners of numerous other disciplines if they are to achieve their goals, and it is the premise of this book that one of those necessary disciplines is theology.

Why Dialogue?

Why is it really a good idea, indeed a necessary idea, for environmental science to enter into a dialogue with theology? From the scientific side of the table, well-reasoned calls for such a dialogue, coming from influential scientists and proponents of environmental sustainability, have become increasingly numerous and urgent. E. O. Wilson, perhaps the best known biologist of his generation, wrote a book entitled *The Creation: An Appeal to Save Life on Earth,* which presents itself as a letter written to a Southern Baptist pastor about the need for a common front between science and theology. Early in the book Wilson says,

Let us see then, if we can, and you are willing, to meet on the near side of metaphysics in order to deal with the real world we share. I put it this way because you have the power to help solve a great problem about which I care deeply. I hope that you have the same concern. I suggest that we set aside our differences in order to save the creation. The defense of living Nature is a universal value. It doesn't rise from, nor does it promote, any religious or ideological dogma. Rather, it serves without discrimination the interests of all humanity.... You may well ask at this point, Why me? Because religion and science are the two most powerful forces in the world today, including especially the United States. If religion and science could be united on the common ground of biological conservation, the problem would soon be solved. If there is any moral precept shared by people of all beliefs, it is that we owe ourselves and future generations a beautiful, rich, and healthful environment.[1]

Twenty years before writing *The Creation*, Wilson was one of thirty-two prominent scientists who in 1990, in an effort spearheaded by noted cosmologist and astrophysicist Dr. Carl Sagan and Nobel laureate in physics Dr. Hans Bethe, sent an appeal for dialogue to the religious leaders of the Earth, presented at the Global Forum of Spiritual and Parliamentary Leaders Conference in Moscow, Russia. In this appeal to religious leaders, they said,

We are now threatened by self-inflicted, swiftly moving environmental alterations about whose long-term biological and ecological consequences we are still painfully ignorant.... We are close to committing — many would argue we are already committing — what in religious language is sometimes called Crimes against Creation.... Problems of such magnitude, and solutions demanding so broad a perspective, must be recognized from the outset as having a religious as well as a scientific dimension. Mindful of our common responsibility, we scientists, many of us long engaged in combating the environmental crisis, urgently appeal to the world religious community to commit, in word and deed, and as boldly as is required, to preserve the environment of the Earth.... As scientists, many of us have had profound experiences of awe and reverence before the universe. We understand that what is regarded as sacred is more likely to be treated with care and respect. Our planetary home should be so regarded. Efforts to safeguard and cherish the environment need to be infused with a vision of the sacred. At the same time, a much wider and deeper understanding of science and technology is needed. If we do not understand the problem, it is unlikely we will be able to fix it. Thus, there is a vital role for both religion and science.[2]

This initial approach from the scientific community led to a science-theology summit held at the American Museum of Natural History and the Cathedral of St. John the Divine in New York City in 1991 and to a joint statement. This joint statement was written and signed by both scientific and religious leaders. Called the "Joint Appeal by Religion and Science for the Environment, 'Declaration of the Mission to Washington'" it was released in 1992.[3] Consider the stature and accomplishments of some of the scientists who acted as signatories to this document. Aside from the scientists already mentioned, among others too numerous to list distinguished signatories included:

Dr. James Hansen, director, Goddard Institute for Space Studies, and one of the leading voices in the world on issues of climate change

Dr. Henry Kendall, Nobel laureate and Stratton Professor of Physics, Massachusetts Institute of Technology, and chairman of the board, Union of Concerned Scientists

Dr. H. Ronald Pulliam, director of the Institute of Ecology, University of Georgia, president of the Ecological Society of America, and one of the most respected ecologists in the United States

Dr. F. Sherwood Rowland, Donald Bren Professor of Chemistry, University of California at Irvine, president, American Association for the Advancement of Science, Nobel laureate for discovering that CFCs were destroying the stratospheric ozone layer

Dr. Stephen H. Schneider, head of the Interdisciplinary Climate Systems Section, National Center for Atmospheric Research, who served as a consultant to federal agencies and White House staff in the Nixon, Carter, Reagan, George H. W. Bush, Clinton, George W. Bush and Obama administrations

Dr. Stephen E. Schwartz, senior physical chemist, Brookhaven National Laboratory, one of the leaders in developing our understanding of acid rain.

Scientific leaders from a variety of disciplines came together with theologians in this effort, the content of which will be dealt with later in this volume. The scientists had initially called for dialogue, and even more of them came and productively engaged in the dialogue with theologians.

For some scientists, spirituality and the natural world are inextricably linked, and the links become stronger as their scientific endeavors bring them into more intimate contact with nature. A conversation between environmental science and theology is a path to incorporate these primary experiences of the spiritual into an enriched worldview. Jane Goodall, the best known primate biologist of her generation, writes

Scientists are continually providing facts and figures that can be used to explain the importance, to ourselves and our future, of preserving ecosystems. But the natural world has another value that cannot be expressed in materialistic terms. Twice a year I spend a few days in

Gombe — that's all the time I have. Of course, I hope that I will see the chimpanzees. But I also look forward to the hours I spend alone in the forest, sitting on the peak where I once sat as a young woman and looking over the forested valleys and vast expanse of Lake Tanganyika. And I love to sit absorbing the spiritual energy of the Kakombe water-fall as it drops eighty feet to the streambed below. . . . No wonder this was one of the sacred places where the medicine men, in the old days, would come to perform their secret rituals.[4]

In an effort to promote dialogue between scientists and theologians, Ecu-menical Patriarch Bartholomew I initiated a series of symposia known as the Religion, Science, and the Environment Movement. This movement has brought scientists and theologians together in a series of meetings and cruises, and notable scientists have traveled together with theologians on research voyages beginning in 1995. These now stretch out over a decade and a half to the waters of the Aegean, the Adriatic, the Danube, the Black Sea, the Amazon, and the Arctic. Scientists taking time for these dialogic trips have included some of the best-known researchers in the world. A visit to the website of this organization[5] and perusal of the participant lists and presentations over the years will rapidly convince the visitor that the dialogic approach already has many well-known proponents willing to invest their time and energy in promoting environmental science–theology interactions.

Academic organizations or societies whose members are working to inte-grate thought and produce an interdisciplinary vision of the relationship between humanity and nature (we will deal with that false dichotomy later in this volume) include the Association for Environmental Studies and Sciences[6] and the Interdisciplinary Environmental Association.[7] Both of these organi-zations welcome dialogue between theology and environmental science and count the humanities and sciences as parts of their core constituency. Mean-while, on the religion-theology side of the table the American Academy of Religion[8] maintains a Religion and Ecology Group and a Sustainabil-ity Task Force; the Catholic Theology Society of America has Theology and Science Topic Sessions;[9] and the College Theology Society[10] maintains a sec-tion on Theology, Ecology, and Natural Science. Many other examples of the impetus to interdisciplinary dialogue between environmental science and theology exist, as research by any interested reader will reveal.

An interesting view on this is offered by Paul Hawken, one of the earliest and most influential proponents of economic reform leading to sustainabil-ity. Hawken, who comes from the world of commerce, stepped onto the world environmental stage with his book *The Ecology of Commerce: A Declaration of Sustainability* in 1993. He went on to write other highly influential books, including *Natural Capitalism: Creating the Next Indus-trial Revolution* in 1999. In a recent book, *Blessed Unrest: How the Largest Movement in the World Came into Being and Why No One Saw It Coming* (2007), he chronicles the varied components of the global social movement working for sustainability, which he calls the largest mass movement in human history. He is neither a scientist nor a theologian, but as a third-party observer of the religion-science dialogue he offers a unique perspective and provides an enumeration of organizations identified across the spectrum of the movement toward sustainability. In *Blessed Unrest,* under the general category of "Religion, Ecology, and Sustainability," he indicates that at that moment globally there were 138 organizations dedicated to *ecopsychology,* 842 organizations dedicated to *environmental ethics,* 16 organizations dedicated to *religion and ecology,* and 920 organizations dedicated to *sustainability, religion, and spiritual issues.* Hawken continues to work with the *WiserEarth* website[11] to provide updated individual listings of these organizations.[12]

The modern dialogue between environmental science and theology was presaged by Aldo Leopold's *A Sand County Almanac* and his *Round River,* originally published posthumously in 1949 and 1953, respectively, and still in print. Leopold (1887–1948), whom many scientists consider the first proponent of ecosystem-level planning for biological conservation, as well as the first environmental ethicist, spoke for the importance of a detailed understanding of ecological interactions and complexity, for the importance to the future of conservation, and for the relationship of these things to ethics and religion. Leopold's themes seem current today. He wrote,

> What value has wildlife from the standpoint of morals and religion? I heard of a boy once who was brought up an atheist. He changed his mind when he saw that there were a hundred-odd species of warblers, each bedecked like to the rainbow, and each performing yearly sundry thousands of miles of migration about which scientists wrote wisely but did not understand. No "fortuitous concourse of elements" working blindly through any number of millions of years could quite account for why warblers are so beautiful. . . . I dare say that this boy's convictions would be harder to shake than those of many inductive theologians.[13]

Taking a developmental view of the very tentatively emerging ecological consciousness he saw in his day, Leopold noted,

> Individual thinkers since the days of Ezekiel and Isaiah have asserted that the despoliation of the land is not only inexpedient but wrong. Society, however, has not yet affirmed their belief. I regard the present conservation movement as the embryo of such an affirmation.[14]

Many conservationists believe that Leopold's summation of this work articulated the classic environmental ethic of an American environmentalist. He wrote:

> Examine each question in terms of what is ethically and esthetically right, as well as what is economically expedient. A thing is right when

it tends to preserve the integrity, stability, and beauty of the biotic community. It is wrong when it tends otherwise.[15]

The contemporary environmental science-theology dialogue is clearly a continuation of the themes raised by Leopold. It is engaged with issues of the meaning of the ongoing and sometimes accelerating environmental degradation, the nature of the inherent value of the Earth, the ethical imperative for the present generation to do something effective, and an overarching context of what environmental sustainability looks like and how it might be achieved.

Taking all of the evidence presented above into consideration, we believe that a conversation between environmental science and theology is clearly under way, the dialogue exists, and the question is not whether it is appropriate or happening but whether or not to join in. We will attempt in this volume to explore these concerns and indeed to describe a deeper level of collaboration between environmental science and theology that we believe has the potential to provide an ethical compass to steer real-world questions of environmental policy.

Clarifying Terms

From the religious-theological side of the aisle a good place to begin the conversation is to clarify some language. Religion can be defined in a variety of ways, which include substantive approaches that attempt to define what religion is in itself, that is, its essence, or it can be defined from a functional view that focuses on how religion addresses human needs, or a combination of both. Taking a substantive approach, Will Deming defines religion as "orientation to ultimate reality" and theology as the "attempt to reflect on, articulate, and systematize that orientation."[16] Additional ways of speaking about "ultimate reality" have included such terms as "sacred reality" and "the holy," and if we were to embed these general terms in a particular religious tradition like Christianity, we would be talking about God and how Christians experience, understand, and define God. Taking Deming's definition, Christian theology is the "attempt to reflect on, articulate, and systematize" the Christian experience of God.

At the level of higher education these religious issues are typically approached and critically examined in one of two ways: in departments of religious studies or in departments or schools of theology. Undergraduate or graduate programs in religion or religious studies are usually broad-based and will often examine the full range of religious traditions, including those that arose out of the ancient Middle East such as Judaism, Christianity, and Islam as well as Asian religions such as Hinduism, Buddhism, and Taoism. Departments or schools of theology on the other hand are more focused and grounded in a particular religious tradition like Christianity. These programs may even be further defined by a particular attachment depending on whether the institution is Methodist, Lutheran, Roman Catholic, or some other Christian denomination. An important point here is that theology, regardless of where it is done, usually assumes faith in a particular religious tradition.

Historically, from a Christian perspective, St. Anselm's definition remains remarkably useful — that theology is "faith seeking understanding." Given the focus of this book we might enlarge Anselm's definition to say that Christian theology is faith seeking understanding in light of the environmental crisis, which leads to another important observation about theology: it never occurs in a social or cultural vacuum.

Theology as Contextualized

In other words Christian theology has always been contextualized. From the very beginning of the biblical narrative to the present, theology has always been enculturated, rooted in a given culture utilizing its language, symbols, and modes of thought, as well as its political and economic structures to create a theologically meaningful world. For example, the social, cultural, and historical world of the Bible is significantly shaped by a patriarchal-hierarchal social structure and the political economy of monarchy, giving rise to such basic characteristics as referring to God as "Lord" or "King of the Universe," and also Jesus' proclamation of the "kingdom" of God.

Given the fact that contextual enculturation in theology is inevitable and unavoidable, what Stephen Bevans calls a "theological imperative," this text highlights three compelling characteristics of the contemporary human world that arise from the dialogue between environmental science and theology.[17] First, humanity's self-perception and its way of perceiving the natural world and the universe beyond are largely defined by a *scientific worldview*. To borrow language from the sociology of knowledge, modern science is a primary "symbolic universe of meaning" through which humanity seeks to understand itself and its relationship to the biophysical world. Without question this is one of the hallmarks of our contemporary thought-world.

The second feature of our contemporary world, which follows from the first, is that humanity is at an *ecological crossroads* in its existence on this planet. Never before has humanity been faced with the extent and magnitude of ecological problems that will very likely define the major issues of the twenty-first century. What may have begun as local or regional issues (such as urban pollution) are now global (including global climate change), threatening to seriously undermine global productivity and stability. The globalization of ecological degradation and the human response are probably best exemplified by the U.N. Environment Programme and its collaboration with the World Meteorological Organization to create the Intergovernmental Panel on Climate Change (IPCC), an international body that collects, collates, and disseminates the research and findings of approximately three thousand experts worldwide on the phenomena of global warming and climate change.

The third characteristic, what may be viewed as the theological-ethical "bottom line" of this text, is the argument that the first two characteristics of the modern world must be viewed from the reality that *our world is a torn and divided one,* reflecting dehumanizing and egregious social and economic inequalities. The numbing poverty and socioeconomic instability of many in the developing world will be exacerbated by ecological problems like global climate change. It is clear from the IPCC's *Fourth Assessment Report* (2007) that the most vulnerable human populations and the ones most likely to be negatively impacted by climate change are the poor in developing countries.

The impact scenarios for developing nations detailed in the *Fourth Assessment Report* are to a large extent caused and compounded by patterns of overconsumption in developed countries. For example, according to environmental scientist Daniel Chiras, a typical U.S. or Canadian citizen "uses twenty to forty times more resources than a citizen of the less developed world and has twenty to forty times the environmental impact."[18] If we scrutinize the disparity further we find that the United States, with less than 5 percent of the global population, uses about a quarter of the world's fossil fuel resources — burning up nearly 25 percent of the coal, 26 percent of the oil, and 27 percent of the world's natural gas. This consumptive appetite for energy resources produces about 25 percent of the world's carbon dioxide emissions — the largest share of any single country — and it will be the poor of the world who will "pay" for this inequality. This issue alone underscores the necessary intersection of social and ecological justice and serves to punctuate the moral and ethical dimension of our ecological situation.

The three points noted above are the aspects of our contemporary cultural context that this text addresses. But what exactly does a contextualized theology mean? According to Stephen Bevans a contextual theology takes into consideration four main elements: (1) the gospel message, (2) the tradition of the Christian people, (3) the culture in which one is engaging in theological reflection, and (4) the changes occurring in that culture "whether brought about by western technological process or the grassroots struggle for equality, justice, and liberation."[19] Given this general description of contextual theology, the specific task of this volume is to investigate in some detail the scientific and ecological changes that are currently underway locally and globally and to explore the ramifications of doing Christian theology in response to this contemporary context. In other words, we propose to explore how theology has responded to the environmental crisis through a process of re-formulation, a process that can best be described as a dialogue between environmental science and theology. The relationship between science and theology and the posture of dialogue will be more fully explored in the next chapter, with important methodological implications for ethically concerned scientists and theologians.

Theology in Dialogue: A Brief Historical Summary

Is this endeavor really new in the history and tradition of Christian theology? The answer lies somewhere between yes and no. It is new to the degree that the extent and range of the ecological "signs of the times" — to borrow a phrase from Pope John XXIII (1881–1963) — is a new development in human history, and a collaboration between theology and science is, while not unknown, certainly atypical as a response to the environmental crisis.[20] On the other hand, it is not new insofar as theology has always been in conversation with its cultural surroundings.

As noted above, biblical theology was shaped by its cultural context. Take St. Paul, arguably the first theologian, as an example. Contemporary Pauline research clearly shows that Paul often drew upon cultural resources that were available to him as a Hellenistic Jew, most notably the popular Greek philosophers of his day such as the Stoics and Cynics. New Testament scholar Abraham Malherbe makes a compelling point when he states that "There can no longer be any doubt that Paul was thoroughly familiar with the teaching, methods of operation, and style of argumentation of the philosophers of the period, all of which he adopted and adapted to his own purposes."[21]

Largely due to Paul's efforts, Christianity became well established in the Greco-Roman world of Imperial Rome, and the tendency of Christian theology to draw upon cultural sources, particularly philosophy, accelerated. The Christian Apologists, those who explained and defended the Christian faith to a largely hostile culture, began to use Platonic and then Neoplatonic philosophical categories in their attempt to justify Christianity to their Greco-Roman audience. Neoplatonism, the philosophical system of Plotinus (ca. 205–270), held the view that all reality was an emanation from one ultimate source — the One — and that the individual human soul could achieve union with the One through reasoned contemplation.

Augustine

Perhaps the best example of an early Christian theologian much influenced by Neoplatonic philosophy was Augustine (354–430), who made an enormous and permanent contribution to the development of Christian theology during the patristic period. While in Milan in 384, Augustine reveals in his *Confessions* that reading the "books of the Platonists" seriously reoriented his thinking, what amounted to an intellectual conversion.[22] He credits the Neoplatonists, most likely the writings of Plotinus, with completely changing his view of the spiritual nonphysical world, which would later become the metaphysical basis for his theological ontology and anthropology.

Aquinas

By the medieval period, however, Augustine's creative dialogue with Neoplatonism began to be overshadowed by the work of Thomas Aquinas

(1225–1274), who is arguably the most significant example of theology in dialogue during the early period of Christian theology. While the influence of Neoplatonism was not totally eclipsed, especially in the theology of Bonaventure, Aquinas's dialogue with Aristotle began to move theology in a new direction. Aquinas singlehandedly reformulated Christian theology using the rediscovered philosophy of Aristotle; Aquinas's *Summa Theologiae* represented his attempt to provide a systematic integration of medieval knowledge. Anachronistically speaking, this may have amounted to a theological version of unified field theory.

The influence of Aquinas, especially in the Roman Catholic tradition, lasted well into the twentieth century due to the neo-Scholastic movement also known as neo-Thomism. Neo-Scholasticism was a revival of Aquinas's philosophy during the nineteenth and twentieth centuries that attempted to revitalize and apply his doctrine to the contemporary world and show in particular that it was compatible with modern science. While the impact of Aquinas may be said to be permanent, his influence began to wane around the mid-twentieth century during the aftermath of the World War II.

Søren Kierkegaard

A devastating event of unprecedented magnitude, World War II opened a fissure of evil the likes of which humanity had never before witnessed. The enormous loss of life combined with the Holocaust seriously challenged the prewar assumptions of European Christian theology and forced theologians to consider why such heinous events occurred. The impact of the two world wars produced a theological "turn to the subject" in both Protestant and Catholic theology, shaped in large part by a dialogue with existentialist philosophy and characterized by the search for meaning.

This development, which occurred first in Protestantism as a result of the social, economic, and political upheaval of World War I, can be traced to the Danish existentialist Søren Kierkegaard (1813–1855). Writing in a Lutheran context (although he was extremely critical of the Danish church), Kierkegaard emphasized "inwardness" and believed that truth was essentially subjective. In the face of fear, anxiety, and uncertainty, one must make a bold "leap of faith" in the religious pursuit of meaning. When done with complete commitment, this leap of faith is one of the highest expressions of individual and personal freedom.

Kierkegaard's philosophical theology influenced other Protestant theologians, most notably Emile Brunner (1889–1966) and Paul Tillich (1886–1968), and began what was known as the neo-orthodox movement in Protestantism. In keeping with Kierkegaard's insights, neo-orthodoxy emphasized the existential dimension of subjective experience in religious faith and how this subjective experience could be transformative for the individual believer. Neo-orthodoxy sought a shift away from historical propositions of Christian faith to the personal inward grasp of these truths.

Karl Rahner

In the Roman Catholic tradition the theologian who most notably exemplified this transition was the Jesuit Karl Rahner (1904–1984), perhaps the most important Catholic theologian of the twentieth century. Rahner began to draw upon additional philosophical sources besides neo-Thomism, particularly the philosophies of Immanuel Kant and Martin Heidegger. Consequently, Rahner established a dialogue between theology and philosophy that resulted in a new approach and method in Catholic theology. His theological innovations elevated the primacy of subjective human experience and human history to foundational categories in his theological method. Rahner's new theological approach, what came to be known as the transcendental-anthropological method, was initially viewed with suspicion by the Vatican, and he was temporarily censured before being exonerated by Pope John XXIII in 1963. He was then appointed as one of the theological experts at the Second Vatican Council (1962–1965), where he had considerable influence.

The Second Vatican Council, the twenty-first ecumenical council of the Catholic Church, was convened by Pope John XXIII in 1962 and concluded in 1965 under Pope Paul VI. This largest gathering of any ecumenical council in Roman Catholic history was characterized by two significant developments. First the council utilized theological consultants, or "experts," who became quite influential, and, second, Christians from Eastern Orthodox and Protestant traditions were invited to attend as observers. While it is difficult to summarize the importance of Vatican II in a few words, it can be said that the council marked a significant development within Catholicism to assess and respond to contemporary developments in the world of human affairs.

Karl Rahner's theological "fingerprints" are noticeable in a number of Vatican II documents, but especially in *Lumen Gentium,* the Dogmatic Constitution on the Church. The importance of Rahner's influence and the significance of the Second Vatican Council cannot be overstated as they mark a major development in the history of Catholic theology in dialogue. Vatican II revealed a willingness of the entire institutional church to be in dialogue with the modern world, which is best expressed in *Gaudium et Spes,* The Pastoral Constitution on the Church in the Modern World. As the document states, *Gaudium et Spes* seeks to address "the whole of humanity. For the Council yearns to explain to everyone how it conceives of the presence and activity of the church in the world of today."[23] This document validated Pope John XXIII's phrase "the signs of the times," which signaled the church's sincere desire to address and respond to the prevailing problems and issues humanity faced in the latter half of the twentieth century.

Johann Baptist Metz

The Second Vatican Council resulted in the development of multiple theological approaches that can be described as the emergence of theological pluralism, which began to take theology in new and diverse directions with new partners in dialogue. One such theology, which came to be known as *political theology*, was formulated by Johann Baptist Metz. A student of Rahner and a theologian in dialogue with the critical theorists of the Frankfurt School, a neo-Marxist think tank, Metz moved beyond Rahner's transcendental-anthropological method and initiated a "turn to the world" in Catholic theology. Metz began to establish practical, fundamental categories for theological reflection grounded in such experiences as suffering, solidarity, dangerous memory (the memory of suffering and freedom), narrative, and praxis.[24] As a theologian who was a veteran of World War II, Metz was highly critical of the modern idea of progress in history and argued that "progress" and "history" mask the reality of its victims. Metz's theology sought to emphasize the suffering of the victims of history and develop a strategic theology, in other words, a theology that would not only address the world but could also assist in transforming the oppressive conditions under which people suffer. Metz's theology is political not because it is partisan in nature but because it seeks to challenge and transform the social-political structures that dehumanize and oppress people.

Liberation Theology

While European political theology gained momentum during the late 1960s and early 1970s, new theological voices emerged from Latin America, epitomized by Gustavo Gutiérrez's book *A Theology of Liberation* (1973). Gutiérrez and other theologians such as Juan Luis Segundo (1925–1996), Jon Sobrino, and Leonardo Boff—to name only a few—began to seriously challenge the prevailing assumptions and methodologies of theology produced in the economically developed world.[25] These liberation theologians made the radical claim that the first step of theology must be a commitment to and dialogue with the poor, or as Leonardo Boff and his brother Clodovis titled the first chapter of their book *Introducing Liberation Theology* "How to Be Christians in a World of Destitution."[26]

The primary social context of this theological dialogue was the basic Christian communities that flourished in Latin America. Essentially, basic Christian communities were small communities of poor committed Christians attempting to live out their faith under oppressive and sometimes hostile conditions. According to Dean William Ferm, the basic Christian communities "are the very stuff out of which liberation theology grows, for they are the 'poor in action' of which liberation theology is but a reflection."[27] This commitment to the poor as the first step in liberation theology, the "preferential option for the poor," was eventually affirmed in official Catholic social teaching, particularly in the social encyclicals and apostolic exhortations of Pope John Paul II.[28]

In addition to dialogue with the poor, liberation theologians also engaged in risky and controversial dialogue with Marxist theory and socialism. However, few if any liberation theologians embraced Marxism as an ideological political platform; instead they utilized the approach of social analysis and — given the capitalist social-economic structure that produced the chasm between the haves and the have-nots in the vast majority of Latin American countries — certain aspects of Marxist theory became functional and instrumental "tools" of critical reflection. According to the Boff brothers, "liberation theology uses Marxism as an instrument. It does not venerate it as it venerates the gospel."[29]

Along with social analysis, liberation theologians also gleaned the notion of praxis from their dialogue with neo-Marxist sources and especially from the work of the Brazilian educator Paulo Freire. At the risk of oversimplification, praxis can be defined as reflective activity, and the Christian faith is then understood as the praxis of faith emphasizing the active ethical dimension of living faithfully. Consequently, as defined by liberation theologians such as Gutiérrez, theology is "critical reflection on praxis" in light of the gospel and in the interest of social justice; its overarching aim is to engage in liberating activity in solidarity with the oppressed poor.[30]

Given the primacy of praxis and the preference for the suffering poor in theological reflection and action, a commonality of purpose and vision can be seen in both Latin American liberation theology and European political theology. These post–Vatican II theologies made and continue to make important and novel contributions to contemporary theology. Stephen Bevans recognizes "the praxis model" as one of the major methodological efforts in contextual theology in contemporary Christianity, and this praxis model will serve as a foundational basis for discussing the interdisciplinary method for engaging science and theology in the second chapter.

Readers should bear in mind that liberation theology is active today across denominational boundaries, from the sometimes-challenging vision of black liberation theology, to the Evangelical Lutheran Church in Brazil, whose president, Rev. Dr. Walter Altmann, has said:

> Latin America being predominantly a "Catholic" continent, the new theological approach was widely linked with pastoral and theological developments within the Roman Catholic Church, although it was from the very beginning an ecumenical endeavor. The very term "liberation theology" was proposed almost simultaneously by the Roman Catholic priest Gustavo Gutiérrez, from Peru, and the Presbyterian theologian Rubem Alves, from Brazil.[31]

It is then no surprise that in the 1970s and 1980s liberation theology had a strong influence on the ecumenical movement, including the World Council of Churches (WCC). Widely recognized is the relevancy of its actions in supporting struggles for human rights under military dictatorships in Latin America, in developing effective methods of overcoming illiteracy (a focus of the exiled Brazilian pedagogue and WCC education adviser Paulo Freire), and in combating racism, mainly in South Africa. As a contextual approach, aimed at critically reflecting on the praxis of God's people, liberation theology was never intended to become a static, dogmatic theoretical construction. Its intention was not to highlight a neglected theological theme, but rather to propose a new way of doing theology. It naturally underwent changes over the decades. At the outset it focused on the living conditions of the poor, and it later incorporated other issues, such as the needs of indigenous peoples, racism, gender inequalities, and ecology.

Feminist Theology

A development parallel to liberation theology in the aftermath of World War II was the emergence of feminist theology, another important example of twentieth-century theological pluralism. While there are clear similarities between feminist and liberation theology — particularly their mutual emphasis on liberation and their use of the praxis model of theology — the distinctive feature of the feminist project was and continues to be focused on the oppression of women combined with a sustained and justified critique of patriarchal and androcentric institutional structures in church and society. According to Rosemary Radford Ruether,

> Feminist theology takes feminist critique and reconstruction of gender paradigms into the theological realm. They question patterns of theology that justify male dominance and female subordination, such as exclusive male language for God, the view that males are more like God than females, that only males can represent God as leaders in church and society.[32]

Feminist theological voices, as for example, Elizabeth Cady Stanton (1815–1902), were present prior to World War II, but the major emergence of feminist theology did not occur until the 1960s and 1970s, what some have referred to as "second wave" feminist theology. In addition to Ruether, significant second wave feminist theologians within the Roman Catholic tradition are Elisabeth Schüssler Fiorenza, Mary Jo Weaver, and Elizabeth Johnson. From the Protestant tradition came Letty Russell, Beverly Harrison, Carter Heyward, and Sallie McFague. Some of these women are the ones who crafted the method and process of contemporary feminist theology framed by their interest in promoting dialogue with marginalized women, a position that Anne Clifford calls "reconstructionist Christian feminist theology."[33] According to Clifford, "a reconstructionist theology praises some theologies, critiques others, and draws into discussion the voices of women long ignored to forge not only new feminist theologies but also transformed societies marked by equality and mutuality of women and men."[34] Clifford offers an excellent summary of the significance of dialogue within the three praxiological movements of reconstructionist feminist theology:

1. Attending to experience(s) of patriarchy and androcentrism by listening attentively to one's own experience and that of other women and/or subjugated men

2. Bringing these experiences into dialogue with a feminist reading of the Bible and/or other Christian texts

3. Developing strategies for transformative action or praxis that are liberating[35]

Feminist theology has continued to evolve into a "third wave" development becoming broader and more inclusive and characterized in particular by the emergence of feminist voices from developing countries. According to Clifford, "In the third wave of Christian feminist theology, partnership transcends more than denominational lines; it stretches across the lines of race, class, sexual orientation, and religion. Christian feminist solidarity envisions these lines not as ones of demarcation, but rather as respectful acknowledgment of difference."[36]

A significant trajectory within feminist theology that includes dialogue with ecology has been the emergence of an ecofeminist perspective, which recognizes the intrinsic link between the oppression of women and the degradation of the natural world. Both of these assaults on creation are seen as the by-product of patriarchal and androcentric social and economic institutions. One could argue that the ecofeminist position within Christian feminist theology has been present since the beginning of the "second wave" movement typified by Ruether's theology and Sallie McFague's work. We will explore McFague's contribution to the ecology-theology dialogue more fully in chapter 8. An important contribution from this body of Christian ecofeminist analysis is the focus on the sacramentality of creation, a frequent theme in contemporary ecotheologies.

Process Theology

While political, liberation, and feminist theologies were taking shape in Europe, Latin America, North America, and elsewhere, another novel theological trend during the latter part of the twentieth century was a keen interest in reformulating Christian theology in response to pivotal developments in science. As noted above, our contemporary world is in large measure shaped by a scientific worldview. The onset of this worldview can be traced to two monumental discoveries in biology and physics:

1. the idea of emergent *evolution* based on Darwin's theory of evolution by natural selection

2. the new scientific *cosmology* based on Einstein's theory of general relativity and Niels Bohr's advances in quantum mechanics

These two scientific developments shattered the human perception that the natural world was a static fixed entity; it was instead seen as the result of a longstanding dynamic process of speciation with an underlying subatomic world of particles, energy flux, and a complex system of interrelationships. These scientific advancements provided the framework for an emerging dialogue between theology and science that came to be called process theology.

These theological perspectives were also influenced by the evolutionary-theological vision of Pierre Teilhard de Chardin (1881–1955), a French Jesuit priest-paleontologist.

Process theology was the direct offspring of process philosophy, the systematic and comprehensive attempts by Alfred North Whitehead (1861–1947) and Charles Hartshorne (1897–2000) to produce a new metaphysics consistent with the new scientific paradigms in biology and physics. Whitehead, a famous British mathematician and philosopher, desired to produce an all-encompassing model that would explain the basic process of reality for all entities from the smallest subatomic particle to God. He called these entities "actual occasions" or "actual entities." In his major work, *Process and Reality*, Whitehead referred to actual occasions as "drops of experience."[37] Simply put, an actual entity is the moment-by-moment process of experience. Thomas Hosinski writes,

> If we can think of a human life as a series of moments of experiences stretching from conception to death, and if we take a cut or slice through this life, we will encounter a single actual entity, a single moment of experience. This single moment is complex, because it bears within it relationships to all the moments that occurred before it and to all the moments that occurred after it in that person's life.[38]

Central to Whitehead's process metaphysics is the role of God, the ultimate ground of possibility, order, and actuality for all actual occasions in the universe because God is present-in-the-process of all actual entities, past, present, and future.[39] According to Hosinski, "Whitehead did not introduce the concept of God into his philosophy because he had some hidden religious agenda; he introduced it on rational grounds because it was necessary for the consistency and coherence of his philosophy."[40]

Following Whitehead's lead, Charles Hartshorne produced a fuller explication of the theological implications of Whitehead's process metaphysics, and he is often credited as the key agent in the development of process theology. In the years that followed and up to the present, many theologians would utilize process philosophy as a major dialogue partner in the effort to redefine central doctrines of Christian faith, particularly the doctrines of God and Jesus Christ.

While some Catholics were influenced by process thought, the vast majority of process theologians worked out of the Protestant context, including such names as Norman Pittenger, Daniel Day Williams, David Ray Griffin, Jay B. McDaniel, and John B. Cobb Jr. Of this group of distinguished process theologians, Cobb is one of the most prolific. Representing the United Methodist tradition, Cobb was a pioneer in the attempt to rearticulate basic Christian doctrines, especially the doctrine of God, using Whitehead's process philosophy. In one of his earlier works, *A Christian Natural Theology: Based on the Thought of Alfred North Whitehead* (and dedicated to Hartshorne), Cobb claimed "Whiteheadian cosmology...does more justice to the natural sciences and creates new possibilities of Christian understanding of man, God, and religion."[41]

In a later work, *God and the World,* Cobb departed from explicit Whiteheadian terminology and sought alternative metaphors for describing God. For example, Cobb likened God to a subjective energy event, saying that "when we think of a moment of human experience as an energy event . . . we think of it from the inside as it feels to itself, for we are thinking of those events which constitute our own existence." If we think of God in this manner, "as an occurrence of thinking, willing, feeling, and loving, then we are close to the heart of Biblical faith."[42]

Cobb addressed the environmental crisis from the view of process thought. He was convinced that Whitehead's thought was inherently ecological and that "Whitehead's philosophy pictures for us a world filled with real events, each having its own intrinsic value."[43] Reflecting on the universal process and the emergence of life, Cobb states:

> If this process is what we mean by "nature" or "life," then we can and should view "nature" or "life" as sacred. But it will be better to speak of it as Creative Process or God. To commit ourselves to God, understood in this way, would be to seek to promote life in its variety and intensity as well as in its consciousness and love.[44]

According to Cobb, if Christians committed themselves to this understanding of God, "it would keep us sensitive to the total ecological consequences of our acts."[45]

Pierre Teilhard de Chardin

In addition to process theology, the thought of Pierre Teilhard de Chardin was and continues to be an important "nexus" for the dialogue between theology and science. In fact, it can be said that Teilhard, a rare and complex individual who was a Jesuit priest, scientist, poet, and mystic, was the quintessential embodiment and personification of the theology-science dialogue. Very revealing of Teilhard's scientific-theological vision is a short passage at the beginning of his book *How I Believe,* in which he writes, "I believe that the Universe is an Evolution. I believe that Evolution goes toward Spirit. I believe that the Spirit achieves itself in the Personal. I believe that the Personal Supreme is the Universal Christ."[46]

For the better part of his life and most especially in his hallmark publication *The Phenomenon of Man,* Teilhard attempted to integrate his scientific-theological vision. In *The Phenomenon* Teilhard articulated the various stages of cosmic evolution. Beginning with cosmogenesis, the origin of matter, the universe unfolds, leading to the evolution of earth (geogenesis), the evolution of life (biogenesis), the emergence of human consciousness (noogenesis), and beyond, converging in future unity, which Teilhard called the "Omega Point."

Underlying Teilhard's view of evolution is the assertion that the elemental "stuff of the universe" has consciousness or psyche, what he called the "within of matter."[47] Teilhard's vision of the universe had serious implications for neo-Scholastic theology and created — in no small way — serious consternation among his superiors and Vatican officials.[48] Nevertheless, while there were official misgivings about Teilhard's thought, John Haught makes an insightful observation and assessment: "He [Teilhard] became convinced that evolution is not a stumbling block to Christian faith but the most appropriate framework available for clarifying its meaning." "Teilhard's writings," he says, "have made it possible for many scientifically educated people to remain Christian."[49]

John Haught is an excellent contemporary example of a theologian who epitomizes theology in dialogue with science, drawing from the insights of process theology and Teilhardian thought. Haught's contribution to interdisciplinary dialogue will be explored in the next chapter. Before turning to interdisciplinary in dialogue, however, it is important to trace the historical roots of theology's dialogue with ecology and environmental issues.

Theology in Dialogue with Environmental Issues

Joseph Sittler

In the United States the first person to seriously consider the importance of ecology and the natural world for theological reflection was Joseph Sittler, a systematic theologian at the Lutheran Theological Seminary in Chicago. According to environmental historian Roderick Nash, "Sittler was one of the first professional theologians in the United States to attempt to base an environmental ethic on Christian faith."[50] Sittler began his foray into ecotheology with a 1954 article, "A Theology for Earth," and went on to produce a number of important essays that "set the table" with a range of important theological issues that are still relevant today.

One in particular, addressed in his 1970 essay "Ecological Commitment as Theological Responsibility," was his argument that the natural world was within the scope of salvation as envisioned in the Bible. More will be said about Sittler's contribution to ecotheology in chapter 6, but it is important to note that he inspired a group of young Protestant theologians to deal with environmental problems; some of these theologians became involved in the Faith-Man-Nature Group that included Richard Baer, Daniel Day Williams, and H. Paul Santmire.

The personal force behind the formation of the Faith-Man-Nature Group was biologist Philip N. Joranson, who brought theologians and scientists together to discuss environmental issues.[51] Before it disbanded about a decade later, the group hosted forums and conferences on the environment. For his part Richard Baer wrote essays for the *Christian Century* in which he argued that abuse of land was a theological concern and that it was a theological imperative for the church to develop a land ethic.[52]

H. Paul Santmire

Baer's colleague H. Paul Santmire, a Lutheran theologian and pastor, went on to produce several texts on the issue of ecology and Christianity, beginning with the publication of his Harvard Divinity School dissertation in 1970: *Brother Earth: Nature, God, and Ecology in Time of Crisis*. In it Santmire affirmed the Christian idea of stewardship but argued that the practice of stewardship should not be for humanity's sake but for the well-being and "fulfillment" of the natural world itself.[53]

In his next work, *The Travail of Nature: The Ambiguous Ecological Promise of Christian Theology*, dedicated to Joseph Sittler, Santmire produced a hermeneutical analysis, that is, an interpretive assessment of some of the major players (for example, Origen, Augustine, Aquinas, Luther, Calvin) in the history of Christian theology on their theological understanding of nature. Santmire's analysis is grounded in two theological motifs. The first, the "spiritual motif," is driven by "the human spirit rising above nature in order to ascend to a supramundane communion with God."[54] The second one, the "ecological motif," affirms the natural world and the interrelatedness "between God, humanity and nature."[55]

As the title suggests, Santmire's analysis indicates that the ecological promise of Christian theology is ambiguous; however, his last chapter, "An Ecological Reading of the Bible," strongly suggests that the ecological reformulation of contemporary Christian theology is not only possible but desirable. That is exactly what Santmire attempts to do in *Nature Reborn: The Ecological and Cosmic Promise of Christian Theology*. As Santmire sees it there have been three religious-theological responses to the environmental crisis. The first, which he calls the "reconstructionist" approach, does not see any hope for the ecological rehabilitation of traditional Christian thought. Santmire says that "these thinkers take it as a given that traditional Christian thought offers no — or few — viable theological resources to help people of faith respond to the ecological crisis."[56]

The second group of thinkers is called the "apologists." They are defenders of Christian theology who emphasize Christian teaching on stewardship and frame the response to environmental issues in the language of social justice. However, they do not push the envelope of revising Christian theology to the next level — what Santmire calls the "revisionist" approach. Santmire traces the revisionist response to Sittler, and he includes in this category people like United Methodist James A. Nash, Lutheran biblical scholar Terence Fretheim, and Denis Edwards, an Australian Catholic theologian — all theologians whose insights we will discuss in later chapters. For Santmire the key to the revisionist approach is the willingness to "revise the classical Christian story to identify and to celebrate its ecological and its cosmic promise."[57] He argues that "the ecologically and cosmically rich thought of traditional Christianity . . . must be reformulated in the context of our own cultural situation and in our own public language, so that we can indeed make it our own, both practically and reflectively."[58]

On the basis of the brief historical summary of Christian theology outlined above, we can conclude that theology has been and continues to be in dialogue with its cultural context. In light of Santmire's statement that Christian theology "must be reformulated in the context of our own cultural situation," it is our position that dialogue with ecology and environmental science is imperative for the twenty-first century. But this claim raises an important question when considering environmental science and theology in dialogue: To what degree can this dialogue be considered interdisciplinary?

Multidisciplinary, Interdisciplinary, and Transdisciplinary

Interdisciplinarity

The answer to the question above is complex, and the answer would be determined by the person responding. Some would argue that the practice — not the idea — of interdisciplinarity is actually quite old, perhaps extending back as far as Plato. Central to interdisciplinary practice is the attempt to integrate and synthesize knowledge. According to Julie Thompson Klein, a contemporary leader in interdisciplinarity, "Plato was the first to advocate philosophy as a unified science and, correspondingly, named the philosopher as the one who is capable of synthesizing knowledge."[59]

Given this perspective we would have to say that, yes, Christian theology in dialogue has to some degree been interdisciplinary. As already noted, theology from the beginning has been contextual, drawing from and in dialogue with its cultural resources. On the other hand, one could argue that the concept of interdisciplinarity is a modern twentieth-century development insofar as it connotes the intentional crossing of the boundaries between disciplines with highly specialized knowledge. While the practice of interdisciplinarity may be ancient, the actual term and idea of the "disciplines of knowledge" arose during the Middle Ages. Klein states that "by the late Middle Ages, the term *discipline* was being applied preeminently in three instances: at Paris, to theology and the arts; at Bologna, to the law; and at Salerno, to medicine."[60]

As societies became more socially and economically diverse (for example, following the Industrial Revolution and the emergence of a middle-class intelligentsia) the production of knowledge, the division of labor within the production of knowledge, and its compartmentalization became more sophisticated and institutionalized. It is Klein's view that the modern understanding of disciplinarity is a nineteenth-century phenomenon propelled by a spectrum of historical factors such as "the evolution of the modern sciences, the general 'scientification' of knowledge, the industrial revolution, technological advancements, and agrarian agitation."[61]

As the twentieth century unfolded, punctuated by two world wars, the diversification and specialization of knowledge accelerated, leading to the creation and proliferation of subdisciplines of knowledge. This, of course, has had an enormous impact on higher education. Take theology, for example. A student does not simply do theology in general but rather specializes in a spectrum of subdisciplines such as biblical theology, historical theology, systematic theology, moral theology, and so forth. It can even be argued that one of the most recent developments is the creation of ecotheology as a legitimate subdiscipline. The sciences are even more institutionalized and complex, whether within biology, chemistry, or physics. Crossover within the sciences (*intra*disciplinarity) began early on, creating subdivisions such as biochemistry. Suffice it to say that the idea and terminology of interdisciplinarity is a twentieth-century phenomenon contextualized by the specialized divisions of knowledge that characterizes the curricula of colleges and universities.

For this text, the issue is important because we intend to take an interdisciplinary approach to the world's ecological degradation. We also intend to make the exchange between theology and science intentional, explicit, and as transparent as possible. A legitimate question, however, is why engage in interdisciplinarity in the first place, and how does the language of interdisciplinarity differ from the language and practice of *multi*disciplinarity and *trans*disciplinarity?

It is our conviction that the extent and the magnitude of the world's current environmental crisis is such that it requires — at the very least — collaboration among the various disciplines of knowledge. An interdisciplinary collaboration between science and theology is viable and necessary because the environmental crisis is scientific in nature but any solution will require an ethical, strategic praxiological response. This does not mean that the current state of global ecology is only a scientific and theological problem — it is not. It is also a social, political, economic, philosophical, pedagogical, technological, and medical problem.

Today the world is experiencing an increase in infectious and vector-borne diseases related to global climate change, and the impact on health of environmental toxins is becoming more obvious. According to Klein, the emergence of interdisciplinarity results from the need to answer complex questions, address broad issues, explore disciplinary and professional relations, solve problems that are beyond the scope of any one discipline, and achieve a unity of knowledge, whether on a limited or grand scale.[62] It is our view that the environmental crisis poses a thicket of complex questions, that it is certainly a very broad issue in its global dimensions, and, most importantly, that it is a problem whose solution is beyond the scope of any single discipline.

Multidisciplinarity

To answer the second part of the above question (the differences between interdisciplinarity, multidisciplinarity and transdisciplinarity) requires a brief foray into their different languages and practices. To begin, one could take a multidisciplinary approach to the environmental crisis through the lenses of separate disciplines, as, for example, political science, economics, and philosophy. Each discipline would bring to bear its own set of questions, methods, and tools of analysis and would most certainly increase our knowledge and information about the environmental crisis. The disciplines, however, would remain separate.

Klein indicates that a multidisciplinary approach "juxtaposes disciplines" and that the "individuals and groups work independently, the existing structure of knowledge is not interrogated, and the disciplinary elements retain their original identity."[63] Moving beyond multidisciplinarity, the key to interdisciplinary exchange is the attempt to integrate knowledge by synthesis and convergence. Klein writes that "when integration and interaction become proactive, the line between *Multidisciplinary* and *Interdisciplinary* is crossed."[64]

Transdisciplinarity

Within the range of crossdisciplinary activity, transdisciplinarity is the most recent development, and it may very likely be the logical outcome of interdisciplinary practice. Klein has defined transdisciplinarity "as a common system of axioms that transcends the narrow scope of disciplinary worldviews through a comprehensive and overarching synthesis, such as anthropology construed as the science of humans."[65] Good candidates for transdisciplinarity that are relevant to this book are ecology and environmental science. Ecology is transdisciplinary because it spans the distinct categories of biology, chemistry, and physics. Think for a moment of the term "biogeochemical cycle" — to be explored in some detail in subsequent chapters. The term itself reflects three scientific disciplines: biology, geology, and chemistry, and it strongly suggests the complexity of Earth's operating systems and cycles that are being significantly impacted by human activity.

Environmental science is also transdisciplinary because it not only integrates knowledge from the scientific disciplines, including ecology, but also from the social sciences (such as political science, sociology, economics) and even the humanities, as environmental science texts often address philosophical and ethical matters. These transdisciplinary sciences are extremely important to theology, particularly ecotheology, which intentionally attempts to analyze, address, and respond to the environmental crisis. Such an approach would not be possible if it were not for the theological commitment to engage in interdisciplinary dialogue with ecology and environmental science and for a supportive and nurturing academic context — a context that should arise out of the ethos of Christian institutions of higher learning.

The Need for Interdisciplinarity in Faith-based Institutions

Under the auspices of the Carnegie Foundation for the Advancement of Teaching, the Boyer Commission on Educating Undergraduates in the

Research University issued a report in 1998 entitled *Reinventing Undergraduate Education: A Blueprint for America's Research Universities*. The report made ten recommendations for reforming undergraduate education that are applicable to many, if not most, colleges and universities. One recommendation relevant here was to "Remove the Barriers to Interdisciplinary Education." The document stated:

> In the years since World War II the continuing appearance of new departments and new programs that merge fields has proven repeatedly the permeability of the lines between disciplines. Individual researchers find that pushing the limits of their fields takes them into new territories and that the work they are doing may have much more in common with that of colleagues across the campus than with members of their own departments.[66]

We have found this last sentence to be especially true. It is our view that removing the barriers to interdisciplinary education and collaboration is important for faith-based colleges and universities that are often challenged to find ways to integrate a faith perspective into the various disciplines of knowledge.

This challenge was recently addressed by Doug Graber Neufeld, chair of the Department of Biology and Chemistry at Eastern Mennonite University (EMU). The mission of EMU, a university in the Anabaptist tradition, clearly identifies "passionate Christian faith," "scholarly inquiry," and "care for God's creation" as important institutional commitments.[67] In 2008 Neufeld, a biologist working with EMU's environmental studies program, was asked by the university faculty conference to tackle the question: "The Word via the World: How does faithful teaching and science make visible the relationship between the created world and the incarnated Word of God?"[68]

Neufeld identified three challenges related to "Creation Care and the Challenge to Anabaptist Educators": "The Environment," "Effective Education in a Changing World," and "The Church's Faithful Response to Environment Crises."[69] Neufeld determined that science needs to cross borders and in particular the border between science and religion. He suggests that the point of contact is the *scientific knowledge* of the human place in nature and the *religious insight* that humans find their place in nature with a sense of purpose. He suggests the need for dialogue and the importance of "listening to each other." He states, "Science hasn't always done a very good job of listening, which is part of what I'm trying to convey by saying we need to cross more borders."[70] Neufeld's idea of crossing borders is akin to what we mean by interdisciplinary dialogue and collaboration.

The need to cross disciplinary barriers is also an important issue in the Roman Catholic tradition, and it was specifically addressed by Pope John Paul II (1920–2005) in *Ex Corde Ecclesiae* (1990), also known as "From the Heart of the Church." In what amounts to a blueprint for Catholic universities as well as a theology of higher education, *Ex Corde* is a significant affirmation of theology in dialogue and interdisciplinarity. Several important points in the document merit discussion. First of all, the document addresses the mission of the Catholic university, part of which is to be of service to church and society. Scholars at a Catholic university are expected to "scrutinize reality" and study "serious contemporary problems." Accordingly, *Ex Corde* states that the study of contemporary problems should occur in such areas as

> the dignity of human life, the promotion of justice for all, the quality of personal and family life, the protection of nature, the search for peace and political stability, a more just sharing in the world's resources, and a new political and economic order that will better serve the human community at a national and international level.[71]

On the matter of serious contemporary problems — the environmental crisis among them — the document encourages the investigation of root causes with an emphasis on ethical and religious dimensions.

Second, *Ex Corde* endorses interdisciplinarity and the integration of knowledge. While recognizing the "rigid compartmentalization" of knowledge institutionalized in academic disciplines, the document stresses the importance of integrating knowledge for the purpose of working toward a "higher synthesis" of knowledge.[72] Consequently interdisciplinary studies are encouraged: "While each discipline is taught systematically and according to its own methods, interdisciplinary studies, assisted by a careful and thorough study of philosophy and theology, enable students to acquire an organic vision of reality and to develop a continuing desire for intellectual progress."[73]

Finally, *Ex Corde* identifies the promotion of "dialogue between faith and reason" as one of the important functions of a Catholic university. Central to this dialogue and the search for "a synthesis of knowledge" is the discipline of theology. The document suggests that theology assists other disciplines in the search for meaning but that the dialogical exchange enhances theology as well, "offering it a better understanding of the world today, and making theological research more relevant to current needs."[74] *Ex Corde* suggests that science and technology are particularly relevant in the dialogue between faith and reason in order to fully explore the theological and ethical implications of scientific research. However, the dialogue between theology and science, while encouraged in *Ex Corde,* begs an important question: How have theology and science related to each other and what exactly are the prospects for dialogue, interdisciplinarity, and the integration of knowledge? It is this question that we must now consider.

Questions for Discussion

1. E. O. Wilson, in his book *The Creation: An Appeal to Save Life on Earth,* writes as though the book was a letter written to a Southern Baptist pastor about the need for a common front of science and theology. Speaking from the voice of your religious tradition, what would you say to your own pastor, rabbi, priest, or spiritual advisor about why he or she needs to engage with the environmental crisis?

2. Jane Goodall and Aldo Leopold (presenting himself perhaps as "a boy") both sound a bit like mystics when they are describing the relationship between people and the environment. Do you think that this is an intellectually supportable approach to talking about the relationship between science and theology in the environmental arena? Have you had any experiences similar to that of Goodall and Leopold?

3. If Christian theology were to be "contextualized" in your local community, city, or state, what dominant issues — environmental and otherwise — would need to be addressed?

4. Using environmental science, political science, and theology as examples, discuss the meaning and nature of multidisciplinary, interdisciplinary, and transdisciplinary teaching and learning.

5. What opportunities for interdisciplinary teaching and learning exist at your institution? Based on your experience, what value do you see in approaching a contemporary social problem from an interdisciplinary perspective?

Active Learning Exercise

♦ In collaboration with fellow students or a student organization, plan, execute, and evaluate a multidisciplinary or interdisciplinary faculty panel on an important environmental issue or a significant problem in your local community. Once completed evaluate the process and outcome of the event and present your findings to your class or student organization.

Recommended Reading

Bevans, Stephen B. *Models of Contextual Theology.* Maryknoll, N.Y.: Orbis Books, 2002.

Boff, Leonardo, and Clodovis Boff. *Introducing Liberation Theology.* Maryknoll, N.Y.: Orbis Books, 1992.

Clifford, Anne M. *Introducing Feminist Theology.* Maryknoll, N.Y.: Orbis Books, 2001.

Goodall, Jane, et al., *Hope for Animals and Their World: How Endangered Species Are Being Rescued from the Brink.* New York: Grand Central Publishing, 2009.

Kenney, W. Henry, S.J. *A Path through Teilhard's Phenomenon.* Dayton: Pflaum Press, 1970.

Klein, Julie Thompson. *Interdisciplinarity.* Detroit: Wayne State University Press, 1990.

Parsons, Susan Frank, ed. *The Cambridge Companion to Feminist Theology.* Cambridge: Cambridge University Press, 2002.

Teilhard de Chardin, Pierre. *How I Believe.* Trans. Rene Hague. New York: Harper and Row, 1969.

Wilson, Edward O. *Biophilia: The Human Bond with Other Species.* Cambridge, Mass.: Harvard University Press, 1984.

———. *The Creation: An Appeal to Save Life on Earth.* New York: W. W. Norton, 2006.

2

The Relationship between
Science and Theology
A Strategic Collaboration

The relationship between science and theology is, to say the least, quite interesting. Historically, one needs only to recall Nicholas Copernicus (1473–1543), the Polish priest-astronomer who initiated the Copernican heliocentric revolution, or Galileo Galilei (1564–1642) and how the Roman Catholic Church responded to his groundbreaking ideas. The intent of this chapter, however, is not to provide a detailed historical analysis of the relationship between science and theology but to highlight several twentieth-century developments that elucidate the science-theology relationship, especially in terms of the environmental crisis, and to examine contemporary thinking on the models of science-theology interaction.

It is our view that an analysis of the types of interaction between science and theology will assist the reader by providing the basis and framework for understanding the functioning of dialogue. The chapter will conclude with a model of strategic interdisciplinarity and the methodology that seeks to integrate the scientific and theological analyses of ecological problems.

Lynn White Jr. on the Ecological Crisis

It is fitting to begin with the famous or infamous — depending on one's ideological position — article by Lynn White Jr. (1907–1987), "The Historical Roots of Our Ecologic Crisis," which appeared in the journal *Science* in 1967; this was an intriguing venue for a medieval historian from the University of California Los Angeles.[1] Considered by many to be a defining moment in the discussion of Christianity's impact on the developing environmental crisis, White's article ignited a polemical firestorm between his defenders and his detractors. The crux of his argument is really quite simple: historically Christianity, the primary reason for the emergence of Western science through the desacralization of nature, is largely to blame for the environmental crisis. Consequently, in White's perspective, "Christianity bears a huge burden of guilt" and "we shall continue to have a worsening ecologic crisis until we reject the Christian axiom that nature has no reason for existence save to serve man."[2]

Over the years White's critics have mounted compelling counterarguments, including the observation that White's historiography is overly simplistic.[3] In reducing the environmental crisis to one single cause, White overlooked the complex range of historical reasons that conspired to produce the current environmental situation.[4] Others have challenged White saying that if Christianity is the underlying cause, then how can one explain the fact that pre-Christian and non-Christian cultures have also despoiled their environments? For example, anthropologists, environmental historians, and analysts of ancient pollen grains have provided evidence of wide-ranging pre-Christian environmental degradation that includes the deforestation of Easter Island, agricultural soil depletion of the American Southwest in the era of the now lost Anasazi people, deforested Mayan lowlands, and salinized farmland in ancient Mesopotamia.[5]

In spite of the arguments for and against White's thesis, it is our position that while White's argument is simplistic, we must acknowledge that since the Industrial Revolution Christianity has, at the very least, legitimated the rapacious Western industrial assault upon the natural world. In fact we would suggest from a theological perspective that White's article raised three important issues. First, in making his case for Christianity's responsibility for the environmental crisis, White drew upon biblical creation theology, particularly the creation stories in chapters 1 and 2 of Genesis. He wrote:

> Christianity inherited from Judaism not only a concept of time as non-repetitive and linear but also a striking story of creation. By gradual stages a loving and all-powerful God had created light and darkness, the heavenly bodies, the earth and all its plants, animals, birds, and fishes. Finally, God had created Adam and, as an afterthought, Eve to keep man from being lonely. Man named all the animals, thus establishing his dominance over them. God planned all of this explicitly for man's benefit and rule: no item in the physical creation had any purpose save to serve's man's purposes.[6]

White's rendition of Genesis 1 and 2, which was not a carefully informed analysis of the original stories, quickly got the attention of biblical scholars, who seriously questioned the veracity of White's interpretation. Long before White's article was written, biblical scholars using historical-critical methods of studying the Bible had produced the Documentary Hypothesis — the theory based on historical and linguistic evidence — that the Torah, the first five books of the Old Testament, was written over time by four authors or groups of authors and then edited. Scholars such as Julius Wellhausen (1844–1918) identified these four sources as the Yahwist (J), Elohist (E), Deuteronomist (D), and the Priestly (P) "authors."

From the view of the Documentary Hypothesis, White mixed together two separate creation narratives, the Priestly version found in Genesis 1:1– 2:4a and the Yahwist version found in Genesis 2:4b–25. Each of these creation narratives, written at different times in biblical history, has its own literary and theological integrity, much of which White failed to mention. For example, his interpretation does not mention that the poetic refrain in the Priestly version that "God saw that it was good" was repeated five times and then followed by "God saw everything that he made, and indeed it was very good." This is an important oversight because the Priestly creation narrative provides us with an interesting anthropological and theological "window" into ancient Israel's valuation of creation that directly challenges White's interpretation.

In light of White's treatment of the Bible's creation narratives, his critics raised the important issue of biblical hermeneutics: the process and procedure of interpreting an ancient text like the Bible for the contemporary world. As deficient as White's interpretation was, some scholars saw it as a catalyst to take a new look at the Bible in light of the ecological problem. Shortly after the appearance of White's article, during the decade of the 1970s and beyond, biblical scholars began to reassess biblical creation theology with renewed interest and energy.

Prior to the 1970s, the dominant view among Old Testament scholars — a perspective promoted by the great German scholar Gerhard von Rad (1901–1971) — was that ancient Israel's creation theology was a later development and secondary to its theology of historical redemption, which is central to such Old Testament writings as the Book of Exodus. This hermeneutical position for interpreting Old Testament theology, known as salvation history, remained the dominant view for many years until the 1970s when biblical scholars Claus Westermann (1909–2002) and H. H. Schmid claimed that creation theology is not peripheral but rather fundamental to the biblical horizon of faith.[7]

Along with Westermann and Schmid, other biblical scholars joined the challenge and made the compelling and successful argument that, in fact, creation is not ancillary to historical salvation but rather should be given elevated status in biblical theology. Commenting on this paradigm shift from salvation history to creation, the American Protestant biblical scholar Walter Brueggemann notes:

> The recovery of creation as the horizon of biblical theology encourages us to contribute to the resolution of the ecological crisis. New investigations in creation faith and its complement, wisdom theology, suggest that the environment is to be understood as a delicate, fragile system of interrelated parts that is maintained and enhanced by the recognition of limits and givens and by the judicious exercise of choices.[8]

As we shall see in chapter 7, biblical creation and wisdom theology can and must provide a cornerstone for a contemporary Christian theological response to the environmental crisis.

The second issue raised by White follows from the first, wherein his article boldly claimed that "in its Western form, Christianity is the most anthropocentric religion the world has seen."[9] It is true that Christianity is anthropocentric, but all religions are insofar as they are focused on the human condition and the quest for meaning and are interested in the question of salvation. This view is affirmed by cultural anthropology and is consistent with the work of anthropologist Clifford Geertz (1926–2006), who saw religion as a powerful cultural symbolic system that influences human behavior and provides human beings with an ordered and meaningful existence. Even Buddhism, which is often seen as an ecologically friendly religion, is concerned with the individual quest for salvation: enlightenment and the release from suffering.[10]

Nevertheless, White's claim of Christian anthropocentrism does raise an important question for biblical hermeneutics and theology: Have Christians been overly anthropocentric in interpreting the biblical text as if only humans mattered? Take, for example, the issue of redemption. Until recently the standard approach has been to interpret the biblical view of salvation, as symbolized in Jesus' proclamation of the reign of God, in exclusively human terms as if creation was unimportant. Biblical scholars and theologians now recognize the Bible's perspective is more comprehensive and inclusive, and its salvific horizon of hope in human redemption also includes the renewal and restoration of all creation.

A third issue, also linked to the aforementioned points, is the question of creation's value. In his use of Genesis 1–2 to make his case, White interpreted the creation stories to mean that "no item in the physical creation had any purpose save to serve man's purpose." In other words White argued that according to the biblical view of creation, the natural world is completely reduced to its instrumental value, that is, its use value for human purposes, and that aside from this creation has no value.

White's analysis, as noted above, failed to consider the important refrain in the Priestly account of creation in Genesis 1 that "God saw that it was good" or note that this valuation of creation had no parallel in the ancient Middle Eastern world. Often referred to as axiology — the assessment or study of values — in theology and philosophy, the value of creation in ancient Israel's creation theology is an essential characteristic that contemporary Christian ecotheology must retrieve from the biblical source. Nonetheless, in spite of White's glaring oversights, his claim that the instrumental valuation of creation was a "Christian axiom" forced theologians to reconsider our culture's axiological assumptions about the natural world and how the natural world was valued in the Bible. The result has been a far more careful and incisive analysis of the Bible's view on the value of creation and our own presuppositions regarding the natural world and our use of it. The axiological question, that is, the question of nature's value, may be the most important issue of the three because from an ethical point of view, particularly a deontological one, the valuation of something is the basis for moral obligation and duty.[11] In other words, we humans tend to care for and protect what we love.

The issue of creation's value is also important in the contemporary dialogue between theology and science as both disciplines attempt to address the deterioration of the Earth's biosphere.

Theology and Science:
From Conflict to Collaboration

The relationship between theology and science can be accessed from a number of perspectives, but two in particular stand out for their clarity and insight. The approaches of Ian G. Barbour and John F. Haught have proposed typologies of the religion-science relationship. Barbour and Haught both prefer the term "religion," a broader term than theology, yet when we review their positions both men appear quite comfortable within the Judeo-Christian theological tradition from which they draw frequent examples. Haught occasionally does make reference to the Abrahamic faith traditions of Judaism, Christianity, and Islam. This text prefers "theology" because theology assumes a faith commitment within a given religious tradition and because this book's project is, in some small way, an example of what St. Anselm called "faith seeking understanding."

In his book *Religion in an Age of Science* published in 1990 and later revised and updated in 1997 as *Religion and Science: Historical and Contemporary Issues*, Barbour proposed a fourfold typology to describe the range of possible relationships between theology and science, which he named *conflict, independence, dialogue,* and *integration.*[12] Building on Barbour's classification, Haught altered Barbour's framework with his own language and thematic content and proposed the typology of *conflict, contrast, contact,* and *confirmation.*[13]

Conflict

On the category of *conflict,* Barbour's and Haught's perspective are virtually identical and reflect the position that the relationship between theology and science is — to use Haught's language — "fundamentally irreconcilable," with no room for agreement and significant potential for open hostility.[14] The classic flashpoint for this conflictual relationship is the divergent extremes over the Darwinian theory of evolution by natural selection. On the scientific side of the fault line are the scientific materialists who, according to Barbour, accept two basic principles: "(1) the scientific method is the only reliable path to knowledge; (2) matter (or matter and energy) is the fundamental reality in the universe."[15]

This view is underscored by two tendencies. The first is *reductionism,* the tendency to reduce the full range of physical reality and existence to the fundamental laws of science (biology, chemistry, and physics), and the second is the tendency of scientific materialists to engage in philosophical speculation on the materialistic implications of scientific research and discovery.

Essentially, *scientific materialism,* also known as scientism, is an ideology, a philosophical extrapolation that originates in science but goes beyond it. Scientism purports to offer an all-embracing definition of reality. Scientists and philosophers who hold this position include a list of notable personalities including the late Stephen Jay Gould, Steven Weinberg, Francis Crick, Daniel Dennet, and Richard Dawkins. Dawkins's book *The God Delusion* makes it quite clear that there is no room for spirit or God in the materialist's universe.

On the theological side of the chasm are the biblical literalists who flatly reject the notion of biological evolution based on their belief in the inerrancy of scripture, an interpretation of scripture suggesting that God dictated the Bible word for word. Also known as fundamentalism, *biblical literalism* has a long history and can be traced back to the Protestant Reformation. Unlike most contemporary mainline Protestant denominations and the Roman Catholic Church, biblical literalists also reject the use of critical-historical methods in researching the Bible. Simply put, from the biblical literalist perspective the Bible stands as it is; because evolutionary theory contradicts the literalist interpretation of the biblical creation stories found in Genesis 1 and 2, it must be rejected.

Moreover, in recent years the biblical literalist view has coalesced into an organized attempt to refute the claims of evolutionary biology, developing what has been called "scientific creationism" or "creation science." In some school districts, adherents of this theological perspective have advocated that creation science be taught alongside evolution in high school science curricula. Advocates of this strategy were successful in the states of Arkansas and Louisiana, leading to court battles in 1982 (*McLean v. Arkansas*) and 1987 (*Edwards v. Aguillard*). The *Edwards v. Aguillard* case is particularly interesting. In the early 1980s the state legislature of Louisiana passed the "Balanced Treatment for Creation-Science and Evolution-Science in Public School Instruction Act" requiring that when evolution was taught in public schools creationism had to be taught as well. The case was argued before the U.S. Supreme Court, and in 1987 it ruled, in a seven to two majority, that the law was unconstitutional because it violated the First Amendment. In other words Louisiana's "Balanced Treatment Act" violated the separation of church and state.[16]

The most recent permutation on the theological side of this conflict has been the idea of creation by intelligent design, a concept developed and packaged by the "Discovery Institute." Intelligent design argues that the structure and complexity of the universe indicate that intelligence is behind the process and that this is a superior explanation for the existence of life than the Darwinian theory of evolution by natural selection. Intelligent design proponents claim that it is science, but many others see it as a repackaged form of creationism. The conflict reemerged in 2004 when the school board of Dover, Pennsylvania, voted to require a statement — supportive of intelligent design — be read by teachers of ninth-grade biology classes at Dover High

School. In 2005 eleven parents of students at Dover High School sued the school district (*Tammy Kitzmiller et al. v. Dover Area School District et al.*). The plaintiffs were successful in arguing that intelligent design was a form of creation science and the judge in the case ruled the Dover requirement unconstitutional.[17]

Independence/Contrast

In the second classification of the relationship between theology and science, the hostility of conflict gives way to a more benign approach, which Barbour calls "independence" and Haught calls " contrast." Basically *independence* represents the view that theology and science have their own unique linguistic and methodological domains and should be kept separate, without interference in the business and workings of the other. Barbour puts it this way: "Proponents of this view say there are two jurisdictions and each party must keep off the other's turf."[18] According to Barbour, the underlying motivation for this position is not just avoiding conflict but "the desire to be faithful to the distinctive character of each area of life and thought."[19] From a strategic and collaborative perspective this is a valid point. When theologians and scientists make "contact" and engage in "dialogue" and move toward "integration" and "confirmation," they must venture beyond their disciplinary comfort zones — a potentially daunting enterprise but, as we will argue later, a necessary venture if strategic collaboration is desired.

John Haught prefers the language of *contrast* for this theology-science relationship but it is extremely similar to Barbour's notion of independence. According to Haught, "Contrast envisages science and religion as independent, autonomous ways of knowing. Only by putting them in separate camps, it insists, can we prevent eventual warfare between them."[20] Haught affirms Barbour's view that science and religion have their own distinct language and methods of inquiry and that it is best to keep them separate to avoid problems. Haught, however, adds the issue of "conflation" to the independence/contrast equation. Conflation is the process of reducing or eliminating the distinction between the disciplines in such a way that the differences disappear or are ignored. According to Haught, "Conflation...is an unsatisfactory attempt to avoid conflict by carelessly commingling science with belief. Instead of respecting the sharp differences between science and religion, conflation weaves them into a single fabric where they fade into each other, almost to the point of being indistinguishable."[21] Haught makes a compelling case that the idea of "creation science" from the biblical literalists and the view of "scientism" from the scientific materialists are examples of conflation.

Dialogue/Contact

The third classification of the theology-science typologies is called "dialogue" by Barbour and "contact" by Haught. According to Barbour, "Dialogue starts from general characteristics of science or of nature" and takes shape in three categories: limit questions, methodological issues, and nature-centered spirituality.[22] Limit questions are queries raised by the scientific method but not interrogated by the scientific process itself. A good example of this would be the ethical and public policy implications of the complex data sets that provide the scientific basis for an understanding of global warming and climate change. Many scientists are quite leery about engaging those questions because in their view these questions fall outside the purview of their disciplinary focus. On other hand, from a theological perspective, when one reads the detailed analysis of the impact and vulnerability scenarios on human beings reported in the *Climate Change 2007* report (see volume 2), the ethical implications are glaring if not staggering. The ethical question then becomes a potential opportunity for conversation.

The emergent field of *postnormal science* represents the attempt by some scientists to employ the precautionary principle ("do no harm") when uncertainties or the stakes in policy decisions are very high, as in the case of global climate change.[23] At present this is a nascent movement among a limited number of scientists, involving a broad dialogue with social scientists and various other stakeholders.[24] While theologians are not currently involved in this dialogue, postnormal science may be an appropriate avenue for dialogue on such issues as climate change, endangered species recovery, deforestation, the bioaccumulation of persistent toxins, and other related environmental issues facing humanity.

The second category for dialogue in Barbour's analysis is on *methodological issues*. A good example lies in the issue of scientific data. According to Barbour, "Scientific data are theory-laden, not theory-free. Theoretic assumptions enter the selection, reporting, and interpretation of what are taken to be data."[25] Barbour rightly points out that similar aspects are present in the process of theological inquiry, one of which is the process of hermeneutics — the interpretation of not only an ancient text like the Bible but the interpretation of the dominant themes, developments, and problems of contemporary human existence. These methodological questions also provide a rich possibility for creative dialogue between scientists and theologians.

The third example of dialogue for Barbour is *nature-centered spirituality.* This is, for the most part, a very contemporary development, although one could trace its nascent beginnings to the New England transcendentalists and the musings of John Muir.[26] The central issue here is the way one lives in relation to sacred reality and in relation to the natural world, particularly in response to a natural world under serious duress. It is Barbour's view that nature-centered spirituality lends support to the ethical questions raised by the relatively new discipline of environmental ethics. This issue is, for obvious reasons, especially significant to the ethical horizon embodied in this text.

Haught, preferring the term "contact" for this designation of the theology-science relationship, provides a simple but cogent description of this classification. He writes that contact "agrees that science and religion are logically and linguistically distinct, but it knows that in the real world they cannot be as easily compartmentalized as the contrast position supposes."[27] The contact position is characterized by an openness to and appreciation for scientific discoveries and developments with an eye for their theological implications. Simply put, theologians must "pay attention" to the scientific enterprise because, as noted in chapter 1, science is one of the dominant characteristics of our contemporary world. According to Haught:

> Contact proposes that scientific knowledge can broaden the horizon of religious faith and that the perspective of religious faith can deepen our understanding of the universe. It does not strive to prove God's existence from science but is content simply to interpret scientific discoveries within a framework of religious meaning.[28]

An excellent example of dialogue/contact among theologians and scientists occurred in 1992 with the Joint Appeal by Religion and Science for the Environment known as the "Declaration of the Mission to Washington" issued on May 12 of that year. The two-page document begins with the recognition that while science and religion have not always seen eye-to-eye historically, the prevailing exigencies of environmental degradation have facilitated a convergence of interests. The opening paragraph reads:

> We are people of faith and science who, for centuries, often have traveled different roads. In a time of environmental crisis, we find these roads converging. As this meeting symbolizes, our two ancient, sometimes antagonistic, traditions now reach out to one another in a common endeavor to preserve the home we share.[29]

A review of the Declaration makes clear that the underlying motivation for this example of contact is not theoretical, methodological, or epistemological but practical — or praxiological — because its intention is to impact U.S. national policy on the environmental crisis. As noted in chapter 1, interdisciplinary collaboration is often motivated by mutual pragmatic concerns such as the search for solutions to problems larger than any single discipline. The primary focus of dialogue in this document is the shared moral concern for the environmental condition of the earth. The signatories state:

> We believe that science and religion, working together, have an essential contribution to make toward any significant mitigation and resolution of the world environmental crisis. What good are the fervent moral imperatives if we do not understand the dangers and how to avoid them? What good is all the data in the world without a steadfast moral compass?[30]

Putting their differences aside, the scientists and theologians who produced this document signal the hopeful emergence of collaboration in an ecological era revealing "a deep sense of common cause."[31]

Integration/Confirmation

The final category of the science-theology typology is what Barbour calls "integration" and Haught calls "confirmation." This classification takes dialogue/contact to a new level of discourse. According to Barbour, "The relationships between theological doctrines and particular scientific theories are more direct than in any of the forms of Dialogue."[32] Barbour sees three examples of this classification: *natural theology, theology of nature,* and *systematic synthesis.*

Natural theology is the theological perspective that evidence of God can be detected in the design of the natural world — a world that has been and is explicated by the natural sciences. This view has a long history within the Judeo-Christian tradition, and it can be argued that it extends back to the biblical period, particularly in Old Testament texts and the Wisdom literature. As a historical example of natural theology, Barbour identifies Thomas Aquinas. Drawing on Aquinas's cosmological and teleological arguments for the existence of God, Barbour states that Aquinas

> offered several versions of the *cosmological argument* for a First Cause (or a necessary being on whom all contingent beings are dependent). He also presented the *teleological argument* for the orderliness and intelligibility of nature in general and the evidence of design in particular natural phenomena.[33]

Barbour also claims that "reformulations of the teleological argument are common in Roman Catholic thought, where natural theology has traditionally held a respected place in preparation for the truths of revealed theology."[34]

In contemporary thought, Barbour suggests that the anthropic principle — the view that the universe from the moment of the Big Bang was designed to produce intelligence — is a modern form of the teleological argument. (The anthropic principle, an idea produced by astrophysicists, will be more fully examined theologically in chapter 6.) For now the important idea underlying natural theology is that its starting point lies in observation of the natural world, which in its modern form could be greatly assisted by scientific theory and discovery.

A *theology of nature,* on the other hand, does not begin with observation of nature but with doctrinal formulations (for example, God as creator) of theological traditions. The primary task of a theology of nature is to reinterpret and rearticulate traditional doctrinal formulations through the hermeneutical lens of the sciences, including cosmology, biology, chemistry, ecology, and the environmental sciences. The goal is to produce a more informed and consistent understanding of humanity, God, Jesus Christ, and so forth in light of new and compelling insights from scientific research as well as to provide the theological basis for ethical engagement in response to the environmental crisis.

Perhaps one of the most influential and respected contemporary examples of a theology of nature is the work of Arthur Peacocke (1924–2006). A biochemist and theologian, as well as an ordained priest in the Anglican Church, Peacocke believed that science and theology are not opposed but are two equally important pursuits of the human quest for knowledge and meaning. According to the journal *Zygon*, Peacocke believed that "any theology is doomed unless it incorporates the scientific perspective into its 'bloodstream.' "[35] According to Barbour, Peacocke

> discusses at length how chance and law work together in cosmology, quantum mechanics, nonequilibrium thermodynamics, and biological evolution.... God creates through the whole process of law and chance, not by intervening in gaps in the process. God creates "in and through" the process of the natural world that science unveils.[36]

In addition to theological reformulations based on scientific insight, Barbour believes that a contemporary theology of nature must "provide motivation for action to preserve the environment of our endangered planet."[37] Barbour offers four specific examples of this project: (1) stewardship of nature, (2) celebration of nature, (3) a sacramental view of nature, and (4) the Holy Spirit in nature.[38] These theological "projects" will be taken up and discussed in chapters 6 and 7, which will provide examples of how several ecotheologians have addressed the environmental crisis from within the Christian theological tradition.

Barbour's final example of integration is *systematic synthesis,* which amounts to a complete overhaul of the philosophical and metaphysical foundations of contemporary theology. In our current scientific, philosophical, and theological world, a prime candidate for integration is *process theology.* As discussed in chapter 1, process theology arose from Whitehead's process philosophy, was nurtured by Hartshorne, and further developed by theologians like John Cobb and David Griffin.[39] In the process perspective God is not the "Absolute" of Greek philosophy or the "Unmoved Mover" of Aristotelian metaphysics. Rather God is "dipolar," meaning that God is immanent within creation and also transcendent from creation. In this construct God is related to all that occurs and acts upon the world through persuasion rather than compulsion or, in other words, God is the ultimate reality that lures all creation forward into novelty.[40]

Some contemporary theologians see process theology as a more adequate understanding of God because, on the one hand, it is responsive to our scientific evolutionary worldview, and, on the other hand, it is a creative way of dealing with the tension in the biblical narrative between God's transcendence (God is above, other than, and distinct from all creation) and immanence (nearness). Process theology will be described in more detail in chapter 7 and, as we shall see, this theological position holds interesting possibilities for an ecotheological interpretation of God and God's relationship to creation.

The final classification in Haught's typology is *confirmation*. Essentially confirmation is the theological posture that seeks to endorse the entire project we call science and, in particular, the underlying and fundamental human desire to know the world. Haught offers a very succinct description of confirmation:

> The confirmation approach may be stated as follows: religion's claim that the universe is a finite, coherent, rational, ordered totality, grounded in an ultimate love and promise, provides a general vision of things that consistently nurtures the scientific quest for knowledge and liberates science from associations with imprisoning ideologies.[41]

Haught makes a compelling case that science itself could not take flight were it not for "a kind of a priori 'faith' that the universe is a rationally ordered totality of things."[42] We take this to mean that "faith" is an anthropological necessity grounded in the human capacity for critical reason that seeks to render the biophysical world an intelligible coherent reality through which human beings construct a meaningful existence in the universe. Haught argues that "religion by its very nature is concerned that we put our trust in reality's overall rationality. And in this sense religion is much more intimately connected to the epistemological *roots* of scientific inquiry" than the preceding classifications of the science-religion relationship that have been discussed.[43]

In Haught's view the convergence of science and theology is grounded in the mutual trust and "confirmation" in the intelligibility of the universe.

A Model for Strategic Interdisciplinarity: The Iterative-Praxiological Method

The science-theology typologies of Barbour and Haught provide a cogent and insightful description of the range of past and current interactions between theology and science, and we wholeheartedly endorse the *dialogue/contact* and *integration/confirmation* classifications of their typologies. In fact we claim that the model and method of *strategic interdisciplinarity* that we are about to articulate is preconditioned on *contact*, on the sincere desire to engage in interdisciplinary *dialogue* with a genuine trajectory toward mutual *confirmation* and a desire to seek *integration* between theology and science. This perspective is rooted in our collaboration on the salmon crisis in the Pacific Northwest through which we discovered a pragmatic working relationship that we call *strategic interdisciplinarity*.[44]

We define *strategic interdisciplinarity* as the collaborative attempt to address a complex problem utilizing scientific and theological-ethical analysis with the goal of producing ethical norms for action, strategic solutions, and public-policy guidelines. The primary focus of this interdisciplinary model is contextual and not theoretical or abstract, and its outcome is practical (or praxiological), seeking to shape both our actions and public policy. In other words the overall aim is to assist in the transformation of social, economic, and political institutions in the interest of Earth, social-environmental justice, and a healthy ecology for present and future generations of human and nonhuman life.

One significant outcome of our collaborative dialogue on issues related to salmon recovery has been the development of an interdisciplinary process for analyzing ecological conditions, specific environmental problems, and their underlying social context while at the same time promoting ethical engagement and public policy action. We call this the *iterative-praxiological method*. Methodologically, the key is the "wedding" of the iterative process from science and the praxis model of contextual theology.

The *iterative process* is essentially a circular method of gathering information, modeling it, empirically testing it through field research, and, as new data are acquired, assessing possible outcomes or actions, and then beginning the process anew. Likewise, the *praxis model*, described below, is also circular. Our interdisciplinary analysis of salmon in the Pacific Northwest produced a method that combined scientific and theological analysis in a collaborative manner for the purpose of impacting public policy and promoting a vision for transforming the complex social, economic, and political factors that underwrite the Pacific salmon crisis.

Historically the theological foundation for the *iterative-praxiological method* was the praxis model of contextual theology (see chapter 1) that was produced by Latin American liberation theologians. They profoundly challenged the traditional methods of the dominant Euro-American theologies by arguing that the first step in theological reflection was a commitment to the experience of the poor; consequently, theology must include critical reflection on the praxis of faith in the interest of social transformation and justice. According to theologian Stephen Bevans, the "central insight" of the praxis model "is that theology is done not simply by providing relevant expressions of Christian faith but also by commitment to Christian action."[45] Bevans claims:

> The praxis model is a way of doing theology that is formed by knowledge at its most intense level — the level of reflective action. It is also about discerning the meaning and contributing to the course of social change, and so takes its inspiration neither from classical texts nor classic behavior but from present realities and future possibilities.[46]

A good example of the genesis of the praxis model as well as its iterative or circular nature is Juan Luis Segundo's description of the "hermeneutical circle" in liberation theology. The context for the hermeneutical circle is twofold. On the one hand, it is the experience of the poor given expression in Latin America's basic Christian communities and, on the other hand, it is the way that that community of the poor read and interpret the Bible in light of their experience. Segundo writes:

Here is a preliminary definition of the hermeneutical circle: it is the continuing change in our interpretation of the Bible which is dictated by the continuing changes in our present-day realities.... And the circular nature of this interpretation stems from the fact that each new reality obliges us to interpret the word of God afresh, to change reality accordingly, and then to go back and reinterpret the word of God again, and so on.[47]

Segundo's definition of the hermeneutical circle includes two necessary ingredients or preconditions. First, there must be the critical analysis of social reality — or a particular aspect of it — as it currently exists. Second, from this analysis comes a new interpretation of the Bible that has been shaped by critically scrutinizing society. In the case of our science-theology collaboration, the aspect of society under examination is ecological degradation as the result of human activity, and our critical analysis is guided by the environmental sciences and the Christian theological tradition. Our theological reflection, however, is not exclusively biblical, although the Bible is essential in interpreting the ecological crisis and vice versa; we draw upon the Bible as well as theological voices that have taken up the environmental crisis as a particular focus for their theological work.

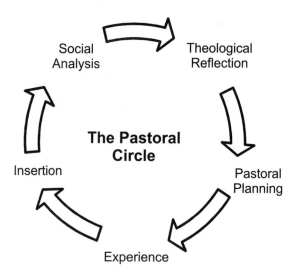

As Segundo's definition of the hermeneutical circle suggests, the overall goal is not an endless circular process of analysis and biblical interpretation but a commitment "to change reality accordingly." In other words, the ultimate outcome is social transformation resulting from the ethical engagement necessary to produce the desired changes to society. We will argue that the necessary social transformation as the result of our scientific-theological analysis is best characterized by sustainability, the topic of the final chapter.

The praxis model of theology received further refinement and articulation for a North American context by Joe Holland and Peter Henriot. In their book *Social Analysis: Linking Faith and Justice,* Holland and Henriot proposed a compact description of the praxis model, calling it the "pastoral circle" or the "circle of praxis," which they envisioned as an iterative process with five components, as shown on the facing page.[48]

Utilizing this as a prototype, the *interative-praxiological method* is also composed of five components, or movements, that unfold in an iterative manner. Sequentially the five components are (1) the environmental crisis, the issue under examination; (2) social analysis, (3) scientific analysis, (4) theological-ethical analysis, and (5) strategic planning oriented toward producing ethical commitment, public policy action, and ultimately a sustainable society.

THE ITERATIVE-PRAXIOLOGICAL METHOD

We applied this *iterative praxiological method* to attempts to restore salmon runs in the Columbia Basin. We offer this environmental issue as a case study for two major reasons, in addition to our location at the University of Portland. First, the salmon crisis in the Columbia Basin, which is also occurring on the Pacific coast of North America from British Columbia to California, is a regional example of the global phenomenon of declining fisheries and the loss of marine biodiversity. The Food and Agriculture Organization of the United Nations estimates that "over seventy percent of the world's fish species are either fully exploited or depleted."[49] The Columbia Basin salmon problem also exemplifies all of the major underlying causes of the world's accelerating loss of biodiversity — a subject treated in chapter 4.

The second reason that makes the Pacific salmon crisis a good case study is that beginning in 1991 many Columbia Basin salmon were listed under the Endangered Species Act (ESA), and in 1997 the Roman Catholic bishops within the basin initiated the Columbia River Pastoral Letter Project (CRPLP), a significant initiative for several reasons. First, the process that led to the publication of *The Columbia River Watershed: Caring for Creation and the Common Good* in January 2001 was atypical for an episcopal letter.[50] Rather than commissioning a "ghost writer" to prepare a draft of a letter, the CRPLP, led by Bishop William Skylstad of Spokane, began the process with a series of listening sessions throughout the Columbia Basin to garner input from all interested parties with a "stake" in the basin's rivers and land. Only after information was gathered did drafts of the letter begin to circulate.

Second, the project was attentive to scientific input, and the steering committee that actually drove the process included two scientists (one was co-author Kolmes, and co-author Butkus provided theological input as a member of the resource committee). In other words the CRPLP is an example of interdisciplinarity and collaboration between science and theology. Finally, the project and published letter involved an international process as it included the diocese of Nelson in British Columbia.

The Salmon Crisis — The Case Study

Some historical background is necessary before applying the interative-praxiological method to this case study of salmon depletion. Salmon runs in the Columbia Basin have been dwindling for approximately 150 years, but the severity of the salmon crisis up and down the West Coast was brought home by the 1991 report by Nehlsen, Williams, and Lichatowich entitled "Pacific Salmon at the Crossroads: Stocks at Risk from California, Oregon, Idaho, and Washington."[51] The report declared that of 214 native, naturally spawning runs of salmon, steelhead, and sea-run cutthroat trout, 101 were in extreme risk of extinction, 58 at moderate risk, and 54 of concern.[52] They also identified 106 other runs that were already extinct. During that same decade salmon and steelhead runs in the Columbia River began to be listed as threatened or endangered under the ESA. To date there are thirteen separate salmon and steelhead runs (identified as Evolutionarily Significant Units or ESUs) within the Columbia Basin listed under the ESA. The task of managing this crisis fell to the fisheries unit at the National Oceanic and Atmospheric Administration (NOAA Fisheries, formally known as the National Marine Fisheries Service) and it has become the lead federal agency in the matter.

Social Analysis

With this information in mind, social analysis is the first movement of a broader critical analysis. According to Holland and Henriot, "Social analysis examines causes, probes consequences, delineates linkages, and identifies actors" related to the issues under investigation.[53] In other words, social analysis critically examines the historical, institutional, and structural aspects of the problem with the aim of uncovering the economic, political, cultural, and social etiology (or causes) of environmental conditions.

For our case study, the process of social analysis is twofold. First it must identify the major players in salmon recovery, that is, the people and organizations typically identified as "stakeholders," the groups who may either benefit from maintaining the status quo or benefit from changing it. Although there is not exclusively an economic benefit or loss, such issues often have a very significant economic component. In the case of salmon recovery in the Columbia Basin, the spectrum of stakeholder groups is truly mind-numbing, a situation we have referred to in past publications as the "bureaucratic conundrum."[54]

Nevertheless, a snapshot of the stakeholders in salmon recovery on the U.S. side of the border includes: (1) government agencies that encompass federal (this includes a range of agencies as well as the Bonneville Power Administration), state (Washington, Idaho, Montana, and Oregon), and local municipalities; (2) Native American tribes (the confederated tribes of Warm Springs, Umatilla, Yakima, and Nez Perce), who hold treaty rights dating back to 1855; (3) industrial, agricultural, and related user groups such as recreational, sport, and commercial fishing interests; (4) a host of non-governmental organizations (NGOs)[55] that often reflect environmental and conservation interests; and (5) legal institutions, particularly federal courts, because contentious litigation continues to be an issue. Bear in mind that all of the above groups must deal with political realities — for good or for ill — depending on what political party occupies the White House and what party controls Congress.

The second layer of social analysis is assessing the human activities — often reflected by the organized stakeholder groups — that impact and/or are directly linked to the underlying causes of the salmon crisis. To simplify this analysis we refer to the acronym HIPPO, proposed by Harvard University biologist E. O. Wilson and others to identify the primary causes of the loss of biodiversity.[56] The following are the underlying causes of the salmon crisis directly related to human activities (HIPPO):

- H habitat destruction (by channel simplification, constructing dams and dikes, water withdrawals, and riparian deforestation, for example);

- I invasive species (including smallmouth bass, walleye, New Zealand mud snails, Eurasian watermilfoil, and approximately eighty others);

- P pollution (including pesticide and fertilizer runoff, municipal effluents containing pharmaceuticals, heavy metals, cleaners, and industrial effluents containing a wide variety of synthetic organic compounds and metals);

- ◆ **P** population density (with a regional population poised to more than double within one generation); and

- ◆ **O** overharvest and overconsumption (including the commercial harvest of fish, the negative impact of hatcheries on wild stocks and other development and construction that converts productive land into retail space, parking lots, and other impervious surfaces).

This leg of social analysis leads directly to the next phase of the *iterative praxiological method,* which is scientific analysis.

Scientific Analysis

In the case of salmon recovery in the Columbia Basin, scientific analysis is also governed by a twofold movement. First, critical scientific analysis questions the prevailing scientific rationale that is the basis of current assessment and modeling in salmon recovery science. From a theological perspective, this appeared to be a highly technical but fascinating foray into the documents and heuristic models that are in current use in salmon recovery science. For example, our analysis indicated that the primary document governing regional salmon recovery planning was the "Viable Salmonid Populations and the Recovery of Evolutionarily Significant Units," or VSP paper.[57] Basically the document argued that salmon recovery efforts must occur at the level of independent populations of salmon and steelhead. An independent population is a geographically limited group of salmon or steelhead, meaning that their life history, including spawning and rearing, is defined by a particular watershed usually a tributary of the Columbia River.

Our analysis revealed two glaring problems with the VSP approach. First the VSP concept failed to take sufficient account of the habitat requirements — directly linked to human activity of land use — for salmon recovery. VSP criteria focuses on fish production, growth, and recruitment, rather than the fragile and complex types of habitats salmon require as they spawn in shallow cold gravel beds, rear at various locations between their spawning grounds and the estuary, grow to maturity at sea, and then migrate back to their natal streams.

Second, the criterion embraced in the VSP process (reducing the risk of extinction of an individual population to 5 percent or less over the next one hundred years) is an example of something that sounds scientific but has no basis in experimentation, observation, or theory. A value of 5 percent is simply what scientists conventionally use as an arbitrary cut-off delimiting statistical significance when they are using a statistical test to evaluate the reliability of an apparent difference between two groups. This cut-off point may appear to have a reasonable level of assurance but in reality it has neither theoretical nor empirical support for choosing a 5 percent extinction rate over 6 percent, 1 percent, or .001 percent. Close examination of current salmon recovery planning indicates that the assumptions of the mathematical models being used take on the unwarranted mantle of being "scientific facts," and this process has serious ethical implications that should be subject to careful scrutiny.

The second leg of scientific analysis must attend to ongoing research related to salmon recovery. New scientific insights and developments can always potentially impact any policy decisions that must be made. A recent example was a study conducted by researchers at Oregon State University that determined that hatchery-produced salmon and steelhead released into the wild carried genetic traits that were detrimental to wild fish that spawned naturally in Columbia Basin rivers.[58] This study seems to affirm longstanding suspicions within the scientific community of the negative impact of hatcheries on wild salmon and steelhead populations, but it also has huge social and economic implications because there are approximately two hundred state, tribal, and federal hatcheries within the Columbia Basin. In light of ongoing scientific research on Pacific coast salmon, this is a good juncture to discuss the role of iteration in science.

In salmon science, iteration is a process where background information is initially gathered, hypotheses or models about how the physical world operates are generated, and evaluations or assessments of these models or hypotheses via experiments or monitoring programs are conducted to provide new data for the planning process. As this new information is gathered, new hypotheses or models for salmon recovery planning are generated. Essentially this is a cyclic scientific process, without attention to a distinct stage of ethical or social reflection. The process as envisioned by NOAA Fisheries was succinctly stated in 2003 by Bob Lohn, the administrator for the NOAA Fisheries Northwest Region:

> The initial rounds of local recovery planning are not expected to be perfect. Initial rounds need to be based on existing information. As we do assessments, we will find that existing information leaves us with critical uncertainties and data gaps. Research and monitoring needs to be directed toward filling those gaps. Also, as the ESU scale of recovery planning evolves, it will provide additional context for the subbasins and the independent populations. Local recovery plans should be viewed as iterative documents that can adapt to new information and that will become more sophisticated with time.[59]

Theological and Ethical Reflection

The third movement of the iterative-praxiological method is theological-ethical reflection on the issue under examination. As noted above, a very fortuitous event occurred when salmon and steelhead were being listed under the ESA: the publication of *The Columbia River Watershed: Caring for Creation and the Common Good.* While the document took a broad-based look at the Columbia River Basin that included social, economic, ecological, cultural, and theological perspectives, it specifically addressed the salmon crisis.

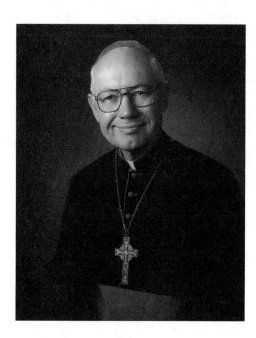

William S. Skylstad is Bishop Emeritus of the Roman Catholic Diocese of Spokane, Washington. A former president of the United States Conference of Catholic Bishops, he retired on June 30, 2010.

For example, in the section called "The Rivers of Our Vision," which offers a *future vision* of hope for the Columbia region, the bishops stated:

> In the vision fish populations are abundant, responding to human ingenuity and mutual cooperation. Commercial, recreational and private fishers continue to enjoy opportunities for providing a family meal, family livelihood or a family outing. People realize the interconnectedness of rivers and ocean and understand their individual and community responsibilities to exercise proper stewardship for both. Negative impacts on fish populations from irresponsible commercial and industrial operations are no longer seen.[60]

Three comments on this document are relevant to the example of salmon recovery. First, the document draws upon biblical creation theology, developing the concept of stewardship and the principle of sacramentality (the belief that creation — the physical universe — is imbued with the hidden presence of God) as the theological foundation for Christian ethical action in the Columbia Basin. Second, the document utilizes key concepts of Catholic social teaching, especially the principle of the common good, and apply it to the Columbia River Basin, defining the common good by an ecological region. Third, the pastoral letter concludes with ten norms for

Sacred scripture provides a rich foundation of imagery and theological reflection on the stewardship of our environment. That imagery in the Old Testament offers numerous reflections on the beauty of the Earth and the need to use that gift as a source of gratitude to God and an encouragement of responsibility for it and for one another. The prophet Ezekiel speaks of the flowing river, where "every sort of living creature that can multiply shall live, and there shall be abundant fish, for wherever this water comes, the sea shall be made fresh" (Ezek. 47:9–10). The Canticle of Daniel describes in a vibrant manner the blessings of nature about us.

Jesus is baptized in the River Jordan and speaks frequently of images from the land and water. The vine and the branches and the nonproducing fig tree provide valuable moral lessons through earthly symbols with which we are most familiar. The elements of the earth like water, oil, bread, and wine provide wonderful symbols in liturgical celebrations. The cleansing and life-giving nature of water, the bountiful earth, and all growing things remind us of the awesome creation on this planet.

The Earth on which we live, the Word of God, and the liturgical celebration led us to theological reflection and application. More recently, Pope John Paul II's World Day of Peace message in 1990 focusing on environment and its relationship to peace seemed to be a significant breakthrough in continuing theological reflection. In 1991 the U.S. Catholic Bishops published a pastoral letter, *Renewing the Earth: An invitation to Reflection and Action on the Environment in Light of Catholic Social Teaching,* which was a significant contribution to this new awareness. In addition, the Columbia River pastoral issued by the Catholic bishops of the Northwest in 2001 as well as the teaching of Pope Benedict XVI on the environment continue the reflection and dialogue.

Having grown up on an apple farm next to a fast-flowing river (the Methow) a few miles from the Columbia River in north central Washington, I find the continuing reflection, appreciation, and concern about the stewardship of our planet exciting and timely. There is nothing like the cycle of the river system, the climate, and the liturgical seasons that keep in touch with the magnificent world in which we live. We can only thank our Creator and take up our responsibility for this world in which we live.

— Bishop William S. Skylstad

ethical consideration, one of which was "Conserve and Protect Species of Wildlife."[61]

In this phase of analysis, the primary task of theological reflection is to examine and interpret the problem in light of *lived faith, biblical theology,* and *Christian social and environmental ethics*. In the case of salmon recovery, the challenge is to define the contextual meaning of stewardship and sacramentality and develop the specific ethical implications — norms — for guiding salmon recovery. In other words, the objective is to create an ethical framework for action that will guide salmon recovery and impact the creation of public policy to attain a measure of social and environmental justice. One concrete example of an ethical norm in salmon recovery would be to identify, preserve, and restore critical spawning habitats for salmon and steelhead, without which the species cannot survive.

Engage in Strategic Planning

The fourth movement of the *iterative-praxiological method* is the overall goal — to engage in strategic planning that promotes committed ethical engagement, political action, and sound public policy guided by the norms of social and environmental justice and the ethical horizon of sustainability. The strategic decisions that are made should impact the personal, private, and public sectors. At the personal level, the response to the salmon crisis for individuals includes a range of possible actions such as reducing or eliminating the use of pesticides and herbicides within one's watershed, buying locally produced organic and salmon-safe food, driving less, and participating in stream restoration opportunities. The private sector is institutional and may involve private homeowners, businesses, parishes, or universities that make collective choices to alter the culture of their enterprise in the direction of sustainability.

One such example that is gaining popularity in the Pacific Northwest and elsewhere is the decision of growing numbers of home and business owners to opt for "green power," energy that is produced by wind, geothermal, or solar facilities. Another good example at this level is the decision to build green according to standards set by groups such as the U.S. Green Building Council using LEED (Leadership in Energy and Environmental Design) criteria.

The public sector refers to actions taken by individuals and groups oriented to impact public policy in the area of salmon recovery. Such actions could include participation in or support for NGOs that lobby or litigate for sound salmon policy, voting, contacting one's congressional representatives, and participating in public hearings designed to elicit public response to policies about to be enacted. Stated differently, the public sector involves grassroots democratic action aimed at changing the status quo of salmon recovery by either preventing a worsening of the present situation or by improving the prospects of genuine salmon recovery in the Columbia Basin.

A particular strength of the iterative-praxiological method is that its flexibility makes it applicable to any environmental or social issue at the local, regional, national, or global level that a community of faith and action wishes to examine. It can be utilized by people in a parish, school, or university context who seek to impact their local ecology and social institutional structures. A key requirement of this method is ecological literacy. Consequently readers are invited, in the chapters that follow, to venture into the transdisciplinary sciences of ecology and environmental science to examine the basic principles and processes of ecology and the primary environmental issues of our day and age.

Questions for Discussion

1. What is your view of Lynn White's assertion that Christianity is the primary cause of the environmental crisis?

2. Does the relationship between religion and science differ from the relationship between religion and the social sciences such as economics, political science, anthropology, or sociology? Can you find support for your opinion by reading a local or national newspaper or from other media sources?

3. Is there an environmental issue in your local area or region that might be amenable to analysis using the iterative-praxiological method? If so, who are the stakeholders that might need to be consulted in the social analysis phase?

4. Choose an example of a topic that has caused conflict between science and religion and then research that topic in order to decide what led to the conflict and whether that conflict was inevitable, given the divergent perspectives involved.

Active Learning Exercises

- Select a non-Christian religion and research what has been written about the relationship between religion and science in that context. Find at least three independent sources for your writing, and produce a two-page paper citing materials appropriately. Relate what your research uncovers to the categories of religion-science interaction developed in chapter 2.

- Choose one of the following environmental issues and research it in your library and online using reputable sources. Include in your research the scientific, economic, theological, and ethical aspects of the issue. Write a two-page paper on how the relationship between science and theology has played out to date in terms of this issue. Topics to choose among are mountaintop removal coal mining, natural gas extraction via hydraulic fracturing, the development of genetically modified livestock, organic farming, and free trade coffee production.

Recommended Reading

The Columbia River Pastoral Letter Project, *The Columbia River Watershed: Caring for Creation and the Common Good, An International Pastoral Letter by the Catholic Bishops of the Region.* Seattle, Wash.: Columbia River Pastoral Letter Project, 2001.

Haught, John F. *God after Darwin: A Theology of Evolution.* Boulder, Colo.: Westview Press, 2000.

———. *Science and Religion: From Conflict to Conversation.* Mahwah, N.J.: Paulist Press, 1995.

Lichatowich, James. *Salmon without Rivers: A History of the Pacific Salmon Crisis.* Washington, D.C.: Island Press, 1999.

Merchant, Carolyn. *The Death of Nature: Women, Ecology and the Scientific Revolution.* San Francisco: Harper and Row, 1980.

Muir, John. *A Thousand-Mile Walk to the Gulf.* San Francisco: Sierra Club Books, 1991.

Wilkins, Thurman. *John Muir: Apostle of Nature.* Norman: University of Oklahoma Press, 1995.

Wilson, E. O. *The Creation: An Appeal to Save Life on Earth.* New York: W. W. Norton, 2006.

3

Ecological Foundations
for Environmental Science
Principles and Processes

It is generally accepted that one of the compelling characteristics of the twenty-first century is that humanity is at an ecological crossroads in its existence on this planet. Consequently, an understanding of ecological processes is essential both for achieving ecological literacy and for establishing rational public policy to conserve resources and develop a sustainable economy. Humans evolve and exist in the biosphere, the thin layer of life-supporting elements consisting of a mixture of air, water, plants, microbes, and animals with which humans interact and to which they are connected in intimate ways. Ecology is the examination of these ecosystems and the complex network of interactions among species and their biophysical environments. Ecology, therefore, provides insights into the nature of human relationships that impact and interact with the natural world.

Ecology and the Scientific Principles of Sustainability

Natural systems such as forests, oceans, lakes, and the atmosphere have been in decline for over two centuries due to the economic activities or simple thoughtlessness of human beings. During the late 1980s and early 1990s, this ecological degradation began to surface as an issue of great theological and ethical concern in a number of Christian denominations. Consider the following denominational statements and developments.

The American Baptist Churches, USA said in its *American Baptist Policy Statement on Ecology: An Ecological Situational Analysis* (1988) that "the study of ecology has become a religious, social, and political concern because every area of life is affected by careless use of our environment. The creation is in crisis. We believe that ecology and justice, stewardship of creation and redemption are interdependent."[1]

In 1990 the Presbyterian Church U.S.A. issued its institutional report, *Restoring Creation for Ecology and Justice,* stating that

Creation cries out in this time of ecological crisis.

+ Abuse of nature and injustice to people place the future in grave jeopardy.
+ Population triples in this century.
+ Biological systems suffer diminished capacity to renew themselves.
+ Finite minerals are mined and pumped as if inexhaustible.
+ Peasants are forced onto marginal lands, and soil erodes.
+ The rich-poor gap grows wider.
+ Wastes and poisons exceed nature's capacity to absorb them.
+ Greenhouse gases pose the threat of global warming.[2]

Also in 1990, representatives of Eastern Orthodox tradition, in *An Orthodox Statement on the Environmental Crisis,* declared:

> Throughout the world, forests are being destroyed by fires and logging; wetlands are being drained for development and agriculture; species are disappearing as a result of greed and ignorance; natural resources are being wasted faster than they are being replenished; waters are being soiled and skies polluted. The global crisis is threatening the very world upon which we human beings depend.[3]

In the Roman Catholic tradition, Pope John Paul II referred to "the ecological question" for the first time in Catholic social teaching (CST) in the papal encyclical *Centesimus Annus* (1991).[4] Discussing the impact of the consumption of resources and the destruction of the world's natural environment, the pope's inclusion of the "ecological question" into CST signaled an important evolution and expansion of CST and the growing influence of ecology on this body of social ethical teaching.

The "ecological question" as expressed from a scientific vantage point is a series of three questions:

1. What are the processes by which ecosystems naturally operate?
2. What is the current status of ecological systems worldwide, and at what rate are things changing due to the activities of human economies?
3. What would human social and economic activities have to look like for us to achieve a sustainable relationship with the natural world so that future generations will have sufficient resources to meet their needs and fulfill their human potential?

The first question will be addressed in this chapter, and the second question will be addressed in chapters 4 and 5. The final chapter of this book will discuss the third question and the issue of sustainability as a strategy for restructuring human systems to promote both the present common good and the common good of future generations.

Ecology: A Historical Retrospective

The science of ecology is transdisciplinary in the sense that it incorporates elements of biology, chemistry, geology, and physics. Its emergence as a field of study was a slow development over the course of approximately a century. Ecology is also integrative in the sense that it attempts to understand the dynamics of not one species, but an assemblage of species interacting in space and time. A historical "tour" of the origins of ecological thought will help to contextualize the current state of the science.

The word "ecology" was coined by Ernst Haeckel (1834–1919), an outspoken German proponent of Charles Darwin's theory of evolution. The word "ecology" is based on two ancient Greek words, *oikos* (a house or dwelling) and *logos* (ultimate truth, answer, principle, scientific knowledge). Haeckel's most widely cited definition of ecology is this:

> By ecology we mean the body of knowledge concerning the economy of nature — the investigation of the total relations of the animal both to its inorganic and its organic environment; including, above all, its friendly and inimical relations with those plants and animals with which it comes directly or indirectly into contact — in a word ecology is the study of all those complex interrelations referred to by Darwin as the conditions of the struggle for existence.[5]

The concept of an *ecological niche,* the set of habitat characteristics, including competitors, predators, food sources, and shelter needs of an organism, dates back to the early days of the twentieth century to a field biologist named Joseph Grinnell (1877–1939). Understanding niches has become crucial to understanding the effects of occurrences such as habitat loss and invasive species. In his classic paper describing the California thrasher's natural history, its relationships with other organisms, and the way they fit together to produce the assemblage of organisms known as a chaparral, Grinnell wrote:

> These various circumstances, which emphasize dependence upon cover, and adaptation in physical structure and temperament thereto, go to demonstrate the nature of the ultimate associational niche occupied by the California thrasher. This is one of the minor niches which with all of their occupants all together make up the chaparral association. It is, of course, axiomatic that no two species regularly established in a single fauna have precisely the same niche relationship.[6]

Defining Ecosystems

The origin of the concept of an *ecosystem,* in which groups of organisms are viewed as a whole system at a level above that of individual niches, goes back to A. G. Tansley (1871–1955), who observed in 1935 that the more fundamental conception is, as it seems to me, the whole *system* (in the sense of physics), including not only the organism-complex, but also the whole complex of physical factors forming what we call the ecology of the biome — the habitat factors in the widest sense....

It is the systems so formed which, from the point of view of the ecologist, are the basic units of nature on the face of the earth....

These *ecosystems,* as we may call them, are of the most various kinds and sizes.[7]

Related to understanding the concept of an *ecosystem* is a recognition of the *ecological services* that ecosystems provide. This notion has gained increasing appeal among some contemporary environmental scientists who, living in a commodity culture such as the United States, want to make a strong case for the value of preserving ecosystems. At first sight, the commercial value of ecosystems may not be obvious, so proponents highlight the essential "goods and services" of ecosystems upon which human existence is dependent.

A prime example is the supply of fresh drinking water that comes from intact watersheds whose surface water and aquifers have been protected from industrial or residential development. This is far less expensive water to provide to a community than drinking water that is the result of waste removal and filtration from contaminated rivers or polluted underground aquifers. This lesson has been learned from coast to coast in the United States, from the Croton and Catskill systems supplying much of the water for New York City, to the smaller Bull Run Reservoir on the slope of Mount Hood that supplies Portland, Oregon, with drinking water.

Building on Tansley's concept of an ecosystem, the notion of ecological services expresses the value of the long-term stability of ecosystems to humans, and the consequences of naively maximizing the short-term harvest rates of living resources. This concern was articulated in a broad sense by Eugene P. Odum (1913–2002), a leading figure in the development of modern ecology. In 1969, discussing the strategy of ecosystem development, he summarized the idea of ecological services:

Man has generally been preoccupied with obtaining as much "production" from the landscape as possible, by developing and maintaining early successional types of ecosystems, usually monocultures. But, of course, man does not live by food and fiber alone; he also needs a balanced CO_2-O_2 atmosphere, the climatic buffer provided by masses of vegetation and clean (that is, unproductive) water for cultural and industrial uses. Many essential life-cycle resources, not to mention recreational and esthetic needs, are best provided man by the less "productive" landscapes. In other words the landscape is not just a supply depot: it is also an *oikos* — the home — in which we must live. Until recently mankind has more or less taken for granted the gas-exchange, water-purification, nutrient-cycling, and other protective functions of self-maintaining ecosystems, chiefly because neither his numbers nor his environmental manipulations have been great enough to effect global and regional balances. Now, of course, it is painfully evident that such balances are being affected, often detrimentally. The "one problem, one solution approach" is no longer adequate and must be replaced by some sort of ecosystem analysis that considers man as a part of, not apart from, the environment.[8]

Society needs, and must find as quickly as possible, a way to deal with the landscape as a whole, so that manipulative skills (that is, technology) will not run too far ahead of our understanding of the impact of change.[9]

Ecosystems and ecosystem services are dependent on flows of energy and nutrients from one organism to another in an ecosystem. The presence of a healthy level of biodiversity, typical of an intact ecosystem, provides a level of stability that protects the ecosystem as a whole against natural fluctuations in things like temperature and rainfall, or from anthropogenic stresses like pollution, to which some species will always be far more susceptible than others. G. Evelyn Hutchinson (1903–1991), the great British-American ecologist, recognized the inter-species relationship of *food webs* a half a century ago:

Biological communities do not consist of independent food chains, but of food webs, of such a kind that an individual at any level (corresponding to a link in a single chain) can use some but not all of the food provided by species in the levels below it. It has long been realized that the presence of two species at any level, either of which can be eaten by a predator at a level above, but which may differ in palatability, ease of capture or seasonal and local abundance, may provide alternative foods for the predator. The predator will therefore neither become extinct itself nor exterminate its usual prey, when for any reason, not dependent on predator-prey relationships, the usual prey happen to be abnormally scarce.[10]

Modern ecological theory therefore appears to answer our initial question at least partially by saying that there is a great diversity of organisms because communities of many diversified organisms are better able to persist than are communities of fewer less diversified organisms.[11]

The Impact of *Silent Spring*

In our contemporary world, energy and nutrients are not the only things flowing from one organism to another in an ecosystem; environmental contaminants derived by the uptake of pollutants into plant and animal bodies also flow freely throughout the ecosystem. Rachel Carson's classic work *Silent Spring,* published in 1962, was a defining national moment when growing numbers of U.S. citizens became aware of the extent and implications of toxic exposure. It was the moment we realized that substances like pesticides travel easily from one organism to another in a way that is particularly dangerous for meat-eating animals. *Silent Spring* can be called the moment when the environmental movement was born. Carson (1907–1964) observed:

> These sprays, dusts, and aerosols are now applied almost universally to farms, gardens, forests, and homes — nonselective chemicals that have the power to kill every insect, the "good" and the "bad," to still the song of birds and the leaping of fish in the streams, to coat the leaves with a deadly film, and to linger on in soil — all this though the intended target may be only a few weeds or insects. Can anyone believe it is possible to lay down such a barrage of poisons on the surface of the earth without making it unfit for all life? They should not be called "insecticides," but "biocides."[12]

In 1964, two years after the publication of *Silent Spring*, Rachel Carson died of breast cancer at the age of fifty-six. Her death was prior to the publication of articles linking ongoing exposure to the use of certain pesticides, including dieldrin and DDT, to both breast cancer rates and the aggressiveness of breast cancer tumors.[13] In spite of her early death, Carson, along with those who preceded and succeeded her, made major contributions to the evolving shape and disciplinary context of ecology and environmental science.

The Relationship of Ecology and Environmental Science

While ecology grew as a study of species interactions, matter and energy flows, niches, relationships between the biotic and abiotic world, the behavior of species assemblages, and so forth, environmental science grew as a response to the need to understand deteriorating ecosystemic functions caused by human activities. The study of environmental science requires the mastery of the fundamentals of natural ecology before it can turn to the anthropogenically driven deviations from the normal state.

Environmental science was not wholeheartedly embraced by ecology and, as the new transdisciplinary science emerged, it was first considered an "applied" field rather than a pure science. Gradually, it became clear that if there were to be natural ecosystems to study, then environmental scientists were needed to study, comprehend, and hopefully help design plans to counteract various aspects of ecosystemic deterioration. Today environmental science is a field in its own right that builds upon the principles of ecology to develop new principles that come from the observation and modeling of a rapidly changing world. Ecology itself now has developed into a number of subspecialties, including population ecology, community ecology, and ecosystem ecology, but all are based on the same fundamental principles, and these fields are all in fruitful conversation with environmental science.

A significant issue in the study of ecology is the simple fact that the ecological health of the planet is in serious decline due to human activity. The relationship between widespread ecological deterioration and human actions has been conceptualized in a variety of ways by different authors. Murray Bookchin's coinage of the term "social ecology" inaugurated a school of thought that explains the environmental crisis as a product of human domination over nature, which in turn stems from a society in which humans dominate one another.[14] According to this school of thought, widespread and thorough political transformation is the sine qua non for humanity to find a path that leads away from a downward spiral of ecological loss after loss.

A different approach to the relationship between ecological problems and human society is that of "human ecology," an interdisciplinary movement that brings together geographers, biologists, communications scientists, economists, sociologists, and others to provide diverse perspectives on various elements of our ecological crisis.[15] A good example of this field of ecological research is the perspective developed by Frederick Steiner.[16] Steiner's model of human ecology includes units or levels of human habitation and social experience beginning with one's local habitat and extending outward to encompass community, landscape, region (bioregion or ecoregion), nation-state, and ultimately the entire planet. It is Steiner's view that each of these realms of human experience ought to be considered independent yet interrelated ecosystems.[17] We will provide a visualization of Steiner's model and utilize it more fully in chapter 8, when we discuss in depth the meaning of sustainability. Throughout this book we favor the use of the term "human ecology" to provide the broadest basis for discussion, and to ensure that the necessity of social transformation is not ignored.

Ecosystems and Toxins

Arctic predators like polar bears suffer from the *biomagnifications* of toxins used elsewhere on the planet, including PCBs, DDT, PAHs (polycyclic aromatic hydrocarbons), and others that make up the modern toxic cocktail resulting from industrial processes and inadequate waste treatment. *Bioaccumulation* results when toxic chemicals or heavy metals taken in by animals through their food supplies accumulate in their bodies, generally in their fatty tissues but also in their bones and skin. The related problem of *biomagnification* refers to the progressive increase in the concentration of these persistent toxins in animals as they ascend a food chain. A fish, for example, may contain the persistent toxins from all of the plankton it has eaten, but a seal will contain the persistent toxins from the bodies of all the fish it has eaten, and a polar bear eating that seal will contain a magnified concentration corresponding to the sums of the toxins located lower on the food chain.

This problem occurs in large part because the synthetic organic compounds invented by humans over the last century are typically fat-soluble. Animals are very efficient at absorbing fatty materials from food, allowing them to efficiently gather energy and fat-soluble vitamins, and fat-soluble chemicals in food pass rapidly into body fat. Biological mechanisms can remove water-soluble toxins from our bodies (for example, mixed function oxidases in the liver, selective secretion into urine), but there is no effective way to remove fat-soluble toxins from our bodies. As a result of biomagnification, people eating a meat- and fish-rich diet typical in the United States, like polar bears eating a carnivorous diet in the Arctic, are often exposed to potentially dangerous levels of persistent toxins.

In addition *pathways of exposure* to toxins go beyond what we eat to include exposure by breathing and the consumption of water. Various toxins are taken in across the permeable linings of our lungs when we inhale, through our stomach or intestines as we absorb digested food, and in some cases directly through our skin when toxin molecules can effectively penetrate our body surface.

This leads to related discussions of issues such as the increase in cancer rates among the children of farm workers exposed to pesticides at home. Similarly, people in North America's "cancer alleys" such as areas of Louisiana and the Great Lakes region are impacted by exposure to industrial pollutants like polyvinyl chloride. Lead exposure for poor inner-city children also has neurodevelopmental consequences. This troubling phenomenon of health consequences of toxin exposure is treated at length in chapter 5.

Watersheds

The surface of the Earth's landmass is divided into areas whose topography determines that they share stream and river drainage for water running downhill toward lakes and oceans. Such drainage basins are referred to as *watersheds*. A number of distinctive biological communities exist within a watershed. One common pattern is grassy uplands that give way to forested riparian zones along rivers that are bound together by the common flow of water, life's most fundamental molecule. Humans have settled and developed their large population centers along coastlines, lakes, and rivers, depending on the availability of water for drinking, transportation, industry, irrigation, and waste disposal. Urban growth challenges watersheds around the world, as megacities place huge demands on watersheds that are no longer adequate to meet the needs of ever-growing populations.

The operation of the hydrological (water) cycle is by *evaporation* of water vapor (mostly from the oceans), *condensation* into clouds, *precipitation* as rain or snow or sleet, *runoff* as the precipitated water moves back downhill toward the ocean, and *accumulation* that traps some of the runoff in shallow or deep groundwater. There is only so much fresh water on Earth: rivers can flow only if they have snowmelt or rain to do so, and aquifers recharge at a finite rate regardless of how quickly water is drawn from them for irrigation or drinking.

Watersheds are locally bounded by the terrain and limited by the amount of precipitation falling. Consideration of a watershed's level is crucial, as damaging modifications to one part of a watershed inevitably reverberate throughout the rest of it. Such consideration has generally not been present in the United States, as is shown by the dropping levels of the Colorado River reservoirs that supply water to the agriculturally rich Central Valley of California and the rapidly expanding population of Las Vegas. As the National Research Council of the National Academy of Sciences says,

> Managing water resources at the watershed scale, while difficult, offers the potential of balancing the many, sometimes competing, demands we place on water resources. The watershed approach acknowledges linkages between uplands and downstream areas and between surface and groundwater, and it reduces the chance that attempts to solve problems in one realm will cause problems in others. Watershed management is an integrative way of thinking about all the various human activities that occur on a given area of land (the watershed) that have effects on or [are] affected by water. With this perspective, we can plan long-term, sustainable solutions to many natural resource problems. We can find a better balance between meeting today's needs and leaving a sound resource legacy for generations to come.[18]

Biogeochemical Cycles

The cycles of molecules crucial to life such as carbon (C), nitrogen (N), and phosphorus (P) involve chemistry, biology, and physics interacting on local, regional, and global scales. Human activities have begun to imbalance these cycles. Early local consequences of these imbalances, such as the *eutrophication* (the presence of excessive nutrients) of lakes due to excess N and P from fertilizer use or sewage effluent, have progressed to biogeochemical imbalances on a global scale. Examples include rapidly developing dead zones in oceans, increases in the frequency and severity of blooms of toxic algae worldwide, and the many expressions of global climate change. Imbalanced biogeochemical cycles are now among the most serious threats to our ability to continue as a civilization.

Biogeochemical cycles are complicated. For example, in the carbon cycle, atmospheric carbon present in the form of CO_2 is absorbed by plants in the process of photosynthesis and ingested by animals when they eat plants or other animals. All living organisms release CO_2 as they carry out the metabolic activities that support their lives, and the great majority inhale O_2 and exhale CO_2 as a waste.

CO_2 is also released to the atmosphere when we burn fossil fuels in our homes or industries or for transportation, when we engage in slash-and-burn agriculture in the tropics, when we burn wood as a heating fuel, when cement is drying, and in many other circumstances. Historically, atmospheric CO_2 levels were 280 parts per million (ppm); at the time of this writing they are approximately 392 ppm. This is due to an anthropogenically induced carbon imbalance related to our industry and consumption levels. This is just one example of the operation of a biogeochemical cycle; other important cycles exist for nitrogen, phosphorus, and other materials.

Inherent to these cycles is the concept of limitations. For example, the ocean can absorb only so much N and P before those near-shore oceanic areas where large rivers drain start to seasonally, episodically, or permanently lack oxygen (referred to as anoxia or hypoxia). Likewise, the atmosphere can absorb only so much carbon dioxide (CO_2) before global mean temperatures increase, disrupting Earth's climate.

These biogeophysical limitations have ethical consequences relating to human population, consumption, and waste. The use of fertilizers in one area ultimately affects the N and P levels in the global ocean, and the use of fossil fuels in one country affects the global climate. Questions of human rights emerge as we enter into discussions of biological necessities, appropriate levels of consumption, and the market economy as a global player. These issues will be explored below.

Trophic Pyramids

Life on Earth is ultimately based on solar energy. Plants get their energy from photosynthesis, which requires carbon dioxide, water, chlorophyll, and sunlight. Animals get their energy by eating other animals or plants. As organisms ascend *trophic levels* (the positions they occupy on the food chain) from autotroph (self-feeding, meaning organisms that are photosynthetic) to herbivore, to carnivore, to top carnivore, the available energy diminishes greatly, and each level contains less living material overall than the previous one. This is true in natural ecosystems such as forests and grasslands and in the human-managed systems of farms and orchards. The higher up the trophic level an organism is, the smaller the proportion of the solar energy originally captured in photosynthesis is present.

The loss of energy as we go from one trophic level to another has consequences for human dietary choices. Beef requires 13 kilograms of grain and 30 kilograms of forage per kilogram of meat produced, while broiler chickens require 2.3 kilograms of grain per kilogram of meat. Additionally, beef production requires 57 kilocalories (kcal) of fossil fuel for each kcal of food gained, while broiler chickens have a 4:1 ratio.

The United States grows slightly under 40 million hectares of corn and roughly 25 million hectares of soybeans. A little over half of the corn we grow goes into animal feed. Over half of the soybeans grown in the United States are crushed for soymeal and oil, and approximately 90 percent of the soymeal produced goes into livestock feed to produce meat.[19] The Food and Agriculture Organization of the United Nations (FAO) estimates that cattle-rearing and processing accounts for 18 percent of global greenhouse gas emissions.[20] A lacto-ovo-vegetarian diet of dairy, eggs, and plants also requires animal feed, but about half as much as a meat-heavy American diet. Humans need to consider the implications of trophic levels and available energy in terms of our production of higher trophic-level food sources, such as grain-fed cattle or farmed salmon fed on fish pellets.

The Carrying Capacity of Ecosystems

The carrying capacity of an area is the number of individuals of a given species that the area can support indefinitely. Only a certain number of blue jays can find sufficient food and shelter and nest sites in a stand of trees. Ultimately, the movement of energy into the living world through photosynthesis, the flow of energy through food webs, and nonliving factors like precipitation and temperature combine to produce carrying capacities that are characteristic and stable within a normal range of variation. Carrying capacity obviously depends on a wide array of factors, such as the food supply, the water supply, the availability of shelter, and so forth. As organisms become overly numerous, an array of density-dependent factors produces increased death rates, reduces population levels, and returns the number of individuals to a supportable level. Such density-dependent mortality factors include lack of food, lack of water, increased spread of diseases and parasites, accumulation of waste products, lack of shelter, and increasing populations of predators.

Human beings are not immune to these carrying-capacity dynamics. With a present global population of nearly 7 billion human beings, Earth itself has an ultimate carrying capacity. The answer to the question of how rapidly we are approaching that point is complex, and it includes our birth rates, death rates, and the rates of resource consumption. Consumption of natural resources by humans in the Northern Hemisphere, with typically low birth rates, far exceeds the rate of consumption of people living in the developing Southern Hemisphere. The number of people the Earth can support with our negative ecological impact is not determined just by population levels, but also by how many resources we consume individually and jointly. Technological advances can increase our supplies of food, fuel, fiber, and other necessities, but they cannot be increased infinitely, nor without significant costs in terms of pollution and the loss of natural landscapes.

These are serious ecological and ethical issues; however, they are not reasons to anticipate a bleak future. In this regard, we can look for inspiration to the long Mennonite tradition of crossing the boundaries of the practical and the conceptual, as exemplified by Doris Janzen Longacre's *Living More with Less* and her *More-with-Less Cookbook*,[21] which has already celebrated its twenty-fifth anniversary and insists on bringing the joy of life into solving environmental issues. These works indicate how it is possible to reduce our resource consumption to leave more for others without falling into the trap of envisioning a dim future.

Longacre says, "Cutting back sounds like a dismal prospect. 'Let's splurge just this once' appeals more to North American ears. Put dismal thoughts aside then, because this book is not about cutting back. This book is about living joyfully, richly, and creatively."[22] Longacre exemplifies the Mennonite belief that resource conservation and a zest for life need not be strangers. We can take heart from this perspective and its assumption that human beings can alter our carrying capacity by intentional living, something no other species on the planet could conceivably achieve.

Habitats and Human Development

Habitat continuity and structure is one of the less obvious elements of natural ecosystem function. For example, we take it for granted that woods and forests occur in certain shapes and areas, that rivers have certain courses, and this all seems self-evident rather than profound or significant. Human activities (draining wetlands, straightening stream courses, urban sprawl, cutting down trees, clearing fields for agricultural use, road construction, and so on) diminish the surface area in which natural communities exist and also fragment and alter the shape of existing natural areas.

What results is frequently unconnected "puzzle pieces" that no longer fit together with the connectivity and structure needed for animal migration. On the land, these separated pieces of natural habitat take on many of the characteristics of oceanic islands, with areas of impassible terrain (instead of water) separating them. As habitat fragments grow smaller, species diversity declines. Organisms that require a large home range for foraging or extensive migratory movements lose the ability to complete their life cycles.

In river systems this decrease or fragmentation can be expressed by the loss of side channels to agricultural land and navigation, as in the Willamette River in Oregon. While it looks normal enough to a casual observer, the total area of river channels and islands actually decreased from forty-one thousand acres in 1850 to twenty-three thousand acres in 1995. Much of its structure was removed as side channels and wetlands were converted to farms, and channel alterations were made for the sake of navigation.[23]

The Willamette River is now far less hospitable to migrating salmon, a true regional icon, which have few remaining places to rest or seek refuge from the main channel. There is much debate about optimal habitat fragment size when ecosystem reserves are being set aside for species conservation. It is generally true that as habitat "patches" become larger the number of species they contain increases. Nonetheless, knowledge of the distributions of local species and the use of migration corridors in any area is crucial when reserves are being designed or stream modifications contemplated.

SOIL EROSION

Soil erosion is a crucial environmental challenge that results from many of the issues raised here. Soil erosion is increased by climatic instability, since both floodwaters caused by excessive rainfall and wind erosion associated with droughts cause the loss of productive soils. Large-scale industrial agriculture that involves heavy farm machinery is often associated with the removal of shelterbelts of trees between farm fields, which would help reduce both rain- and wind-driven erosion on smaller fields; similarly, shelterbelts could provide small patches of habitat that would help preserve biodiversity in farming regions.

Consuming a typical American meat-heavy diet requires that much more grain be grown, putting additional pressure on both soil and freshwater resources. Livestock allowed to trample stream banks as they access drinking water greatly accelerate the rate of stream-bank erosion. The conversion of tropical forests into farmland to meet the demand of developed nations for meat exposes soils and increases erosion. Excessive use of herbicides and pesticides can leave a toxic legacy in the soil. In addition, once a cycle of agrochemical use has begun, increasingly impoverished soil loses its natural fertility and needs more and more chemical applications to retain the very high levels of productivity required for industrial agriculture.

In forested parts of the world, lumber operations often clear-cut trees, leaving the soil exposed to rapid erosive loss. The demand for timber products, including wood and paper, is shaped by a consumer society that annually asks for ever-larger houses and more disposable paper and cardboard products.

Farming on steeper slopes or marginal lands — as population growth forces an increasing number of subsistence farmers into areas that previous generations would have considered unsuitable — accelerates the degradation of the land and soil loss. Human population levels and resource-consumption rates that are out of balance with regional land and water resources need to be brought back into balance, and an economic bridge must be built to provide the resources needed by the population.

In summary, if either human population levels or resource utilization rates grow unchecked beyond the capacity of the Earth to support them, soil erosion will prove to be merely one intractable problem among many. However, taking the steps outlined in chapter 8 to move toward sustainability can greatly reduce soil erosion.

A good example of habitat modification involves the winter habitat of the monarch butterfly. Monarch butterflies migrate long distances (up to three thousand miles) in the fall, and butterflies from the states east of the Rocky Mountains winter primarily in an area of oyamel fir and mixed fir-pine forest ecosystem in central Mexico, where specific conditions of altitude and humidity allow them to survive the winter in densities up to 25 million monarchs per acre. The specific areas in which monarchs can survive the winter are very limited, and the region has been rapidly logged over the last forty years, despite receiving legal protection from the Mexican government. What was once a continuous forest that offered a stable area containing a suitable overwintering habitat has become a series of large logged areas containing small islands of hospitable conditions, each one vulnerable to rapid change because of its small size.

As of 2008, the majority of the overwintering eastern monarchs were limited to an area of approximately 12.5 acres. The butterflies also face challenges from development of natural areas in the United States, but the most dramatic threat to their survival is the reduction of their overwintering habitat to a series of isolated retreats, any of which could be decimated in a short time by illegal loggers.[24] It would be a great loss if there were no more monarch butterflies in the eastern United States, although habitat degradation and fragmentation have made that a real possibility.

Energy Consumption: Renewable and Nonrenewable Sources

There is a perpetual balance in the energy use and flow in natural ecosystems (as already noted in the sections on ecological niches, the ecosystem concept, and trophic pyramids) between the energy captured from solar radiation by photosynthesis and the energy utilized in a variety of niches at a variety of trophic levels in an ecosystem. The balance of this process can sometimes include the added complication of biomass, which accumulates as large masses of deceased organisms are not immediately decomposed. An example of this is the enormous layers of planktonic algal remains that sink to the sea floor, are buried at great depth and pressure for millions of years, and eventually are converted into underground petroleum deposits. Similar processes are the sources of coal and natural gas.

When humans entered the equation, at first their sources of energy were part of the normal balance in an ecosystem, such as burning wood for heating and cooking or utilizing windmills or watermills for mechanical energy (originating in solar power converted into air or water currents). Over time people found the long-buried deposits of what we call fossil fuels and began to exploit them at a very rapid pace. This has disrupted ecosystems worldwide. The present imbalance in the carbon cycle has already been noted, and its implications will be discussed later at greater length. This disruption results from using fuel on such a large scale that it does not participate in the typical short-term mass and energy balance of the world. It may be that humans will manage to return to energy sources that are part of the typical short-term balance of energy input from the sun to the earth (wind power, solar power, tidal power, ocean thermal-energy conversion, hydroelectric power) to prevent further damage to the ecosystem. We may also turn to power sources that are not part of the short-term planetary energy balance at all, but that would not unbalance biogeochemical cycles; such sources might include geothermal power, nuclear fission, or nuclear fusion. It is important to consider how these possibilities may relate to energy balances in our ecosystems.

What Is Environmental Sustainability?

The ecological principles outlined above are essential characteristics of a scientific understanding of sustainability, and such environmental sustainability includes concerns related to human ecology as well as natural ecosystems. The following definition of environmental sustainability builds upon an earlier definition of ecological sustainability, but incorporates various elements of human-ecosystem interactions.[25]

Defined environmentally, a sustainable situation exists when an ecosystem's energy flows and nutrient cycles are stable or fluctuating within a normal range of variability; when the species diversity and population levels of organisms are robust and self-supporting; when habitat diversity and the areas and connections of natural habitats allow organisms to carry out all stages of their life cycles; when toxic man-made materials or materials extracted from the Earth's crust are not accumulating in the soil, air, or water; and when ancient energy sources derived from long-deposited and converted biomass are not destabilizing ecosystems through climate change.

Constraints on energy consumption are crucial to environmental sustainability. Human expenditures of energy for transportation, housing, industry, agriculture, and so forth exceed the energy flows of other organisms in the ecosystem. Human energy use produces the greatest imbalance, driving ecosystems toward instability. The preservation or nondeterioration of ecosystems is the hallmark of ecological sustainability.

Even a slow rate of progressive, directional deterioration will eventually overwhelm the capacity of any natural ecosystem to regulate its crucial characteristics within acceptable limits. Slow environmental changes often pass unnoticed because in any one year they are modest; however, an imperceptible downward creep soon produces a shifting baseline that lessens our impression of the significance of the environmental deterioration that has taken place.[26] Over time this becomes what has been called *environmental generational amnesia,* in which every human generation in its youth observes the present stage of the environment, takes it as normal, and interprets future environmental decline against the standard of what is an already degraded starting condition.[27] Only a strict adherence to the principle of environmental nondeterioration can prevent this process from occurring.

Nevertheless, as crucial as the ecological understanding of sustainability is, the whole picture is incomplete without due consideration of human societies and economies and the largely detrimental impact of human activities on natural systems. The human demand and impact on Earth's ecosystems has been referred to as the *human ecological footprint*. First introduced by William Rees in 1992, this concept was further developed by Mathis Wackernagel in his doctoral dissertation at the University of British Columbia in Vancouver. The concept of an ecological footprint has emerged as one of the primary ways of measuring human consumption and its ecological effects, and it is a major component of sustainability analysis.[28] This concept will be discussed in some detail in the next chapter along with the ways humans impact the natural world.

Questions for Discussion

1. How should the concept of carrying capacity be used to inform public policy debates related to environmental issues?

2. Complex systems like biogeochemical cycles play a key role in the environmental crisis. Discuss how this complexity impedes public discussions and what might be done to ameliorate the situation.

3. Should political boundaries between entities like counties and states be redrawn along the lines of watersheds?

4. Is there a true ethical imperative to eat with trophic levels in mind because of the hunger in the world? Do you think that would make any difference?

Active Learning Exercises

♦ Find out what watershed you live in, using the U.S. Environmental Protection Agency's Surf Your Watershed website (*http://cfpub.epa.gov/ surf/locate/index.cfm*). Follow the initial link to see what citizens groups are doing in your watershed, what local environmental websites exist that focus on your watershed, and any assessments of watershed health. Write a two-page reflection on your own watershed and anything you learned about it.

Recommended Reading

Dodson, Stanley I., et al. *Readings in Ecology.* Oxford: Oxford University Press, 1999.

Hawken, Paul. *The Ecology of Commerce.* New York: HarperCollins, 1993.

Leonard, Annie. *The Story of Stuff: How Our Obsession with Stuff Is Trashing the Planet, Our Communities, and Our Health — and a Vision for Change.* New York: Free Press, 2010.

4

The Impact of People
on Ecological Processes
The Harm We Do

A significant issue in contemporary U.S. culture is our apparent inability to discriminate between "needs" and "wants." If we focused our chemical industry, for example, on developing and testing materials we *need* to produce food, fiber, medications, vital metals, and plastics, we would be monitoring a much more reasonable number of novel compounds than the estimated seventy-five thousand in use today. The multiplication of materials being quickly invented to meet the apparently insatiable appetites of excessive consumerism means that we never invest the needed time or resources to consider the consequences of what we synthesize, manufacture, and distribute. Our accelerating consumption potentially poisons us as well as others. Although our consumer goods do not always need to possess the newest metallic colors or LED displays, we have allowed ourselves to be convinced that they do.

Accelerating rates of *consumption* in the Western world and the use of Western society as an economic model for the rest of the planet that determines what is appropriate to consume have unintended consequences as human populations increase in most regions and affluence increases in some areas. The excessive consumption of resources in industrialized societies, which generally have low population growth rates, mean that these regions of the world reap economic benefits through their access to inexpensive goods. Environmental consequences result. These consequences often strike in distant locations, perhaps from where natural resources are being harvested at unsupportable rates, or where the cheapest possible manufacturing processes are used, usually emitting toxins as they produce goods for export. In the West, consumption must be moderated in order to ameliorate the environmental crisis both here and around the world.

High *population growth rates* in regions like sub-Saharan Africa and parts of Asia pose their own challenge to the planet. In those areas, where population may be doubling every twenty or thirty years, people are often living at subsistence levels already, with drinkable water, farmland, firewood, and other resources increasingly scarce. People in these regions cannot decrease their per capita consumption rates significantly, nor can they continue to grow exponentially in their human populations without devastating their local ecologies. Consequently many human communities in Africa, Latin America, and parts of Asia entrapped in a spiral of poverty exemplify the egregious disparity between the world's haves and have-nots.

Moreover, these same populations are extremely vulnerable to a range of environmental problems such as a lack of adequate water resources, deforestation, desertification, and climate change. Take climate change as an example. In *Climate Change 2007,* the Working Group II of the Inter-governmental Panel on Climate Change (IPCC) identified Africa, Asia, and Latin America as those continents containing human communities extremely vulnerable to the negative impacts of climate change and the least able to adapt.[1] The true irony — and injustice — of climate change is that the wealthy of the world produce the vast majority of greenhouse gases and the poor of the world will suffer the greatest consequences.

The ecological impact of a regional population of humans, what we defined in the last chapter as the human ecological footprint, is the product of their numbers multiplied by their individual *consumption rates.* As indicated above, many people living at subsistence levels have far less impact on the planet's air, water, soil, and other natural resources than a few people with an excessive lifestyle. Areas of the globe, including much of North America and Europe, are peopled by societies making enormous demands on a finite global ecosystem as their homes get larger, their cars become bigger, their fashions become more quickly outmoded, and the baseline of appropriate consumption levels creeps insidiously upward. While fifty years ago groups of people were generally referred to as "citizens," now the term generally used is "consumers." These societies must seriously question the culture of "supersizing," based on the generally unspoken premise that increasing rates of consumption are themselves a good thing.

Steps toward recycling, reuse, reduction of demand and consumption, and elimination of waste are needed as economically developed nations strive to become sustainable, that is, to learn how to live more naturally without impoverishing the future. Our dominant economic models are predicated on continual growth in consumption to provide an engine that drives human progress upward and that increases employment, productivity, and afflu-ence. However, these models, strikingly nonecological in their nature, are unsustainable in a finite world.

As noted in the previous chapter, ecosystems are stable because the flows of energy, water, and nutrients are maintained within normal ranges of fluctuation. The *illusion of unlimited economic growth* is based on the premise that an infinitely increasing rate of productivity and the concomi-tant waste production are compatible with a finite global supply of natural resources. Our technological prowess can increase our efficiency of using resources, but it cannot make more air, water, or sunlight. The model pro-vided by overconsuming societies poses a dual threat to ecosystems and to global political stability. Unfortunately, most impoverished societies aspire to emulate over-consuming societies in what they eat and how they live, and this compounds both threats.

If we accept Eugene Odum's observations, noted previously, we as a species have never recognized the complexity of our ecosystems, including the essential services they provide. We have failed to acknowledge the vital need to conserve both living and nonliving ecosystem components for long-term stability, as well as the results of partitioning the world haphazardly by our development activities.

Some environmental impacts are obvious and relatively simple, and some are difficult to discern and complicated. *Biodiversity loss* is sometimes obvious, as, for example, when forests suddenly disappear due to development, and sometimes more subtly as small habitat losses from one year to the next constitute a silent and gradual decline in the variety of plants and animals that share the Earth with us. We have taken for granted that the air will remain breathable, that water will run fresh and clear, that birds will return in the spring, and salmon will return to spawn. If this has not been true in our communities or in our region, we have believed that it was true somewhere.

Today, though, the views of our planet from space show that our complacency is misplaced. *Energy use* and *climate change,* linked like dancers in the history of the twentieth century, have caused energy use in the twenty-first century to become a crucial concern for the continuity of human society. Much of the Northern Hemisphere glows at night as our cities sprawl, while the tropical forests diminish and burn as slash-and-burn agriculture spreads into what were strongholds of rainforest. Meanwhile, microscopic samples of ocean water show algal diversity declining, and our fish communities are diminished as jellyfish and other "inedible" forms replace over-fished commercially valuable species. We must become intentionally engaged with planning and economic activities at every level from the local to the global if the irreplaceable ecosystem services upon which our lives rely are to continue unabated.

Crucial to success in this venture is the realization that human ecology has implications at a progression of levels, from small geographic units to continents. The planning process must be integrated both vertically and horizontally in order to achieve sustainability. This is challenging but comprehensible — and achievable — whether we are planning a new park, a power plant, or a reservoir.

The extraordinary magnitude of our impact on the planet has not gone unnoticed by scientists. In 2002 the Nobel prize–winning chemist Paul Crutzen suggested that, due to the human impact on global ecology, we were leaving the Holocene period (the "recent" geological epoch including the roughly ten to twelve thousand years since the end of the last ice age) and entering the Anthropocene epoch of geologic time (an epoch in which human alterations of the planet have become so dominant that a new era named after our influence is appropriate). While the new term circulated informally within scientific literature for a time, a group of geologists, members of the Stratigraphy Commission of the Geological Society of London, published an essay in 2008 — "Are We Now Living in the Anthropocene?" — in which they argued that the evidence requires serious discussions about formalizing the term Anthropocene. Basing their observations on such scientific criteria as carbon cycle perturbation, a collapse of biodiversity, and ocean changes, the geologists concluded that "sufficient evidence has emerged of stratigraphically significant change (both elapsed and imminent) for the recognition of the Anthropocene — currently a vivid yet informal metaphor of global environmental change — as a new geological epoch to be considered for formalization."[2]

We turn now to a summary of scientific research on the most important human impacts on the ecology of the planet: in other words, the specific results of the human ecological footprint. What were once local or regional environmental problems have — in the last 150 years — taken on global dimensions. We begin with what is arguably the most serious threat to human and planetary well-being — the reality of global climate change.

Climate Change

The initial warning that carbon dioxide (CO_2) levels in the atmosphere were increasing took place over half a century ago. Dr. Charles David Keeling (1928–2005) began to measure atmospheric CO_2 levels in 1958 at Mauna Loa in Hawaii. When he began his work, atmospheric CO_2 was roughly 315 parts per million (ppm);[3] within a few years he demonstrated that the hypothesis of increasing CO_2 levels annually was supported, by means of his upward moving "Keeling Curve," now having reached roughly 392 ppm. Despite the obvious importance of a shifting global atmosphere, Keeling had to struggle to maintain funding to continue the project, which he did, despite one short gap from February to April of 1964. Such measurements continue to be taken today.

In 1981, James Hansen of the NASA Goddard Institute for Space Studies published an article in the journal *Science,* which presented data about global climate change. The paper stated in part that

> The global temperature rose 0.2°C between the middle 1960s and 1980, yielding a warming of 0.4°C in the past century. This temperature increase is consistent with the calculated effect due to measured increases of atmospheric carbon dioxide. . . . The anthropogenic carbon dioxide warming should emerge from the noise level of natural climate variability by the end of the century, and there is a high probability of warming in the 1980s. Potential effects on climate in the twenty-first century include the creation of drought-prone regions in North America and central Asia as part of a shifting of climatic zones, erosion of

the West Antarctic ice sheet with a consequent worldwide rise in sea level, and opening of the fabled Northwest Passage.[4]

Between 1984 and 1988 Hansen testified to the U.S. Senate on three occasions about the significance of global climate change. On the twentieth anniversary of his first testimony, speaking to the House Select Committee on Energy Independence and Global Warming, Hansen recalled the significance of his 1988 testimony:

> On 23 June 1988 I testified to a hearing, chaired by Senator Tim Wirth of Colorado, that the Earth had entered a long-term warming trend and that human-made greenhouse gases almost surely were responsible. I noted that global warming enhanced both extremes of the water cycle, meaning stronger droughts and forest fires, on the one hand, but also heavier rains and floods.[5]

In 1988, Hansen and his coworkers published more detailed predictions derived from modeling in the *Journal of Geophysical Research* in an article that can only be considered prescient today. They stated in part:

> The greenhouse warming should be clearly identifiable in the 1990s; the global warming within the next several years is predicted to reach and maintain a level at least three standard deviations above the climatology of the 1950s.... Regions where an unambiguous warming appears earliest are low-latitude oceans, China and interior areas in Asia, and ocean areas near Antarctica and the north pole.... The temperature changes are sufficiently large to have major impacts on people and other parts of the biosphere.... During the late 1980s and the 1990s there is a tendency for greater than average warming in the southeastern United States and much of Europe.[6]

Hansen summarized twenty years of nonprogress on global climate change in his 2008 House of Representatives testimony. He declared:

> The difference is that now we have used up all slack in the schedule for actions needed to defuse the global warming time bomb. The next president and Congress must define a course next year in which the United States exerts leadership commensurate with our responsibility for the present dangerous situation.
>
> Otherwise it will become impractical to constrain atmospheric carbon dioxide, the greenhouse-gas produced in burning fossil fuels, to a level that prevents the climate system from passing tipping points that lead to disastrous climate changes that spiral dynamically out of humanity's control. Changes needed to preserve creation, the planet on which civilization developed, are clear. But the changes have been blocked by special interests, focused on short-term profits, who hold sway in Washington and other capitals.[7]

Twenty years ago Hansen's warnings could have prevented many of the consequences already caused by global climate change. Today Hansen's warnings might still be able to prevent the loss of coastal regions where millions of humans live, the long-term destabilization of drinking water supplies as we lose the summer melts of glaciers that provide this necessity to much of humanity, and the loss of tens of thousands of species as their natural habitats alter and disappear. The question is, Have we really listened, or are we giving lip service to a crisis that calls for a genuine reorientation of our lives as humans, consumers, nations, and members of faith traditions?

The Evidence

The consensus findings of the scientific community, released in 2007 as *The Fourth Assessment Report of the Intergovernmental Panel on Climate Change* (IPCC), indicates that our society is on a path toward an environmental crisis driven ever more quickly by anthropogenic greenhouse gas emissions. The "Summary for Policy Makers" of *Climate Change 2007: The Physical Science Basis* (February 2007) says, "Warming of the climate system is unequivocal, as is now evident from observations of increases in global average air and ocean temperatures, widespread melting of snow and ice, and rising global mean sea level."[8] In addition, this new "Summary for Policy Makers" reports a "*very high confidence*" that global climate change since 1750 is due to human activities.[9]

Atmospheric carbon dioxide (CO_2), which is the principal gas driving global climate change, is the major combustion product of fossil fuels. The ever-accelerating rate of fossil fuel consumption over the last 150 years, combined with the extensive burning of wood, has raised average atmospheric CO_2 levels from 280 parts per million (ppm) prior to the beginning of the industrial age to roughly 392 ppm. This high level increases global heat retention, since CO_2 allows solar radiation to reach the Earth's surface from the sun, but blocks the natural escape of infrared radiation re-radiated from the Earth's surface to space. More energy arriving with less energy escaping results in a steady buildup of energy on the planet, which we are now experiencing as climatic destabilization and overall warming. The Keeling Curve used to measure CO_2 levels indicates the levels of CO_2 at Mauna Loa, where continuous measurements were first taken (Figure courtesy of the National Oceanic and Atmospheric Administration [NOAA] and the Scripps Institution of Oceanography [SOI]).

Additional greenhouse gases include water vapor and methane (produced by the large numbers of cattle and sheep now being raised worldwide, by rice paddies, and by perhaps by thawing tundra). Methane is a greenhouse gas twenty-three times more potent molecule-by-molecule than carbon dioxide.

If the CO_2, and to a lesser extent methane gas, that we release were the only factors driving global climate change, the prospects would not be so frightening. However, additional processes make global climate change a self-accelerating destabilization of our planet. Destructive feedback loops

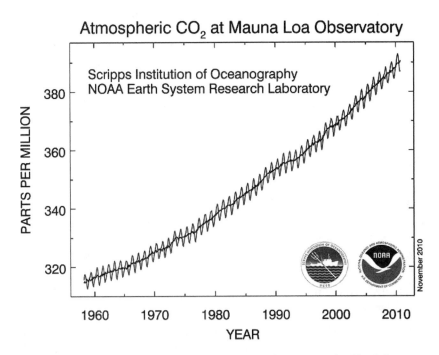

exist and exacerbate global climate change. A *destructive feedback loop* is a process that is self-accelerating with its rate of change increasing over time.[10] The best understood loop is that as the planet warms, melting ice exposes dark surfaces beneath it on mountain ranges and in Antarctica, and these dark surfaces absorb more heat than the ice did, causing further warming, which in turn causes additional ice to melt.

Another example of a destructive feedback loop occurs as the oceans warm, causing more water to evaporate into the atmosphere, which increases the amount of water vapor in the atmosphere. Water vapor is a greenhouse gas, which contributes to the increasing temperature of the planet, including the oceans. This begins a self-perpetuating cycle of warmer air heating the oceans and causing more evaporation, producing yet more atmospheric water vapor, which further increases the greenhouse effect. Warmer water in its liquid form also absorbs fewer gases, so a warming global ocean absorbs less CO_2, leaving more in the atmosphere.

The Impact

The IPCC is clear that the destructive impact of climate change will affect the most vulnerable populations (human and nonhuman) on the planet. The "Summary for Policymakers" of Working Group II states that those with the least resources have the least capacity to adapt and are the most vulnerable. Specific trends highlighted include significant reductions in drinking water supplies due to decreased river runoff and glacial melt; decreases in global food production above a three-degree temperature increase, with immediate decreases in food production at lower latitudes; increased coastal flooding worldwide; negative health effects in developing countries; and decreased productivity of global fisheries.[11]

Four points are particularly important:

1. Increases in average global temperature will produce net economic losses in many developing societies and the greater the degrees of increase, the greater the potential for economic damage.

2. The expected economic impacts of climate change will exacerbate the existing disparity between developed and developing nations, and the global mean temperature at the higher end of the projected spectrum will greatly increase economic disparity.

3. Due to weaker resources for adaptive capacity, developing countries will suffer more adverse impacts than developed nations and within developing nations more people are expected to be harmed by climate change.

4. Finally, developing countries will suffer the greatest in terms of loss of human life.

Worst-case scenarios, in which multiple destructive feedback loops engage concurrently, project temperature and sea-level changes that would be difficult to mitigate by most social systems — and especially by societies with limited resources. While the IPCC impact scenarios have attempted to incorporate or at least acknowledge a wide range of environmental feedback loops, what has not been highlighted is that any social disruption due to climate change, especially in the developing world, is potentially a destructive feedback loop leading to self-accelerating social instability.[12]

Reduction of snow and ice threatens to diminish water supplies for drinking and agriculture worldwide, with the greatest impact on humans in the Himalayas and the Andes. The IPCC estimates that reduction in available water will impact between 75 and 250 million people in Africa alone by 2020.[13] Such a shortage could increasingly pit stakeholders against one another as water supplies diminish. Similarly, self-accelerating social upheaval could accompany projected rising sea levels and the increasing numbers of powerful hurricanes/cyclones in Bangladesh. A similar impact could be anticipated with projected sea level increases in the Nile Delta and elsewhere, which could result in millions of environmental refugees.[14]

The most recent IPCC projections are that sea levels will rise between 0.4 and 1.4 meters, even if we reduce global greenhouse gas emissions by 2050 to between 50 and 85 percent below the year 2000 emissions. There is now a certainty that a large number of environmental refugees will be displaced.[15] Mass movements of environmental refugees will stress the infrastructure in their own countries and neighboring ones, producing the prospect of increased political instability and violence.

Impact scenarios also indicate that food production will decrease and food security problems will increase for many, especially in developing nations. For example, as rainfall patterns shift and petroleum production diminishes, the biofuel industry's demand for biomass feed stocks will compete with the need for food. IPCC estimates that rain-fed agriculture in Africa may experience reductions in crop yields of up to 50 percent by 2020, and warmer nighttime temperatures have been shown to significantly diminish the yields of current varieties of rice crops upon which more than two billion humans depend.[16]

Potential Social Disruptions

These destructive feedback loops toward social disintegration may be mirrored by constructive feedback loops in wealthy developed nations that diminish any social disruptions caused by climate change. The "Contribution of Working Group III to the *Fourth Assessment Report* of the Intergovernmental Panel on Climate Change, 2007" notes that mitigation actions (for example, replacing old coal-fired power plants with clean alternative energy sources) could reduce pollution-related health care costs and act as "near-term co-benefits" that would offset the effects of the mitigation costs.[17]

A decreased need for society to invest in expensive pollution-related health care would be a stabilizing influence to counteract the original economic stress of carbon mitigation investments. Similarly, agricultural productivity may be protected from climate change by intensive research into temperature-tolerant and drought-resistant crop varieties.[18] Given sufficient resources *and* the will to carry out large-scale carbon mitigation and adaptation actions, wealthy human societies could experience increased levels of entrepreneurship, employment, and innovation. An era of investment in new energy technologies could provide enormous economic opportunities.

As the above analysis suggests, societal destabilization, especially in the developing world, ought to be acknowledged as another potential destructive feedback loop and a serious threat to national and international security. Humanity must plan for an uncertain future by realistically assessing the consequences of policy decisions. Preventing a social disintegration destructive feedback loop from causing widespread harm to vulnerable people ought to be a clear priority. Carbon adaptation and mitigation efforts might become a constructive social feedback loop to stabilize societies in the developed world; however, an incapacity to carry these actions out could produce a destructive feedback loop accelerating social disintegration in the developing world. The IPCC has called attention to an adaptive capacity that is unevenly distributed across societies.

The Church Speaks Out

In response to the issue of climate change, in 2001 the U.S. Catholic bishops issued a pastoral letter titled *Global Climate Change: A Plea for*

Dialogue, Prudence, and the Common Good. Taking the IPCC *Third Assess-*
ment Report as its starting point, the bishops declared that "we accept the
consensus findings of so many scientists and the conclusions of the Intergovernmental Panel on Climate Change (IPCC) as a basis for continued
research and prudent action."[19]

The bishops' letter acknowledges the significant disparity between developed and developing nations with regard to the adaptive capacity to respond
to climate change. The bishops make a compelling argument that "developing countries have a right to economic development that can lift people out
of dire poverty" and that "wealthier industrialized nations...need to share
...emerging technologies with the less developed countries and assume more
of the financial responsibility that would enable poorer countries to afford
them."[20] The bishops conclude their reflection by stating that "no strategy
to confront global climate change will succeed without the leadership and
participation of the United States and other industrial nations."[21]

In a more recent statement (February 2007) in response to the IPCC's
Fourth Assessment Report, the U.S. bishops reiterate their moral position on
global climate change but also argue that the "new report demands urgent
action." Bishop Thomas G. Wenski, then chair of the U.S. bishops International Policy Committee, stated in a letter to congressional leaders that
the *Fourth Assessment Report* "has outlined more clearly and compellingly
than ever before the case for serious and urgent action to address the potential consequences of climate change as well as highlighting the dangers and
costs of inaction."[22]

The cost of climate change to the poorest of the poor is highlighted by
perspectives developed within the Evangelical community. Utilizing the concepts of creation care and resurrection, while accepting the scientific reality
of anthropogenic climate change, the Rev. Jim Ball has produced *Global*
Warming and the Risen Lord: Christian Discipleship and Climate Change,[23]
a volume that develops a thoroughly biblical perspective. The Evangelical
Christian understanding of climate change and environmental issues in general has been spearheaded by the Evangelical Environmental Network[24] with
its *Creation Care* magazine; these concerns were highlighted in the words
of the earliest statements stemming from the *Third Lausanne Congress on*
World Evangelization[25] held in Cape Town in 2010:

> We love the world of God's creation. This love is not mere sentimental
> affection for nature (which the Bible nowhere commands), still less is
> it pantheistic worship of nature (which the Bible expressly forbids).
> Rather it is the logical outworking of our love for God by caring for
> what belongs to him. "The earth is the Lord's and everything in it."
> The earth is the property of the God we claim to love and obey. We care
> for the earth, most simply, because it belongs to the one whom we call
> Lord. The earth is created, sustained, and redeemed by Christ. We can-
> not claim to love God while abusing what belongs to Christ by right

of creation, redemption and inheritance. We care for the earth and responsibly use its abundant resources, not according to the rationale of the secular world, but for the Lord's sake. If Jesus is Lord of all the earth, we cannot separate our relationship to Christ from how we act in relation to the earth. For to proclaim the gospel that says "Jesus is Lord" is to proclaim the gospel that includes the earth, since Christ's Lordship is over all creation. Creation care is thus a gospel issue within the Lordship of Christ. *Such love for God's creation* demands that we repent of our part in the destruction, waste, and pollution of the earth's resources and our collusion in the toxic idolatry of consumerism. Instead, we commit ourselves to urgent and prophetic ecological responsibility.

In the fall 2007 issue of the "Creation in the News" section of *Creation Care* magazine (p. 21), a sort of "state of the Evangelicals" poll was reported.

A national poll by Ellison Research, released October 11, found that 84 percent of evangelicals support legislation to reduce global warming pollution levels, and 54 percent are more likely to support a candidate that works toward that end (with only 10 percent less likely to support a candidate who works for global warming action). "What we are seeing is significant support among evangelical Christians for prudent measures that will help stop and reverse levels of global warming pollution and will be consistent with God's call to all of us to be stewards of his incomparable creation," said David Clark, president of Palm Beach Atlantic University, former chairman of the National Religious Broadcasters, and an ECI signatory. The Ellison Research poll found that 70 percent of evangelicals believe global warming will have an impact on future generations, and 64 percent say that action against it should begin immediately. Eighty-nine percent of evangelicals agreed that the U.S. should seek to curb its global warming pollution, regardless of what other nations do.[26]

In the "Written Testimony of the Most Reverend Katharine Jefferts Schori, Presiding Bishop of the Episcopal Church before the Senate Environment and Public Works Committee,"[27] which took place in 2007, in response to the IPCC's *Fourth Assessment Report*, she stated:

The scientific community has made clear that we must reduce carbon emissions globally by 15 to 20 percent by 2020 and 80 percent by 2050 in order to avoid the most catastrophic impacts of climate change. On behalf of the Episcopal Church, as a Christian leader representing today not only the concerns of Episcopalians, but the concerns of the many denominations that are part of the National Council of Churches, I implore you to make these goals a national priority. To my colleagues in the faith community who doubt the urgency of addressing global warming, I urge you to reconsider for the sake of God's good earth. I join many of my colleagues and many of you on this committee in sharing a profound concern that climate change will most severely affect those living in poverty and the most vulnerable in our communities here in the United States and around the world. I want to be absolutely clear; inaction on our part is the most costly of all courses of action for those living in poverty.

Industry Responds

Despite the crucial importance of climate change to the future of humanity, climate change "skeptics" funded by corporate entities in the petrochemical and coal industries have spread misinformation that has significantly delayed the global response to this problem. The most egregious of these public relations processes, carried out by ExxonMobil, used a set of steps originally developed by the tobacco industry in its efforts to deny that second-hand tobacco smoke causes cancer. The basic steps involved in both campaigns involved manufacturing uncertainty by raising doubts about what are unequivocal scientific findings, establishing false front organizations that constitute a very public "echo chamber" to repeat the misinformation endlessly, shifting the focus from solid science that already exists to a delaying call for more research, and promoting often poorly qualified scientific spokespeople to reiterate their opinions over and over.[28]

Incredible as it may appear, some of the staff involved as "climate change skeptics" previously worked with the tobacco industry before it abandoned its efforts to deny the health effects of tobacco. For example, Steven Milloy headed two different lobbying organizations with the acronym TASSC, "The Advancement of Sound Science Coalition," working on behalf of the tobacco industry. When the campaign closed in the face of public exposure as a front organization during the litigation against Big Tobacco, "The Advancement of Sound Science Center" began working on climate change on behalf of ExxonMobil. Milloy also worked with two other ExxonMobil-funded front organizations, Tech Central Station and the Competitive Enterprise Institute.

Another example is Dr. Frederick Seitz, a well-respected physicist in the 1960s, who changed careers to oversee the distribution of large amounts of tobacco industry research funds during the 1970s and 1980s. These funds were made available for work that would not implicate smoking tobacco in health problems. From there Seitz moved to retirement and then back again to active corporate duty in the late 1980s and 1990s when ExxonMobil needed help to promote its agenda of climate change skepticism.[29]

Dr. S. Fred Singer has perhaps the most impressive record as a contrarian, having (to date) denied the role of second-hand smoke in cancer, the role of CFCs in ozone thinning, and the role of fossil fuels in climate change. Singer's most recent venture, the promotion of a group he calls the Nongovernmental International Panel on Climate Change (NIPCC), is an assortment of people who range from a retired professor of welding technology to a spokesperson for the British coal industry, to a board game inventor. Singer's NIPCC is perhaps the epitome of disinformation in efforts to promote confusion by distorting the well-known IPCC acronym.[30]

An excellent report titled *Smoke, Mirrors, and Hot Air: How Exxon-Mobil Uses Big Tobacco's Tactics to "Manufacture Uncertainty" on Climate Change* is available from the Union of Concerned Scientists (see *www.ucsusa.org/*). The entire Union of Concerned Scientists report is well worth reading. ExxonMobil has made its efforts to derail carbon emission mitigation less visible since the unprecedented open letter sent to Exxon-Mobil by the Royal Society, the authoritative scientific organization that has existed in Great Britain for centuries. In 2006 the society admonished ExxonMobil to stop funding disinformation campaigns and to cease making "inaccurate and misleading" statements about climate change.[31] However, despite Exxon's 2007 promise to stop funding climate change denial groups, *The Times* of London reported on July 19, 2010, that Exxon had spent $1.75 million in the preceding year to fund such activities.

A recent analysis published in the *Proceedings of the National Academy of Sciences* of the United States unequivocally shows that there is a remarkably strong consensus among actual climate scientists that anthropogenic climate change is a reality. Among 1,372 active climate researchers, between 97 and 98 percent support the viewpoint that climate change is being driven by human activities, and the few dissenters have substantially less expertise and less prominence among scientists than those who constitute the much larger consensus group.[32] Climate change skepticism is now a manufactured commodity that belongs to the realm of politicians and special interest groups; it is not part of the scientific endeavor.

The "Ozone Hole"

The story of global ozone thinning has a potentially happy ending, due in large measure to the stern warnings of the world's scientific community, which led to the Montreal Protocol in 1987. This was the first effective global environmental accord to address an emerging environmental crisis. A description of the events and the science that led to the most successful international environmental treaty to date is worth considering.

CFCs

Chlorofluorocarbons (CFCs), first patented by Frigidaire in 1928 and rapidly employed by many firms including General Motors, DuPont, and Westinghouse, were an apparent chemical panacea that could provide the capacity to develop modern air conditioners, refrigerators, and spray cans for many products; they were also heavily used in the production of Styrofoam. Believed to be harmless to people and the environment at first, billions of pounds of CFCs were produced, utilized, and released to the atmosphere as a waste gas. By 1970 a million tons of CFCs were used annually.

In the beginning of the 1970s a scientist named James Lovelock traveled around the world on the research vessel *RV Shackleton* to make the first careful measurements of atmospheric ozone. Lovelock's data showed that approximately all of the CFCs ever produced and released remained in the atmosphere of the earth.[33] While there was no proof at that time that the accumulating CFCs would cause any significant problems, two scientists, F. Sherwood Rowland and Mario J. Molina, began to investigate the effects of the growing atmospheric CFC levels. In 1974, a short paper by Molina and Rowland published in *Nature* described how stratospheric CFCs destroy the ozone layer, with each CFC molecule eliminating ten thousand or more ozone molecules.[34]

The *Nature* paper raised no furor, but a subsequent presentation and press conference at the annual meeting of the American Chemical Society, along with a longer paper published in *Reviews of Geoscience and Space Physics,* effectively alerted the media and the world to the dangers of CFCs.[35] Sweden banned CFC aerosol products in 1977, the U.S. Food and Drug Administration banned CFCs in aerosols over a period from 1976 through 1978, but the U.S. government allowed their other industrial uses to continue. Given a rather weak policy response, heavily influenced by the value of CFCs to the chemical industry, little changed.

When CFCs are struck by solar radiation in the upper atmosphere, they release an atom of chlorine that is capable of carrying out a series of rapid reactions, destroying thousand or tens of thousands of ozone molecules for each chlorine atom generated. CFC molecules are remarkably persistent and concentrations in the upper atmosphere diminish very slowly.

A seasonal ozone loss over Antarctica occurs in the springtime because sunlight returns to interact with the CFC molecules that accumulated on atmospheric ice particles throughout the long dark winter months. Wind patterns over Antarctica provide a uniquely stable polar vortex containing stratospheric ice crystals that persist throughout the Antarctic winter and slowly increase their CFC content.

In 1981 the British Antarctic Survey measured a seasonal but huge area of extreme ozone depletion (often called a "hole" but actually an extensive and profound thinning of the stratospheric ozone layer) over the South Pole. The significance of this threat was realized with unusual speed. In 1985 twenty countries signed the Vienna Convention for the Protection of the Ozone Layer, and in 1987 the Montreal Protocol was signed, which essentially banned CFC use internationally by 1996. However, CFCs have an atmospheric life of a hundred years or more, so the ozone "hole" did not immediately begin to diminish.

Some of the largest seasonal Antarctic ozone "holes" have occurred since the CFC ban. A record ozone thinning over Antarctica (both in size and in intensity) was reported by NASA in 2006. In September 2006 the average area of the ozone hole was the largest ever observed, at 10.6 million square miles. Scientists from NOAA's Earth System Research Laboratory in Boulder, Colorado, used balloon-borne instruments to measure ozone directly over the South Pole. By October 9 the total column ozone had plunged to 93 Dobson Units (DU, a measure of ozone concentration) from approximately 300 DU in mid-July. More importantly, nearly all of the ozone in the layer between eight and thirteen miles above the Earth's surface had been destroyed. In this critical layer, the instrument measured a record low of only 1.2 DU, having rapidly plunged from an average nonhole reading of 125 DU in July and August.[36]

Scientists have also concluded that ozone is thinned in the upper atmosphere all around the globe with a concomitant risk of increased skin cancer, albeit not as dramatically as over Antarctica. Some project that it will be roughly a century before stratospheric CFCs slowly diminish and the ozone "hole" repairs itself.

Rowland, along with Molina and Paul J. Crutzen, won the Nobel prize for their work on atmospheric chemistry in 1995, and Rowland summed up his vision of the future in his Nobel address:

> The situation at the end of 1995 is therefore a mixed one. The three most important CFC molecules have atmospheric lifetimes measured from many decades to a century or more, with the consequence that there will be significant quantities of them present in the atmosphere throughout the 21st century. The major springtime losses in the Antarctic will probably continue at least until mid-century. However, because the primary cause of these ozone losses are the man-made chlorine and bromine compounds limited by the Montreal Protocol, the amount of organochlorine in the troposphere will peak soon, if it hasn't already.... The threat of extensive further stratospheric ozone depletion during the 21st century appears to be under control.[37]

The world community, at least in the limited arena of CFC emissions, was capable of responding to scientific knowledge, consulting and reflecting together, and acting for the common good. The levels of atmospheric CFCs are beginning slowly to decline, and recent estimates are that the Montreal Protocol is showing the first signs of success. In fifty or one hundred years the gradual decline of atmospheric CFCs should lead to a fully recovered ozone layer.[38] International cooperation has been successful in this specific regard, but eliminating CFCs is much simpler than replacing fossil fuels.

Ozone Thinning vs. Global Warming

It is worth reviewing a common misunderstanding about ozone thinning, which is often confused with other environmental concerns. Thinning of the Earth's stratospheric ozone layer, which permits excessive amounts of ultraviolet radiation to penetrate the atmosphere and reach the surface of the earth, is too frequently confused with global warming. Ozone layer thinning is a confusing topic for at least three reasons:

1. Ozone thinning is caused by chlorofluorocarbons (CFCs), also a minor component of the greenhouse gases, CFCs are principally significant as an agent of stratospheric ozone thinning.

2. Ozone generated by automobile exhaust and bright sunlight is a pollutant with serious health consequences when present at ground level; however, this differs entirely from the natural ozone layer high in the stratosphere that forms when solar radiation naturally interacts with oxygen to form ozone.

3. People often speak of an "ozone hole" over the Antarctic, while the reality is a significant seasonal thinning of the ozone layer that is most intense over the Antarctic in the spring.

Water

Water and watersheds deserve separate mention in terms of human ecology, because the present patterns of agriculture and development are so peculiarly out of touch with the reality of water supplies. In many locations around the world, crops are being grown that are inappropriate for the local availability of water. For example, rice production in the Central Valley of California is based on subsidized water pumped out of the Colorado River. Such irrigation forms part of a system that almost entirely consumes the water in the river before it reaches the sea. (The last time that rainfall in this region caused dam operators to release a large flow to the Colorado River delta was during the 1980s.)

A particularly devastating example has been cotton production in the Aral Sea region of Uzbekistan and Kazakhstan, where extensive water diversion into unlined irrigation canals led to the death of the Aral Sea, extensive salinization of the surrounding soils, and immense human suffering caused by airborne pesticide-laden dust from the former sea bottom.

In other areas of the world rapid urban growth in arid regions is having a negative impact as human population densities spread over hundreds or thousands of square miles of land surrounding heavily diverted rivers. In the United States, Las Vegas is perhaps the prime example of watershed-blind development that is occurring elsewhere around the globe. Las Vegas grows and grows, as it struggles to obtain more and more water from distant areas to support a population swimming and drinking and playing golf in a desert.

The state of Nevada had 2.7 million residents as of 2008, and fully 70 percent of them live in Las Vegas and the surrounding county. Projections are a state population of 4.3 million in 2026, with almost 80 percent of the population in Las Vegas and the surrounding county.[39] Water for Las Vegas comes primarily from Lake Mead, the largest human-made lake and reservoir in the United States; it is located on the Colorado River thirty miles from Las Vegas. Formed by the Hoover Dam, it runs for 110 miles behind the dam and holds approximately 28.5 million acre feet of water. It is estimated that given the effects of climate change (scientific models predict a reduction in runoff to the Colorado River of between 10 and 30 percent over the next thirty to fifty years) and the burgeoning human population in the region, Lake Mead stands a 50 percent chance of being dry by 2021.[40] Clearly, the water supply will be inadequate to sustain the projected population growth.

Elsewhere, irrigated agriculture that rapidly withdraws underground water is depleting aquifers that have slowly accumulated over thousands of years. A good example in the United States is the accelerating depletion of the Ogallala aquifer that irrigates the agricultural heartland of America.

Barcelona in Spain and Cyprus have begun to bring in tankers of fresh water, while China looks toward the diminishing water supply in the adjacent Himalayas. Desalination plants are springing up in Australia and Florida. Canada's House of Commons has voted a "voluntary" ban on bulk export of its water. However, the North American Free Trade Agreement, which remains controversial in Canada, would have to be renegotiated to ensure the exclusion of large-scale water exports.

Suddenly golf courses and green lawns and swimming pools need to be reconsidered, and what was apparently limitless begins to seem precious. Watersheds are real entities, and our willful ignorance of this fact is a major contributor to the newly minted expression "water will be the next oil."

Water as a For-Profit Commodity

The future of drinking water supplies is also being jeopardized today by the use of drinking water as a for-profit commodity. For-profit corporations have moved on a large scale to operate public water systems, often leading to substantial increases in the cost to the public of drinking water. Internationally, two of the major water companies are the French firms Suez and Veolia, major global players in "the water market." Suez has been criticized for providing poor service, cutting off water supplies to poor people, and suing countries from which it has been expelled for enormous amounts of money. Suez operates drinking water or wastewater facilities in Canada, Mexico, Chile, Curaçao, Brazil, Morocco, South Africa, Senegal, Abu Dhabi, China, Australia, and many other countries. The relations of Suez with customers have been especially contentious in Bolivia and Argentina, where Suez has been expelled or is in the process of being expelled. Wenonah Hauter, executive director of Food & Water Watch, reported at the annual general meeting of Suez in Paris in 2006 that "Suez has placed profit over the human right to water by raising rates, cutting off the water of people unable to pay, refusing to extend services to poor neighborhoods, violating water quality standards, and contaminating public waters."[41]

Bottled water is a second and complex issue. Sometimes it provides the only safe drinking water available in the developing world, but it is a transportable commodity that is heavily marketed to produce demand in the developed world. The production of bottled water often involves taking hundreds of millions of gallons of water from wells in one area and shipping them elsewhere, with results that can be catastrophic in terms of local drinking water or agricultural water supplies. Water bottling facilities remove hundreds of millions of gallons annually from finite aquifers, the bottles require millions of gallons of petroleum to produce and additional energy to transport and deliver, and the use of plastic bottles can expose consumers to phthalates and Bisphenol-A. In addition, bottled water in the United States is much more weakly regulated than municipal drinking water supplies for chemical contaminants and the presence of bacteria. The discarded bottles impose a significant burden in terms of a waste stream to be recycled or land-filled. Finally, bottled water costs much more than tap water, often thousands of times more for the volume purchased.

The growing corporate rush to invest in water rights and develop water delivery systems that remove water from one region and bottle it for the use of wealthier people elsewhere, and also at times to supply drinking water at prices unaffordable to local populations, was part of the motivation behind the U.N. declaration of an International Year of Freshwater in 2003. According to an International Union for Conservation of Nature (IUCN) report, more than 1 billion people lack safe drinking water, and almost 2.5 billion lack access to sanitation. If present trends continue, the IUCN estimates that by 2025 two-thirds of the Earth's population will have serious water shortages or simply have no access to a safe water supply.[42]

Concluding that developing countries lack the infrastructure to develop and manage efficient water systems, the World Bank has insisted on the privatization of water supplies in developing countries — with unexpected results. Many people around the world have objected strenuously to what they consider their water becoming the property of a multinational corporation, and the new corporate owners have often increased prices as a "full economic recovery" strategy. This has led to open rebellions over water in Cochabamba and later El Alto, Bolivia. Movements against privatization have also emerged in India and Africa. Felton, California, recently succeeded in its six-year fight to recover its water supply from a multinational corporation based in Germany. Yet, despite these examples, water system privatization is a rapidly growing trend internationally.

Coping with Water Scarcity, published in 2006 by the United Nations UN-Water Thematic Initiatives Program, states in part:

> It is in the arid and semiarid regions affected by droughts and wide climate variability, combined with population growth and economic development, that the problems of water scarcity are most acute. Water use has been growing at more than twice the rate of population increase in the last century, and, although there is no global water scarcity as such, an increasing number of regions are chronically short of water. By 2025, 1.8 billion people will be living in countries or regions with absolute water scarcity, and two-thirds of the world population could be under stress conditions. The situation will

Maude Barlow, a Canadian author and activist, chairs the Council of Canadians and chairs the board of Food & Water Watch. Called at times "the Ralph Nader of Canada," she is the author of several books, including *Blue Covenant: The Global Water Crisis and the Coming Battle for the Right to Water* (2009).

Water has played a central role in every faith and every culture in the world. Water as a life-giving force provided by the Creator has been universally seen as part of the Commons, belonging to all as a fundamental right of personhood, as well as to other species and the Earth itself.

As recently as two decades ago, large parts of the world still lived off the land, many in complete isolation from the global trade and market system, and billions lived their everyday lives within a Commons framework. The integrity and health of the Commons crashed however, when economic globalization and market fundamentalism were introduced as the only model of development for the world. In several short decades, the notion of water was transformed from an assumed unlimited public asset to a declining and potentially profit-making commodity to be placed on the open market like oil or cars. Billions are now denied water because they cannot afford to pay for it.

As the world rapidly runs out of accessible water, it is urgent that we return to a Commons framework for its equitable distribution or many more will die. Water belongs to the Earth, other species, and future generations. However, it is very important not to return to the notion that the supply is unlimited and anyone can use whatever they want, however they want, whenever they want. A new understanding of the water Commons must be rooted in a sober and realistic assessment of the true damage that has already been unleashed on the world's water resources as well as the knowledge that our freshwater systems must be managed and shared in a way that protects them now and for all time.

The wise use of our water Commons is best based on several principles: that water was put by nature where it belongs and will teach us how to live if we will listen; that water is a public trust that must be protected in law for all people, not just the privileged few, for all time; and that water is a universal human right that must not be denied to anyone because they are poor.

— Maude Barlow

be exacerbated as rapidly growing urban areas place heavy pressure on neighboring water resources.... Poor communities have tended to suffer the greatest health burden from inadequate water supplies and, as result of poor health, have been unable to escape from the cycle of poverty and disease. Thus, growing scarcity and competition for water stand as a major threat to future advances in poverty alleviation, especially in rural areas.[43]

The Church Speaks Out

Archbishop Renato R. Martino, president of the Pontifical Council for Justice and Peace, presented *Water: An Essential Element for Life,* note prepared by the Pontifical Council for Justice and Peace as a contribution of the Holy See to the Third World Water Forum in 2003. It states:

> Water is an essential element for life. Many people must confront daily the situation of an inadequate supply of safe water and the very serious resulting consequences.... The Holy See offers these reflections... to contribute its voice to the call for action to correct the dramatic situation concerning water. The *human being* is the centre of the concern expressed in this paper and the focus of its considerations.
>
> The management of water and sanitation must address the needs of all, and particularly of persons living in poverty. Inadequate access to safe drinking water affects the well-being of over one billion persons and more than twice that number have no adequate sanitation. This all too often is the cause of disease, unnecessary suffering, conflicts, poverty, and even death. This situation is characterized by countless unacceptable injustices.... Communities and individuals can exist even for substantial periods without many essential goods. The human being, however, can survive only a few days without clean, safe drinking water.
>
> Many people living in poverty, particularly in the developing countries, daily face enormous hardship because water supplies are neither sufficient nor safe. Women bear a disproportionate hardship. For water users living in poverty this is rapidly becoming an issue crucial for life and, in the broad sense of the concept, *a right to life issue.*[44]

Ecological and Carbon Footprints

One challenge in making decisions about lifestyle and consumption choices is that the "best way" is not always obvious; instead there are usually trade-offs between options. For example, is it better to live in a small space in a city, where food has to be purchased from a grocery and commuting to work can be done on foot, or is it better to live on a modest-sized farm near the city where a family can grow much of its own food but family members need to commute to work by automobile?

RESEARCH FOCUS: WATER

Many resources are available to help inform you about the present issues surrounding the overuse and privatization of water. Several books and websites worth consulting for further research are listed here. It appears that water may indeed "become the next oil" unless steps are rapidly taken to prevent this.

Web Link Resources

www.foodandwaterwatch.org/water

www.foodandwaterwatch.org/water/bottled/take-back-the-tap/TakeBackTheTap_web.pdf

www.nrdc.org/water/drinking/bw/bwinx.asp

http://lighterfootstep.com/2008/05/five-reasons-not-to-drink-bottled-water/

http://environmentaldefenseblogs.org/climate411/2008/03/26/bottled_water/?gclid=CIDXzIuCwJQCFST7iAod8xD5Tg

http://thegreenguide.com/reports/product.mhtml?id=49

ftp://ftp.fao.org/agl/aglw/docs/waterscarcity.pdf

www.vatican.va/roman_curia/pontifical_councils/justpeace/documents/rc_pc_justpeace_doc_20030322_kyoto-water_en.html

Book Resources

Chamberlain, Gary L. *Troubled Waters: Religion, Ethics, and the Global Water Crisis*. Lanham, Md.: Rowman & Littlefield, 2004.

Snitow, Alan, Deborah Kaufman, and Michael Fox. *Thirst: Fighting the Corporate Theft of Our Water*. New York: John Wiley and Sons, 2007.

Clearly both options have positive features, and only by establishing some sort of common currency of environmental cost and benefit can the two options accurately be compared. This is akin to moving from a barter system to the standardized valuation provided by a currency system: a skein of wool and a quart of milk both have value, but which is worth more? Similarly, eliminating a forty-mile daily commute and becoming largely independent of commercially purchased food are both good, but which provides greater benefit to the environment? Only by establishing some sort of common currency or metric of environmental impact for different choices can this sort of comparison be convincing.

The first publication using the term "ecological footprint," which dealt with the environmental impact of cities, made the case that much of the impact of urbanization was felt outside the borders of a city itself; it consisted of the large surface area of productive land surrounding the city (and elsewhere) that was needed to support the city's inhabitants.[45] This was followed by additional work that explored what was first called *appropriated carrying capacity* and later referred to almost entirely as an ecological footprint. In 1996 a book entitled *Our Ecological Footprint: Reducing Human Impact on the Earth* brought this concept into mainstream intellectual life, and the focus changed to allow individuals rather than communities to examine their environmental impact. Since then, the advent of numerous Internet-based ecological footprint calculators have allowed this practice to become quite widespread.

An ecological footprint expresses the resources an individual uses in terms of the surface area of the earth (acres or hectares) to supply that person with energy, timber, paper, crops, seafood, minerals, space for housing, and so forth.[46] Ideally, we would all use resources in a way that used only our share of the planet's surface, while leaving a significant area unused by people so that natural ecosystems could thrive. Ecological footprints are often expressed in terms of how many Earths would be required if all of the humans alive used the same amount of productive habitat to support their lifestyle. Americans are often surprised to discover that we are living as though we had four or five Earths from which to share resources.

Subsequently, as the crisis of global climate change has moved to center stage, another measure has emerged as a way of expressing the environmental impact of a person's lifestyle on the planet. The second measure is a person's *carbon footprint*. Higher levels of resource consumption (because of a bigger house, less fuel-efficient car, greater consumption of meat, and so on) increases the greenhouse gas emissions needed to support the lifestyle (home heating, gasoline for vehicles, electricity for air conditioning, fertilizer and fossil fuels to raise grain to feed cows, energy to manufacture larger and more numerous possessions and transport them to local shops, and so forth).[47]

As global climate change has become the most pressing environmental concern for many people, the idea of a carbon footprint has emerged as a sound way to express an individual's environmental impact. Carbon footprints are used to explore the possibilities for reducing personal greenhouse gas emissions and also to calculate a carbon offset for unavoidable emissions.

Carbon offsets are a somewhat contentious topic, because the ability to "purchase" our way out of environmental damage by funding reforestation or the construction of wind turbines, for example, can lessen our sense of personal responsibility, and hence our impetus to reduce our resource use. Nonetheless, carbon offsets are at least a response to unavoidable greenhouse gas emissions. Research is now underway to determine which commercially available carbon offsets are well managed and which ones are less effective.[48]

Most recently, as the scarcity of fresh water and its commodification have become a concern in many parts of the world, a new measure, the *water footprint*, has emerged. This measure is based on the recognition that some materials are far more intensively dependent on water for their production than others, and that consumer choices can influence both water use and the flow of materials in trade, particularly if the production of those materials increases water consumption in already water-poor areas.

Initially, the water, although invisible, in goods and services, such as the water expended in the production of rice or coffee or beans, was referred to as *embodied water,* although standard usage today is *virtual water.*[49] Producing a ton of beef requires 13,500 cubic meters of water, while the water required to produce the same amount of other foodstuffs is substantially less (for example, pork requires 4,600 cubic meters; poultry 4,100 cubic meters; rice 1,400 cubic meters; milk, 790 cubic meters).[50] Different human diets require very different amounts of virtual water. A vegetarian will use 2.6 cubic meters per person per day, while a typical American diet takes 5.4 cubic meters per person per day.[51] Virtual water is sometimes divided into different components: green water is soil water taken up by plants, blue water is surface water and groundwater, and so on.

A water footprint is a way of examining a person, corporation, or nation's consumption of water in order to understand the environmental implications of lifestyle choices. Water footprints should help us reduce water demands particularly in arid areas. Water footprint calculators are beginning to appear on the worldwide web.[52] For example, a cup of coffee requires 140 liters of water to produce, while a cup of tea requires 34 liters.[53] Paying attention to these sorts of differences in the future has obvious implications for international trade.

No single one of these measures — an ecological footprint, a water footprint, a carbon footprint — is "right"; instead, they represent different metrics for thinking about the environmental impact of lifestyle choices, and each one presents different avenues for a person to consider in reducing the impact of a chosen lifestyle on the planet. A great many choices we make about where we live, how we travel, what we eat, how warm or cool we keep our homes, what sorts of lights and appliances we use, and how much water we consume have significant effects on our environmental impact however they are measured.

Biodiversity Loss

The stability of our ecosystems is built on biodiversity, the intricate web of interconnections that allow living organisms to adjust as various species temporarily wax and wane in numbers due to environmental fluctuations. Human activities have seriously reduced biodiversity worldwide to such an extent that our effects on the web of life resemble a massive asteroid impact

RESEARCH FOCUS:
CALCULATING YOUR ECOLOGICAL FOOTPRINT

Getting a sense of how many things are worth thinking about is easiest by making use of some of the array of online tools for measuring individual lifestyle choices. Many accessible footprint calculators exist, a number of them that might give you different ideas about how your lifestyle impacts. Web addresses are listed below.

Web Resources

www.nature.org/initiatives/climatechange/calculator/

www.climatecrisis.net/takeaction/carboncalculator/

www.fightglobalwarming.com/carboncalculator.cfm

www.conservation.org/act/live_green/carboncalc/Pages/default.aspx

www.conservation.org/act/live_green/Pages/ecofootprint.aspx

www.myfootprint.org/

www.footprintnetwork.org/en/index.php/GFN/page/personal_footprint/

www.waterfootprint.org/index.php?page=files/home

or an incipient ice age. The importance of biodiversity is stressed in the *Millennium Ecosystem Assessment* report issued in 2005.

Biodiversity — the diversity of genes, populations, species, communities, and ecosystems — underlies all ecosystem processes. Ecological processes interacting with the atmosphere, geosphere, and hydrosphere determine the environment on which organisms, including people, depend. Direct benefits such as food crops, clean water, clean air, and aesthetic pleasures all depend on biodiversity, as does the persistence, stability, and productivity of natural systems.[54]

Humans may have already increased the rate of species extinction by as much as a thousandfold. The International Union for Conservation of Nature (IUCN) estimates that somewhere between 12 percent and 52 percent of species in well-studied higher groups of organisms are now threatened with extinction. Human activities responsible include the destruction of habitats, introduction of nonnative invasive species, deforestation, desertification, overfishing, pollution, and widespread modifications of the environment, including climate change. The IUCN report says:

Among a range of higher taxa, the majority of species are currently in decline. Studies of amphibians globally, African mammals, birds in intensively managed agricultural lands, British butterflies, Caribbean corals, waterbirds, and fishery species show the majority of species to be declining in range or number.... The majority of biomes have been greatly modified by humans.... Tropical dry forests are the most reduced by cultivation, with almost half of the biome's native habitats replaced with cultivated lands. Three other biomes — temperate grasslands, temperate broadleaf forests, and Mediterranean forests — have experienced 35 percent or more conversion. Habitat conversion to agriculture typically leads to reductions in native biodiversity.[55]

A rather bleak vision of the future of oceanic life on earth, if anthropogenic stresses on the oceans' biodiversity are not reduced, was recently published in the *Proceedings of the National Academy of Sciences* by Jeremy Jackson. He wrote,

Today, the synergistic effects of human impacts are laying the groundwork for a comparably great Anthropocene mass extinction in the oceans with unknown ecological and evolutionary consequences. Synergistic effects of habitat destruction, overfishing, introduced species, warming, acidification, toxins, and massive runoff of nutrients are transforming once complex ecosystems like coral reefs and kelp forests into monotonous level bottoms, transforming clear and productive coastal seas into anoxic dead zones, and transforming complex food webs topped by big animals into simplified, microbially dominated ecosystems with boom and bust cycles of toxic dinoflagellate blooms, jellyfish, and disease. Rates of change are increasingly fast and non-linear with sudden phase shifts to novel alternative community states. We can only guess at the kinds of organisms that will benefit from this mayhem.... Halting and ultimately reversing these trends will require rapid and fundamental changes in fisheries, agricultural practice, and the emissions of greenhouse gases on a global scale.[56]

Despite the dire condition of the oceans, the loss of forests, especially species-rich tropical forests, is driving the greatest biodiversity catastrophe now underway. The authoritative report of the World Commission on Forests and Sustainable Development, now a decade old, paints another bleak picture of a future of biodiversity that appears to be just around the historical corner.

Over the last two decades of the 20th century, rapid deforestation has taken its toll — some 15 million hectares of forests are lost annually, largely in the tropics.... Forests have virtually disappeared in 25 countries; 18 have lost more than 95 percent of their forests and another 11 have lost 90 percent. The highest current estimate of the world's remaining forested areas is about 3.6 billion hectares from an originally forested area of more than 6.0 billion hectares....

Forest decline threatens the genetic diversity of the world's plants and animals. The World Conservation Union recently calculated that about 12.5 percent of the world's 270,000 species of plants, and about 75 percent of the world's mammals are threatened by forest decline.[57]

The overall impact on biodiversity can be summarized using the acronym HIPPO, as referred to above: Habitat loss, Invasive species, Pollution, Population growth, and Overharvesting/overconsumption.[58] No individual element of the five-part HIPPO threat is the dominant cause of species extinction, and no individual element of this threat can be resolved to solve the problem. We need to examine *all* that we do across the planet to develop a broad vision of how we contribute to HIPPO and how we might change the path we're on. The biodiversity of the planet is a legacy of enormous value, both intrinsic and anthropocentric, a source of inspiration and relaxation, the origin of new medications and food plants, and the guarantor of ecological stability. We squander it at our own risk.

Energy

In 1956, Dr. M. King Hubbert (1903–1989), a prominent geologist working as the chief consultant for Shell Oil, predicted at the spring meeting of the American Petroleum Institute's Southern District Division of Production, that U.S. oil production would peak in approximately the early 1970s and irreversibly decline rapidly thereafter.[59] Global peak production and a subsequent rapid decline were projected for around the year 2000 in his report "Energy Resources: A Report to the Committee on Natural Resources of the National Academy of Sciences–National Research Council."[60]

Although initially Hubbert was heavily criticized by some other petroleum experts and economists, in 1971 Hubbert's prediction of peak U.S. oil production and subsequent decline came true. Even after U.S. oil production peaked as predicted, national and international leaders promoted policies that did nothing effective to reduce the rapid growth of oil consumption. Our cars and SUVs got larger, our commutes got longer, and our personal dependency on petroleum continued to increase absent any effective and consistent governmental policies to counter the approaching mismatch of supply and demand. Peak global oil production and subsequent decline now appear to have been within a few years of his projection.

Dr. Hubbert's reasoning in 1956 and 1962 was accessible to anyone with a technical background who took the time to examine his work. Despite Dr. Hubbert's prominence in the oil industry, his professional standing as a geologist, and the simplicity of his argument, we have waited over a half century to take seriously the threat posed by a society whose economy is based on inexpensive and readily available petroleum, a commodity that is decreasing. Moreover, if we had acted early to reduce oil consumption the additional benefit would have been dramatically fewer greenhouse gases in the atmosphere that drive our climate to instability with all that entails.

Coal

The story of coal is in some ways the mirror image of oil. We have come to depend ever more and more on coal to produce electricity and fuel our industrial processes, and the supply of coal is enormous. If we increased our coal consumption annually we would not run out of material for centuries. However, coal is used only at a great price. The air pollutants associated with coal-burning include the now well-understood greenhouse gas carbon dioxide, but also the toxins of mercury, radon, and sulfur dioxide (a major source of acid precipitation). In addition, coal mining leaves behind heavily contaminated streams, damaged watersheds, and acid mine drainage.

Our quest for ever-increasing efficiency has led to the invention of mountaintop removal mining, which trades cheap energy for mountains and communities. So egregious is this practice that is has been roundly denounced by Bishop Walter Sullivan, one of the great ethical voices of the last century in the United States. In describing his fact-finding visit to mountaintop removal sites, he states:

> Our program began with dialogue with representatives of the mining industry who emphasized that the "mountain top removal" approach to mining provides jobs for people of an impoverished area, contending also that flattening the mountains makes additional land available for industry. The mining companies claim to do quality reclamation for schools and industry and also emphasize that corporations involved in this kind of mining are paying a 100 million dollars in state taxes.... After two hours of listening and some dialogue, our delegation drove to a site where "mountain top removal" [MTR] is occurring. We saw for ourselves a huge area in which the top of a mountain had literally been lopped off. Rocks, debris, toxic chemicals and trees were simply dumped over the side of the mountain, adding to the devastation of the land and "hollers" below....
>
> That Tuesday evening we heard from those adversely affected by MTR at the foot of the mountains. Dynamiting is the chief way to level mountains. Blasting knocks houses from their foundations and causes contamination to existing wells and drinking water supplies. The clear cutting of trees causes rapid run-off of rain which fills existing creeks and streams with sediment causing extensive flooding in low lying areas....
>
> I should note here that when coal is predominant so is poverty in the lives of people. Central Appalachia is rich in natural resources but poverty and depressed lives exist side by side....
>
> Wells are now becoming toxic and drinking water is a health hazard, especially for children. Increasingly people are being forced to move from their homes with no place to go. Established communities are breaking up and people's lives are being destroyed.[61]

The coal industry is now promoting a "clean coal" agenda with aggressive public relations materials that appear to be reminiscent of ExxonMobil's disinformation campaign.[62] Although an obviously well-funded clean coal website exists, in actuality no clean-coal technology has ever been employed on a large scale. The coal power plants currently under construction or proposed include no large-scale facilities that capture and sequester carbon dioxide (a process at the heart of the promises of the "clean coal" proponents), nor is it clear that this could be done economically or in many areas. Clean-coal technology should continue to be researched as should other potential energy sources, but it should not serve as a smokescreen for the coal industry to continue business as usual. A more thorough treatment of the technical pros and cons of clean-coal technology are outside the scope of this book, but an excellent report on the topic from the Union of Concerned Scientists is easily accessible.[63] It may be that clean coal becomes a valuable reality some day, but at this point it serves as a public relations shield and an avenue for research.

Reducing Energy Consumption

If our future energy solution lies in neither coal nor petroleum and given that natural gas hydraulic fracturing severely impacts ground water, what should we do to balance the needs of humans and of our ecosystem? How can we keep the lights on and still have a planet with a stable climate, clean air and water, and productive ecosystems? A solid part of the answer is conservation. Our energy use has increased dramatically in the past half-century, and we need to become intentional about our level of energy use.

Another part of the answer to the energy challenge lies in the use of different power sources. One group that has attempted to formulate an answer to this question is the Carbon Mitigation Initiative (CMI).[64] A joint venture of Princeton University, British Petroleum, and the Ford Motor Company, the CMI is looking for realistic energy solutions for the future of humans and our planet. The CMI proposes that in order to prevent passing some ecological tipping point (a point of no return) by continuing on our current track and tripling carbon dioxide concentrations in the Earth's atmosphere, we need to stabilize emissions at current levels over the next fifty years and then reduce them.

Stabilizing the output of greenhouse gasses will require reducing carbon dioxide emissions by roughly 7 billion tons per year by 2054, keeping roughly 175 billion tons of carbon dioxide out of the atmosphere. Viewed on an annual basis, this calls for seven "wedges" each capable of reducing annual carbon dioxide emissions by one billion tons. The sum of these seven wedges is what the CMI calls the "stabilization triangle," a triangular shape that fits in between the present upward sloping trend of increasing carbon dioxide emissions and the horizontal line representing stable emissions (see figure 2 at *www.princeton.edu/ cmi/news/CMIinBrief.pdf*).

The CMI believes that *existing technologies* that could contribute a wedge include:

* doubling the fuel efficiency of two billion cars from 30 to 60 mpg
* decreasing the number of car miles driven by half
* using best efficiency practices in all residential and commercial buildings
* producing coal-based electricity with twice the current efficiency
* replacing fourteen hundred coal-electric plants with natural gas facilities
* increasing wind electricity capacity to 2 million large wind turbines
* installing seven hundred times the current capacity for solar electricity generation
* using forty thousand square kilometers of solar panels or 4 million wind turbines to power electric cars
* increasing ethanol production by fifty times using one-sixth of the world's farmland
* eliminating deforestation and doubling the rate of new forest planting
* adopting conservation tillage globally
* doubling the present capacity of nuclear power plants to replace coal-fired power plants.

Unproven technologies that could each provide a wedge include capturing and storing carbon dioxide emissions from eight hundred coal-fired power plants, producing hydrogen from coal at six times the current rate and storing the carbon dioxide produced, and capturing and storing the carbon dioxide from 180 coal-to-synfuel plants.[65] However, recent events involving the Deepwater Horizon must lead us to consider how authentic the commitment of BP actually is to develop a responsible energy future.

The CMI does not even address more speculative large-scale power sources such as ocean thermal energy conversion, tidal power and wave power, nuclear fission, and deep geothermal energy.[66] Hydrogen fuel cells are another energy source well worth developing as a secondary energy transportation system rather than as an energy supply.[67]

Alternative energy futures represent an enormous challenge for the future of humanity: they contain both promise and peril. Given the realities of peak oil production and global climate change, no topic receives more attention than how we will fulfill our energy needs in the future. In the sixth chapter we will turn our attention to the impact these environmental challenges pose to a theology of human existence.

Questions for Discussion

1. Given the global decline in fish stocks and the difficulty in patrolling the open ocean, what should be done?

2. If the Kyoto Protocol set targets for carbon dioxide emission reductions that were too weak to reverse the process of climatic destabilization, should the United States have ratified the treaty anyway? In spite of the U.S. refusal to ratify the Kyoto Protocol, what do you think should be done in this country to combat global climate change and reduce carbon dioxide emissions?

3. Las Vegas, Nevada, combines rapid population growth, an arid climate, and water needs that place demands on the Colorado River, which already supplies water for agriculture in Mexico, Arizona, and California. What process could help find a healthy way forward in this set of circumstances?

4. How can a society that values freedom of speech deal with intentional programs of misleading climate change denial being funded by a few corporations and trade organizations?

5. China, India, and Indonesia are three countries where substantial segments of the population live in poverty; rapidly growing greenhouse gas emissions accompany their economic development. How can this Janus-faced challenge be met?

6. Why was the Montreal Protocol able to reverse the accumulations of CFCs in the stratosphere, while the Kyoto Protocol has been unable to reverse the accumulation of carbon dioxide in the atmosphere?

Active Learning Exercises

• Go online to the Australian Bureau of Meteorology website's Ultra Violet Forecast page (*www.bom.gov.au/uv/*) and click on the Map option that allows you to see the UV map for Australia today. Study the material there, then go back to the home page and click on the link that takes you to the UV Forecast Table and study this material. Once you have thoroughly examined this material, follow the link to the *SunSmart* page run by the Australian Cancer Council. Use this second resource to learn something about the recommended safety procedures for Australians and the risks they face. Write a two-page essay about how the risk of skin cancer due to ozone layer thinning would cause you to change your schedule of daily activities this week if you lived in Australia. Would you exercise at different times, dress differently, carry out activities with friends or family members in a different way?

• Read one week of your local newspaper and make note of all the articles in it that appear to be related to ongoing climatic destabilization due to rising levels of greenhouse gases such as CO_2 and methane. Make a table listing the publication date, author byline (if any), length of article, title of article, and a brief review of the contents of the article. Turn this table in; it will be evaluated in terms of how thorough a job was done.

Recommended Reading

Barlow, Maude. *Blue Covenant: The Global Water Crisis and the Coming Battle for the Right to Water.* New York: New Press, 2007.

Economy, Elizabeth C. *The River Runs Black: The Environmental Challenge to China's Future.* Ithaca, N.Y.: Cornell University Press, 2004.

Hansen, James. *Storms of My Grandchildren: The Truth about the Coming Climate Catastrophe and Our Last Chance to Save Humanity.* New York: Bloomsbury USA, 2009.

Pooley, Eric. *The Climate War: True Believers, Power Brokers, and the Fight to Save the Earth.* New York: HarperCollins, 2010.

The Environmental Signs of the Times
Toxins and Children

Perhaps the most important and unknown environmental sign of our times is the impact of toxic exposures on the lives of infants and children. This story involves long time lags, multiple chemicals and routes of exposure, and materials we cannot easily see or sense that nonetheless diminish the capacities and futures of our own children. The toxic materials involved are astoundingly varied and numerous. The chemical industry worldwide is a multitrillion dollar annual endeavor producing roughly seventy-five thousand different compounds of varying danger. They enter our environment in many ways, from smokestack emissions to intentional widescale applications of sprays.

The need to deal with the detail and complexity of environmental toxicity has prompted us to organize this discussion into three major parts. The first part ("An Overview of the Impact of Toxins on Children") and the third part ("Cost-Benefit Analysis and Discounting Future") provide a general understanding of the impact of toxic substances on our society and the impact that related policy decisions have on children's health. The second part ("The Details of Chemical Exposure"), more difficult in detail and nomenclature, attempts to provide a thorough picture of just how many circumstances promote often-tragic chemical exposures in children, and also of the wide array of industrial and agricultural chemicals that we use or have used with thoughtless optimism as to the eventual outcomes. However, before turning to these three parts, it is important to briefly describe what toxicology is and how toxins are measured.

We hope that most readers will persevere through all three sections of the chapter, but we do not want the intricacy of the details of chemical exposure (the middle section) to become a barrier to anyone who wants to obtain a general understanding of the issues involved in childhood toxin exposures. All are encouraged to at least study the text boxes on pages 114 and 115 in the middle section as they provide useful information on ways to reduce personal exposure to toxins.

What Is Environmental Toxicology?

Scientists generally test their hypotheses by carrying out laboratory experiments using treatment and control groups, but it is clearly impossible to use this approach to examine the effects of toxins on children. Therefore environmental toxicologists must turn to the effects of previous toxin exposures on people or on laboratory animals sacrificed to serve as models for the biological responses of children.

Environmental toxicology is a Cerebrus[1]-headed science, a combination of (1) after-the-fact epidemiological studies of large numbers of people whose lifestyle, location, or occupation led to chemical exposure over periods of time — a process that is generally difficult to document; (2) laboratory studies done on animals to determine the biochemical mechanisms and biological consequences of toxin exposure in order to infer what human responses might be; and (3) studies by psychologists, neurologists, or other research physicians on children or other humans who have been exposed to toxins in order to determine the effects of a demonstrable level of toxin exposure.

How Toxins Are Measured

Rather than the part per million (ppm) measures used in the discussion of CO_2 concentrations in the atmosphere, concentrations in toxicology are based on the weight of materials and are most often expressed as micrograms per deciliter. A microgram is one one-millionth (1/1,000,000) of a gram. A typical paperclip weighs about one gram, so a microgram would be a millionth of that size and quite invisible to the naked eye. A deciliter is about 42 percent the size of a U.S. cup, or roughly three and one-third fluid ounces. A mental image of a microgram (of any material you choose to think about) per deciliter would be a completely invisible particle in a cup of drinking water. However, even five to ten such invisible particles of lead in a cup or deciliter of a child's blood can have significant consequences for his or her mental development and behavior as an adult.

Another set of measures are used to express the sizes of bits of particulate material (PM), most often soot, in the air. PM_{10} particles have a diameter of ten microns, or roughly one-seventh the diameter of a human hair. PM_5 particles are half that diameter, and $PM_{2.5}$ particles a quarter that size. These common particles in urban air pollution are such small particles that our body has no defense against inhaling them deeply, and they then lodge deep in human lungs. Particles this size inhaled by children exacerbate asthma and other respiratory problems; when inhaled by mothers they lead, among other things, to poorer birth outcomes. The smaller the particles the more deeply in the lungs they lodge (and the more health issues they cause).

This book's glossary includes many of the names of chemicals that have negative health effects on children. As the abbreviated forms of the names commonly used (for example, polychlorinated biphenyls are generally referred to as PCBs) can be confusing, refer to the glossary as needed.

An Overview of the Impact of Toxins on Children

Prior to World War II, people possessed a very limited set of chemical tools to use in their various activities. Antibiotics were essentially nonexistent, and most people died of infectious diseases such as tuberculosis. Pesticides to protect crops and stored food supplies were primitive, consisting of materials like lead arsenate. They had high toxicities and were difficult or impossible to wash off produce. The mid-1940s saw a surge in chemical sophistication associated with research during the war, and after World War II antibiotics and the pesticide DDT quickly became widespread.

At first, DDT must have seemed like a miracle, as it and its quickly birthed chemical cousins appeared to be low in toxicity, inexpensive, and highly effective. In the wake of DDT spraying, which readily dispatched both crop pests and biting insects that were nuisances or sources of disease, photographs remain of children playing in the clouds behind DDT sprayers to remind us of the dangers of naive enthusiasm for new solutions that seem almost too good to be true.

By the 1960s the pesticide industry was an economic behemoth, but the environmental dangers of pesticide use were also beginning to be apparent. In 1962, Rachel Carson, a well-known scientist and popular nature writer, reluctantly interrupted her books on the wonders of nature and ecology to publish *Silent Spring.* As we have discussed above, this book sounded an alarm about the ecological impact of widespread pesticide contamination in the environment.[2] The book's title refers to a future spring that might come without birdsong if DDT and other pesticides continued to be used profligately. By that time the poisons were already killing birds that live at high trophic levels such as bald eagles and brown pelicans. The chemical industry attacked Carson as it attempted to protect its sales and profits, but she testified before Congress, and until her death of cancer in 1964 she spoke out on behalf of the health of our ecosystem.

Carson did not advocate banning all pesticide use, but she did call for its thoughtful and carefully managed use. In response to the publication of *Silent Spring,* the public furor that followed, and the subsequent counter-attack of the chemical industry, President John F. Kennedy had his Science Advisory Committee investigate Carson's claims. The committee's 1963 report, which supported Carson's ideas, led to the increased regulation of chemical pesticides. However, such regulation was limited. Since then, industrial chemicals of all sorts are incredibly numerous, and the most vulnerable organisms on the Earth today (including our own children) face a frightening barrage of toxins.

The tens of thousands of synthetic organic compounds used and disposed of in today's industrial society continually surprise us with their persistence, toxicity, penetration throughout the ecosystem, and health consequences for all life forms. This should come as a shock to no one, given the impact of DDT in the 1960s and the events that took place at Love Canal in New

York, the nation's first famous leaky toxic waste dump. These wake-up calls were only partially heeded.[3]

While regulation of the use of pesticides and herbicides as well as other toxic compounds and industrial waste processing has improved since the days of Love Canal, toxins are still licensed for release (by setting acceptable emissions levels for industrial facilities), even though we know very little about the health effects of most synthetic organic compounds before we begin to use them. The cost of investigating the potential health consequences of new chemical inventions by animal testing prior to employing them would be considerable, so there appears to be a tacit acceptance of the Frankenstein-like nature of the synthetic chemical industry. Some chemicals serve us well and some brutally harm us or other life forms. Unfortunately, the costs are often borne disproportionately by workers in the chemical industry and by the poor who live in inexpensive housing near industrial facilities or in developing countries with weak environmental legislation. A particularly vulnerable group of people — due to a range of developmental characteristics — are infants and children.

Pathways of Exposure for Children

Infants and children living in different regions and circumstances all have some things in common. Their vulnerability to toxic exposure begins with the prenatal exchange of materials between mother and child through the umbilical cord and continues through breast-feeding. As infants develop motor skills such as thumb-sucking and crawling, they are exposed to common household contaminants, including dust, and play with toys that often end up in their mouth. The typical activities of children expose them to toxic contamination that includes heavy metals and pesticides.[4] In addition, infants and children grow rapidly, which makes them especially susceptible to acquiring large amounts of toxic material into their developing bodies; they are also susceptible to the development of pediatric cancer. Throughout their infant and childhood years brain development takes place as a rapid and elaborate process that is threatened if neurotoxins are present.[5]

Infants and children are also acutely vulnerable to toxins because their bodily defenses are incomplete. Their immature blood-brain barrier allows toxins to pass from their circulatory system into their central nervous system. In addition, children have lower levels of the chemical-binding proteins that protect the vital organs of adults from toxins. Infant biochemistry is also less capable of detoxifying and excreting poisons than that of an adult. Such developmental characteristics, combined with a child's longer lifespan, increase the time for negative consequences to develop, creating an unusual potential for environmental toxins to impact human health.[6] Wherever infants or children live, they face health risks that result from the thoughtless actions of the past or the reckless actions of the present in the handling and use of toxic chemicals.

The overall vulnerability of children to environmental toxins was recently highlighted by a group of two hundred scientists who gathered in the Faroe Islands for the first International Conference on Fetal Programming and Developmental Toxicity. They released a statement that concluded in part that "the accumulated research evidence suggests that prevention efforts against toxic exposures to environmental chemicals should focus on protecting the fetus and small child as highly vulnerable populations. Given the ubiquitous exposure to many environmental toxicants, there needs to be renewed effort to prevent harm."[7]

Recent groundbreaking research released by the Environmental Working Group (EWG) clarifies the extent to which pre- and postnatal infants are exposed to toxic industrial chemicals, many of which are commonly found in household products. In a follow-up study to its initial research described in *BodyBurden: The Pollution in People* (2003), in July 2005 the EWG released its report *BodyBurden: The Pollution in Newborns*.[8] "Body burden" refers to the toxic burden of pollutants carried in the human body.

Researchers analyzed the umbilical cord blood of ten newborn babies in the United States between August and September 2004, revealing a total of 287 chemicals found in their umbilical cord blood. According to Jane Houlihan and her colleagues, "This study represents the first reported cord blood tests for 261 of the targeted chemicals and the first reported detections in cord blood for 209 compounds."[9] Furthermore they state: "Of the 287 chemicals we detected in umbilical cord blood, we know that 180 cause cancer in humans or animals, 217 are toxic to the brain and nervous system, and 208 cause birth defects or abnormal development in animal tests."[10]

The United States manufactures or imports nearly seventy-five thousand chemicals a year, most of which have never been tested for safety regarding human health. In EWG's judgment, "Fetal exposure to industrial chemicals is quite literally out of control."[11] The health effects of the combinations of chemicals acting together in low doses is poorly understood, but what has been discerned to date indicates that as we learn more about the combined actions of mixtures of environmental chemicals we will have even greater reasons to be concerned for our children.[12]

The Details of Chemical Exposure

Children in Urban Settings

Imagine a child growing up in inner-city Cincinnati, Ohio. Cincinnati is an old city, one with an environmental legacy that goes back to an era when we knew less about toxicology, an era with little regulation of how we built and worked and lived and with no resources available to remediate the misjudgments of the past. This child (let's call him Jimmie to give him a name and perhaps a face) is likely to live in a house old enough to have lead paint on the walls, as did almost half the housing in the country. If the paint is flaking, young Jimmie may eat some of the paradoxically sweet-tasting lead chips. He will undoubtedly be exposed to lead in the soil and the rest of the environment around his home, thanks in part to the decades-long use of leaded gasoline. If Jimmie is exposed to higher lead levels prior to or after birth than most children, his adult brain volume will be smaller than theirs.[13]

Jimmie's race or religion don't really matter as lead toxicity is a very evenhanded tragedy. Jimmie's gender does matter, however, because males display a greater level of neurological damage than females with similar blood lead levels, especially in reduction of the prefrontal cortex, where conceptual thought and analytical reasoning reside. If Jimmie were Suzie, her brain would also be damaged by the lead, but as a male Jimmie will experience even more damage for the same degree of exposure.

Prefrontal cortex damage reduces what is sometimes called "executive functioning," so it is no surprise that higher blood lead levels early in life are associated with an increased diagnosis of conduct disorder as a child and later increases in arrests for violent or serious crimes. Each five microgram per deciliter increase in blood lead levels produces a modest but statistically significant increase in subsequent arrests.[14] All of this paints a picture of what we might call "poor impulse control"; and if Jimmie were Suzie, she would more likely experience a teen pregnancy.

Jimmie or Suzie might have problems other than just impulsiveness. Low-level lead exposure damages children's measured IQs. In a study of 1,333 children, it was found that when blood lead levels went from 2.4 micrograms per deciliter to 30 micrograms per deciliter, IQ decreased by 6.9 points.[15] Such an IQ variation can make a significant difference to the educational experience, life, and prospects of a child. These findings are consistent with earlier studies linking higher lead exposure to lower mental functioning and behavioral difficulties.

There appears to be no "threshold" below which exposure is safe.[16] The Centers for Disease Control defines an elevated blood lead level as anything above 10 micrograms per deciliter, but concentrations well below this have now been shown to reduce IQ at six years of age. Children with blood lead levels between 5 and 9.9 micrograms per deciliter had IQ values measured at six years of age that were 4.9 points lower than children with blood lead levels below 5 micrograms per deciliter.[17] End-of-grade achievement test results confirm the detrimental impact of early childhood blood lead levels.[18]

As a society we have, to some degree, responded to the issue of lead toxicity by reducing sources of lead exposure. In Cleveland in 1997, the percentage of inner-city children examined with over 10 micrograms per deciliter of lead in their blood was 16.5 percent, but in 2006 it had decreased to 2.3 percent.[19] In a sense this is a substantial improvement for society overall, and certainly many children in the United States are exposed to relatively low lead levels now, given the cessation years ago of the use of leaded paint on houses and the demise of leaded gasoline (except for light propeller-driven aircraft). For many parents, especially wealthier parents with more choices in domicile and the wherewithal to pay for domestic lead testing, their children are now relatively safe from this life-diminishing toxin. But for the 2.3 percent, life will not present them with all of its potential promises. This diminution of life from the outset is not something limited to lead exposure; it reaches across a wide range of rarely considered environmental toxins.

As if lead were not enough of a concern for the parents of an urban Jimmie or Suzie, recent evidence collected from inner-city families in which the mother wore a backpack air monitor for forty-eight hours during the last months of her pregnancy show that children exposed in utero to the highest levels of background urban air pollution had 4–5 point lower IQ scores at five years of age. This difference is enough to diminish performance and learning ability in school and concomitantly the ability of the children to achieve their full potential in life compared to children raised with less exposure to urban air pollution.[20]

Cleveland is far from unique in the environmental risks associated with growing up there. In the San Francisco Bay Area, concentrations of heavy metals and chlorinated solvents in ambient air proximate to children's homes were positively associated with the incidence of autism spectrum disorders. Exposure to heavy metals, chlorinated solvents, and DDE (a breakdown product of DDT) is also detrimental to neurological and psychomotor development. Because the levels of various air pollutants are often high in the same areas, the study was unable to identify the specific heavy metals or chlorinated solvents thought to be the probable cause of the increased autism due to prenatal or early childhood exposure.[21] Similarly, in New Bedford, Massachusetts, mothers living near an organochlorine contaminated harbor and Superfund site had infants whose umbilical cord blood had elevated levels of a number of organochlorine molecules. The higher the levels of organochlorine compounds, the lower the infants scored on measures of attention and attention-related skills.[22]

Urban settings contain large numbers of sites listed on the federal Toxics Release Inventory (TRI). TRI sites are federally licensed to release toxins at specified maximum levels, and may be large- or small-scale commercial facilities. A study of childhood brain cancer in the eastern United States compared proximity between the mother's residence during pregnancy and the closest Environmental Protection Agency-regulated TRI site. The study showed increased risks of brain cancer, diagnosed before age five, for children of mothers who lived within one mile of a TRI facility and especially if the TRI facility was releasing known carcinogens.[23]

The nature of work available in urban settings can also place infants and young children at risk. Maternal occupational exposure prior to or during pregnancy to alkanes, mononuclear aromatic hydrocarbons, 1,1,1–trichloroethane, toluene, mineral spirits, and some other solvents found in workplaces are associated with increased frequencies of acute lymphoblastic childhood leukemia.[24] Higher levels of benzene and 1,3 butadiene in Houston, which are common urban air pollutants, are associated with increased rates of childhood leukemia.[25]

An urban Jimmie or Suzie is likely to develop asthma or other respiratory ailments as childhood asthma doubled in the United States between 1982 and 1993.[26] Approximately 2.3 million U.S. children with asthma live in parts of the country with unhealthy ozone levels in the air, 2.1 million children with asthma live in areas with high levels of particulate pollution for part of the year, and 1.3 million children with asthma live in areas with high levels of particulate pollution for all of the year.[27] The higher the zinc concentration of the particulate pollution (a component contributed by incinerators, industrial processes, and motor vehicles), the greater the rate of emergency room visits and hospital admissions among children.[28] Increasing exposure to urban air pollution produces increased frequencies of the onset of asthma and hospital admissions for asthma, especially in younger and poorer children.[29] Even in cities like San Francisco, where coastal breezes produce what is generally thought of as reasonably good air quality, children living in closer proximity to freeways have higher rates of asthma.[30]

It is also known that early-life susceptibility to bronchitis is linked to air pollution, especially that which is related to heavy vehicular pollution, ambient polycyclic aromatic hydrocarbon (PAH), and fine particulate matter concentrations. Preschool-age children are especially vulnerable to illnesses induced by air pollution.[31] Childhood respiratory allergies are also associated with ozone and particulate pollution exposure.[32] Even brief exposures of young children in Montreal to emissions of sulfur dioxide from refinery smokestacks increased rates of asthma-related emergency room visits and hospital admissions.[33]

Jimmie or Suzie would be more likely to experience a premature birth or have a low birth weight if their mother resided in a polluted urban area. Preterm birth in the United States increased 23 percent from the mid-1980s to 2002.[34] In a study of birth records from four Pennsylvania counties, maternal exposure to particulate pollution under ten microns in diameter (PM_{10}) or sulfur dioxide increased the risk of preterm birth.[35] In California, a large study was conducted to examine the relationship between air pollution and undesirable birth outcomes for over six hundred thousand newborns. Researchers used birth certificate data, the addresses of mothers, and levels of carbon monoxide and PM_{10} measured during pregnancy at the closest air monitoring station to the mothers' homes. The prevalence of preterm birth and low birth weight was linked to residence near highways as well as prenatal exposure to high carbon monoxide, PM_{10}, and ozone.[36] Low birth weight in Connecticut and Massachusetts was associated with exposure to common constituents of urban pollution (carbon monoxide, NO_2, SO_2, PM_{10}, and $PM_{2.5}$).[37] Measures of midpregnancy fetal growth obtained during ultrasound examinations were diminished for infants exposed in early pregnancy to greater levels of urban air pollution.[38] In addition, increased exposure to the ozone generated by traffic produces a greater risk of cleft lip and cleft palate in Jimmie or Suzie.[39]

Children in Rural Settings

It isn't only urban children whose health is at risk. The widespread use of pesticides and herbicides can turn a seemingly idyllic, or at least rural, childhood terrain for Jimmie or Suzie into a dangerous place. In the Salinas Valley in California, scientists collected urinary samples from low-income women in agricultural settings and discovered elevated levels of organophosphate pesticides during pregnancy and the breastfeeding period.[40] These highly soluble materials passed to their children before and after birth.

A large study in Washington state concluded that children in agricultural communities had greater levels of pesticide contamination during crop spraying and if they lived with someone who applied pesticides.[41] Farmworker children in North Carolina had higher urine levels of pesticide residues if they had mothers working part-time, or they lived in rental properties.[42] Childhood leukemia has been linked to maternal occupational exposure to pesticides.[43] Pesticides in agricultural communities might be in the air, water, food, on parents' clothing, or concentrated in toxic waste sites. A study of 5,302 fetal deaths in Washington state found no overall relationship between fetal death rates and proximity of the mothers' residences to known toxic waste sites, but for waste sites specifically known to contain pesticides a small but significant increase in fetal deaths occurred when the residence of the pregnant woman was within five miles of the toxic site. The risk of fetal death increased slightly with every mile closer to the waste site.[44] A large-scale study of childhood cancers in the United States found a significantly increased risk for many types of cancer for children residing in counties with 60 percent or more of their total acreage devoted to agriculture.[45]

There are other ways in which life in a rural setting might not protect Jimmie. Birth defects are also linked to pesticide exposure of unborn children. Hypospadia is a birth defect in which the urethra of infant boys develops abnormally, usually on the underside of the penis. Application of certain pesticides has been shown to produce hypospadia in laboratory animals. In Arkansas the presence of the herbicide diclofop-methyl on a field within 500 meters (roughly 500 yards) of a pregnant woman's home during gestational weeks six through sixteen was later associated with an increase in hypospadia.[46]

Another birth defect impacting infant boys is cryptorchidism (undescended testicles). Studies have linked this condition to mothers with higher levels of organochlorine pesticides in their breast milk. The total organochlorine load of the mother, rather than any specific pesticide, seemed to be related to this lack of testicular descent in the fetus.[47] Prenatal exposure to organohalogenated compounds, polybrominated diphenyl ethers (PBDEs), and higher PBDE levels in breast milk increase rates of both hypospadia and cryptorchidism, with agriculture work by mothers highly correlated with these male birth defects.[48]

Pesticide applications are also linked to autism, and Jimmie or Suzie might face an increased risk of this disorder if they were living near pesticide applications in their early life. A recent study indicates that a link appears to exist between the proximity of maternal residence during pregnancy to pesticide applications; increases in autism spectrum disorders are correlated with pesticide drift. Two pesticides, the organochlorine compounds dicofol and endosulfan, are specifically implicated in California's Central Valley.[49] While children living near farms are not uniquely vulnerable to autism, this disorder has increased tenfold from the early 1980s to 1996, and higher ambient levels of heavy metals and chlorinated solvents (more typically urban issues) also increase the number of children born with the disease.[50]

Children in the Suburbs

Life in the suburbs, however, does not insure safety from environmental toxins for Jimmie or Suzie. Perfluorinated compounds (PFCs) are a component of nonstick coatings, fabric, leather, food packaging, and other applications typical of convenience products seen in affluent suburbs. PFC use in the home translates to PFC accumulation in our bodies. PFCs are highly suspect for their effect on human health; they are linked in laboratory animal studies to liver and testicular cancer, immune system disorders, birth defects, and other medical issues. Even relatively low levels of PFCs in maternal blood serum are associated with reduced birth weights.[51] A recent study of the efficiency of PFC transfer between mother and child by breast feeding indicated serious questions of health risks, sufficient for the study's authors to call for an assessment of hazardous exposure via nursing.[52] PFCs give us nothing but convenience. Among the chemical compounds identified in umbilical cord blood at birth are eight PFCs used in fast food packaging and clothing, including PFOA, categorized as a likely human carcinogen by the EPA's Science Advisory Board.[53]

Like their rural counterparts, suburban Jimmie or Suzie will face a greater risk of leukemia if Dad or Mom sprays pesticides in the house, an increased risk of childhood brain cancer if Mom or Dad use herbicides residentially, and an increased risk of leukemia if the level of PCBs in carpet dust (industrial chemicals banned in 1988 but often present indoors where their breakdown by sunlight and water is low) is high in the room where the child spends the most time.[54] Childhood acute lymphoblastic leukemia rates are also increased by postnatal exposure to household air containing paint fumes; even the type of chemical exposure we casually produce by repainting a nursery in a suburban home can have tragic consequences.[55]

An additional health risk for suburban children is the scantily researched health risks associated with chemicals released from the crumb rubber layer in artificial turf playing fields. This cushioning layer is generally made of ground recycled automobile tires, which contain a wide variety of chemical additives and which are considered too toxic to dispose of in normal landfills or by ocean dumping. Early indications are that volatile organic compounds with known health effects are released from the rubber subsurface layer and may pose a hazard to children whose sports or recreational activities bring them into substantial contact with artificial turf.[56]

Another chemical group, known as phthalates, are plastic softening agents generally found in soft toys and flexible bottles, like the ones seen with young families at the sidelines of soccer games. Mothers with higher phthalate concentrations in their breast milk had male infants with altered early sex hormone levels. The early disruption of sex hormone levels can alter important developmental processes and cause significant differences in later stages of sexual maturation.[57] Higher maternal urinary phthalate concentrations are associated with increased likelihoods of preterm birth.[58] Higher levels of prenatal phthalate exposure and phthalate metabolites in urine samples are correlated with lower IQ measures and other measures of cognitive ability.[59]

Bisphenol-A (BPA) is a petrochemical found in food or beverages sold in lined metal cans and in polycarbonate beverage containers (including many baby bottles). BPA is a synthetic estrogen; even in low doses it disrupts development of normal reproductive systems and is also implicated in a host of other health-related issues. A recent study of umbilical cord blood in minority children[60] was the first to demonstrate BPA in the blood of newborns. This would be equally likely in Jimmie or Suzie of any race if they ate or drank from similar baby bottles or canned food sources. Major baby bottle makers and beverage container makers are moving away from BPA following bad publicity about BPA entering formula when baby bottles are heated.[61] Legislation mandating that change is spreading, but plastic linings of metal cans continue to contaminate the food in them with BPA.

Other toxins that might affect Jimmie or Suzie in a modern suburban home include dozens of brominated flame retardants.[62] Brominated flame retardants, also known as PBDEs, are absorbed by mothers and passed on through breast milk. The United States and Canada both allow these toxic materials to be used as fire retardants (in furniture, computers, TVs, automobiles, and so on) despite medical evidence that has resulted in the banning of PBDEs by the European Union. The average level of brominated fire retardants in the breast milk of twenty first-time U.S. mothers was approximately seventy-five times higher than was found in European women.[63]

PBDE concentrations in breast milk in the United States are correlated to concentrations in house dust and increased maternal consumption of dairy products and meat.[64] Research has also shown that PBDEs, which pass to infants via breast milk, cause memory deficits, learning and hearing impairments, and other sensory deficiencies.[65] PBDE exposure at critical moments in prenatal brain development can cause permanent harm.[66] PBDE levels as low as four parts per billion (ppb) in animal brain tissue or twelve ppb in animal brain fat cause permanent brain damage. Thirty percent of U.S. women have more than twelve ppb of PBDE in the fat of their breast milk; it is not known how that corresponds to resulting concentrations of PBDE in infant brain tissue.[67]

PBDEs produce infant developmental deficits by reducing thyroid function in pregnant mothers. Women with low thyroid hormone levels are much more likely to have babies categorized as having IQs of less than 85 and IQs of less than 70. These IQ levels are likely to significantly limit their possibilities for a full life (two-thirds of children dropping out of high school have IQs below 85). PBDE effects on later thyroid function in children exposed before birth may or may not be as permanent as the neurological deficiencies produced.[68]

No Escape in the Arctic

Even if Jimmie or Suzie were children in the Arctic they would not be immune from risk. DDE, a breakdown product of DDT, a pesticide now banned in the United States but persistent, is widely distributed around the world by wind, water, and food chains, and still heavily used around the world, for example, for malaria control in Africa. Fish consumption, especially of predatory fish, is linked to higher maternal tissue and milk levels of DDE as well as other fat soluble contaminants like PCBs. The egregious situation for Alaskan natives and Canadian Inuit is that they have excessive blood DDE levels, associated with their diet of marine mammals and predatory fish, despite the fact that they live in a region that never used DDT to protect crops.[69] DDE passes readily from mother to child through nursing and across the placenta. Inuit women have high levels of PCBs in their bodies and breast milk. Cohort studies of children done elsewhere show that increased prenatal PCB exposure causes decreased IQ at nine years of age; this is a high price for Arctic children to pay for the careless disposal of industrial chemicals.[70]

Regardless of where Jimmie and Suzie live, global events will alter environmental risks when it is time for them to have children. Analyses of the effect of exposure to high ambient temperatures in the second and third trimesters of pregnancy have been combined with modeling of our changing climate. These indicate that if global climate change continues along its present course, the prevalence of low-birth-weight babies (more prone to a wide variety of health problems than larger babies) will increase significantly. Roughly 5 to 6 percent more low-birth-weight babies are anticipated. Should Jimmie or Suzie, as adults, have such an infant he or she will likely have more health and developmental issues to contend with.[71]

Cost-Benefit Analysis and Discounting the Future

Before leaving the topic of environmental toxins, it is important to briefly discuss the scientific and ethical problems associated with policy decisions

REDUCING YOUR BODY BURDEN

According to a study titled "Pollution in People: A Study of Toxic Chemicals in Oregonians," released in 2007 by the Oregon Environmental Council, typical parents can help protect their Jimmie or Suzie from toxins. One of the participants in the study who donated her blood and urine to be tested for the presence of twenty-nine toxic chemicals was a young mother who had decided to reduce her unborn child's exposure to two types of hormone-disrupting chemicals, phthalates (contained in many plastics and personal care products) and Bisphenol-A (found in some baby bottles, plastic toys, and food containers).

She had the lowest number of chemicals detected in her body of any study participant, her total phthalate level was under half of that of the second lowest participant, and her body alone contained no detectable level of Bisphenol-A. The affordable steps taken by this prudent mother (removing a vinyl shower curtain, eliminating plastics from her kitchen and home, choosing nontoxic personal care products for mother and child) were effective even in our complicated contaminated world. A simple action like taking calcium supplements can help reduce blood lead levels in pregnant women. Lead is stored in bones and, like calcium, which is liberated from bones due to the demands of pregnancy, blood lead levels can go up in pregnancy and harm the unborn infant. Simply taking calcium supplements during pregnancy can help reduce blood lead levels by a quarter.

that result from cost-benefit analysis. Cost-benefit analysis is the standard methodology intended to facilitate objective decision making for policies that have both expenses and benefits associated with them. It is clear that without infinite funds, a society cannot simultaneously embrace all the activities that it would aspire to. It is important, therefore, to understand the relative social values of different ways of expending limited financial resources. Cost-benefit analysis is used for this purpose. Unfortunately, it does not achieve complete objectivity because of inherent biases in the system that generally favor shortsightedness and a laissez faire approach to environmental issues.

The three steps of cost-benefit analysis are (1) calculating the monetary value of the benefits that would be produced by a policy decision, (2) calculating the monetary costs of that policy being implemented, and (3) adopting those policies whose benefits (expressed in monetary terms) exceed the costs.

The problems at each step of this process have been described in detail.[72] The benefits associated with cost-benefit analysis of environmental policies

RESOURCES FOR CHOOSING HEALTHY PRODUCTS

To choose healthy products for infants and children

www.chej.org/documents/BabysToxicBottleFinal.pdf

www.oeconline.org/kidshealth/tinyfootprints/Walletcards

www.healthytoys.org/home.php

www.checnet.org/healtheHouse/pdf/plasticchart.pdf

To choose healthy personal care products

www.safecosmetics.org

www.cosmeticsdatabase.com/special/parentsguide/index.php?nothanks=1

To reduce dietary mercury and PCB consumption

www.nrdc.org/health/effects/mercury/walletcard.pdf

www.environmentaldefense.org/documents/1980_pocket_seafood_selector.pdf

www.nrdc.org/health/effects/mercury/effects.asp

are very hard to quantify (what is clean water worth? clean air? forests to hike in?). At the outset, it is not clear that agreeing to monetize these sorts of benefits is even appropriate. The costs of environmental policies are often hard to calculate, and exaggerated costs can provide "cover" for unwilling business interests or for partisan political agendas. Given the difficulty in both determining the value of environmental benefits and any projected costs that depend on potential impacts of environmental policies on business, the third step (decision making) of cost-benefit analysis is extraordinarily difficult to carry out objectively.

Additionally, such a process discounts the future. In standard economic analysis, future costs and benefits are discounted; that is, they are treated as though they are worth less than costs and benefits in the present time. This can be understood perhaps by the following analogy. If you can collect 3 percent interest from a bank annually, the $1,000 you get today is worth more than $1,000 you may get next year. At the very least, you could put today's $1,000 in the bank and collect $30.00 more in the course of a year. Thus, $1,000 given to you next year would be worth $30.00 less than $1,000 obtained now. If the periods of time involved get longer, the effect is magnified. For example, given a 3 percent discount rate, twenty years from now $100 will be equivalent in purchasing power to only $38 at the present time.[73] The ethical implications of discounting the future value of things, which are not clearly monetized in the first place (a long healthy life, clear skies at dawn, a lake you can let your children swim in), are complicated and perhaps not best left to economists and policymakers.

The fundamental concerns about cost-benefit analysis have been expressed eloquently:

> There are no meaningful prices attached to protection of human life, health, nature, and the well-being of future generations, and no end of nonsense has resulted from the attempt to invent surrogate prices for them. The absence of prices is fatal to the cost-benefit project, but it is not the case that unpriced benefits are worthless: what is the cash value of your oldest friendship, your relationship with your children, or your right to vote and participate in a democratically governed country? As the German philosopher Immanuel Kant put it, some things have a price, or relative worth, while other things have a dignity, or inner worth. The failure of cost-benefit analysis, in Kantian terms, stems from the attempt to weigh costs, which usually have a price, against benefits, which often have a dignity.[74]

The world around us today, with polluted lakes, rivers, and oceans, toxins in our air, the marks of bioaccumulation in children's bodies, looks uncomfortably as though we are living in a present whose value was discounted at some time in the past. Does our society today want to ignore that lesson and do the same to generations in the future? This question enters the realm of theology by raising important ethical issues.

Questions for Discussion

1. What is the correct balance to strike between careful regulation of potentially toxic industrial chemicals and economic innovation leading to high levels of employment?

2. What can you currently do to reduce your exposure to harmful human-produced environmental toxins?

3. Can the precautionary principle be incorporated into U.S. environmental laws without shifting substantial resources from the private sector to the public sector, and if not should this be done?

4. Is there an alternative to "discounting the future" that would be a more Earth-friendly vision of evaluating investment opportunities, or is this type of economic analysis by its very nature divorced from environmental concerns?

5. What is the relationship between poverty and exposure to environmental toxins? Does this situation require an imperative for ethical action?

Active Learning Exercises

♦ Where are you from? Go to the U.S. Environmental Protection Agency (enviromapper storefront at *www.epa.gov/emefdata/em4ef.home*). Enter your home zip code and then, using both the "Air, Water, Waste" and "Program Systems" boxes on the left, successively adding all the different polluting entities, examine the maps showing the distribution of each. Print any map you choose from among these views of your home zip code. Notice that you can click on any specific location and follow that link to find out more about the local situation. Write a one-page discussion of what you found out and how it relates to what you expected to find. Is your hometown like you thought it was? In earlier versions of enviromapper there used to be a "social justice" function that allowed you to view the polluting sites in reference to areas with different levels of wealth, education, or the proportion of people of color. This function was discontinued. From what you know of your home zip code, would that have added any more pertinent information to the map?

♦ In groups divide among yourselves and read recent reports on where different environmental toxins exist in the U.S. food supply. Good reports to include are:

– the national Workgroup for Safe Markets, "No Silver Lining, an Investigation into Bisphenol A in Canned Goods" (*www.uspirg.org/home/reports/report-archives/healthy-/healthy-communities/no-silver-lining-an-investigation-into-bisphenol-a-in-canned-foods*)par

– the Environmental Working Group's "Shopper's Guide to Pesticides" (*www.foodnews.org/*) and their "Overexposed, Organophosphate Pesticides in Children's Food" (*www.ewg.org/node/7877*)

– the data base online at What's On My Food (*www.whatsonmyfood.org/index.jsp*).

Many other reports are available.

Once your reading is done, make a trip to a food store and accumulate two theoretical shopping carts, one filled with conventional products and the other with organic/BPA-free foods purchased as locally as possible. Each theoretical cart should contain $75 worth of items bought using the guidelines. Make two tables showing the food items in each cart. Then compare the types and quantity of food bought with each type of diet in mind and write a two-page reflection on the relationship between income level and a family's capacity to adopt a chemical-free diet. Include the two tables along with the reflection.

Recommended Reading

Carson, Rachel. *Silent Spring.* New York: Houghton Mifflin, 1962.

Colborn, Theo, Diane Dumanaski, and John Peter Meyers. *Our Stolen Future: Are We Threatening Our Fertility, Intelligence, and Survival? A Scientific Detective Story.* New York: Plume, 1997.

Shabecoff, Philip, and Alice Shabecoff. *Poisoned Profits: The Toxic Assault on Our Children.* New York: Random House, 2008.

Shrader-Frechette, Kristin. *Taking Action, Saving Lives: Our Duties to Protect Environmental and Public Health.* Oxford: Oxford University Press, 2007.

Theological Reflections on Ecology
and the Environmental Crisis
An Ecotheology of Revelation
and Human Existence

At first glance it appears that the impact of ecology and environmental science on the shape of Christian theology is a relatively recent phenomenon. The majority of what has come to be called ecotheology emerged out of the Judeo-Christian theological tradition in the last twenty to thirty years. Nevertheless, we would be remiss if we did not mention forerunners, historical voices from the recent past that began to presage the full-blown appearance of ecotheology. Walter C. Lowdermilk (1888–1974) is one example. A professional soil conservationist, speaking and writing in Jerusalem in 1939, Lowdermilk proposed the "Eleventh Commandment":

> XI. Thou shall inherit the earth as a faithful steward, conserving its resources and productivity from generation to generation. Thou shall protect thy fields from soil erosion and thy hills from overgrazing by thy herds, so that thy descendants may have abundance forever. If any shall fail in this stewardship of the land, his fertile field shall become sterile stones and gullies, and his descendants shall decrease and live in poverty or vanish from the face of the earth.[1]

Lowdermilk went on to suggest that all nations have a "Moses of land conservation to instill in the national consciousness the principle of an Eleventh Commandment to regulate man's relation to the holy earth as a faithful steward."[2]

As engaging as Lowdermilk's eleventh commandment was — and still is — the first systematic attempt in the United States to reshape Christian theology in the direction of ecotheology was the Lutheran theologian and pastor Joseph Sittler (1904–87). In his 1954 essay, "A Theology for Earth," Sittler declared that "man is no longer related to nature in God's intended way" and that "the largest, most insistent, and most delicate task awaiting Christian theology is to articulate . . . a theology of nature as shall do justice to the vitalities of earth."[3]

Sittler proceeded to devote the better part of his life to this task, producing some of the first and best insights for the emergence of ecotheology.

Sittler was one of the first to initiate dialogue between ecology and theology by proposing what he called "a theology of ecology" in which he recognized the nexus between ecology and theology: the primacy of relationship.[4] Sittler argued that ecology required theologians to begin thinking in terms of relationality, and he declared that the only adequate basis for theological reflection in an ecological age was what he termed "ontology of community."[5] It is interesting to note that Sittler and Lynn White Jr. were contemporaries, both having died in 1987. Unfortunately, White's critical essay bears no evidence that he read Sittler's work. If he had, his essay might have been a more balanced assessment of Christianity and the ecological crisis.

The importance of relationship is by no means new to the Judeo-Christian theological tradition; it extends back to the biblical narrative, where the term "covenant" is commonplace for naming the relationship between God and God's people. It highlights what scripture scholar Carol Dempsey calls the biblical mandate of "right relationship."[6] From the beginning of the New Testament writings, it is clear that theologians like the apostle Paul were very concerned with "right relationships" within the church, particularly within the fledgling communities that he helped establish. Since then people-to-people relationships, especially in subdisciplines like theological ethics, have dominated theological reflection.

What is new is the extent to which theology has had to broaden its horizon of relatedness to include not only the biophysical world of Earth but the cosmos itself and the genesis of the project we call life. What is also new is the incisiveness with which ecology has become a predominant hermeneutical lens for interpreting the entire range of theological categories in what is typically referred to as systematic theology. Systematic theology, also known as constructive theology, attempts to provide a systematic, comprehensive, and often sequential treatment of the major doctrines and aspects of the Christian faith tradition. Usually beginning with human existence (also known as theological anthropology), systematic theology proceeds to offer a theological analysis of God, Jesus Christ, church, theological ethics and morality, spirituality, and so on. Ecotheologians have taken up this task by providing an interpretation of these essential components of Christian faith through the lens of ecology and environmental science.

Because the previous two chapters have dealt with the extent and the growing severity of the environmental crisis, we begin our theological reflection with the question: What does the environmental crisis mean theologically and how should we interpret it? Because of the scope and magnitude of the ecological degradation that has occurred thus far, it is our conviction that this is a revelatory moment in the history of our planet and species.

Simply defined, revelation, or the doctrine of revelation, refers to the self-disclosure of God in human experience. An ecotheology of revelation must be anchored in four essential aspects of the dialogue between ecology and theology: (1) the Bible and the biblical theological tradition, (2) history and culture, (3) creation and the natural world, and (4) environmental science and ecology.

The Biblical Theological Tradition

At the risk of stating the obvious, the Bible is indispensable for any Christian theological endeavor. It contains the roots of the Christian tradition and the earliest attempts to interpret the meaning and nature of human existence, the encounter with God, and for Christians, the encounter with and interpretation of Jesus of Nazareth. The Bible as a book, composed in human language, contains the self-communication of God and is considered by Christians and Jews alike to be a primary medium of divine revelation.

It is important to note, however, that the theological term "revelation" does not occur in the Bible. Nevertheless, the biblical story, framed between the creation narratives in Genesis and the eschatological renewal and restoration of creation in the Book of Revelation, is all about God's self-communication. The idea that the Bible is revelatory of God is central to biblical theology and hermeneutics, and it indicates that God's self-disclosure occurs through a variety of mediums. Four of those mediums, to be addressed in some detail in the next two chapters, are history, creation-Wisdom theology, God, and Jesus Christ, who for Christians is the apex of God's self-disclosure.

Within the range of the world's major religions, the Bible is a unique document insofar as it represents one of the earliest attempts of a religious culture — ancient Israel — to produce a religious historical narrative that is replete with a variety of literary forms that communicate the many ways the ancient Israelites encountered and interpreted divine reality. Central to their encounter and interpretation is the novel idea that God is revealed in and through historical events and historical people. It is a novel idea, given the religious landscape of the ancient Middle East, where the majority of ancient Israel's neighbor's encountered divine reality in and through natural events expressed through a polytheistic religious worldview. Israel, on the other hand, associated God's self-communication with covenant relationships with particular people, such as Abraham and Moses, and historical events, such as the Exodus. This set the stage for the historical foundations of the Abrahamic religions in which history and the prophet archetype became central to Judaism, Christianity, and Islam, which are often referred to as "religions of the book."

One might ask at this point what this has to do with the environmental crisis. First, as earlier chapters have made clear, one of the primary tasks of theology is to scrutinize the historical "signs of the times," of which a major sign today is our environmental predicament. Second, any attempt to provide a theological interpretation and response to this crisis must include the biblical tradition in the search for relevant theological motifs and principles that can be applied to our contemporary situation. In keeping with the biblical narrative and the importance of history, we are challenged to ask how we should theologically interpret the environmental crisis. Our response, given the size and significance of this crisis, is that it must be considered a major revelatory event in our time and space.[7] To borrow an idea from John Haught, the environmental crisis is a major "interruption" for humanity and for the typical, taken-for-granted way our species has done business on this planet.[8]

We propose four ways of seeing our ecological crisis as revelatory of God. First, drawing upon the important work of the late Cardinal Avery Dulles (1918–2008) in his book *Models of Revelation,* the environmental crisis must be seen as *an opening to new awareness.* Dulles states that new awareness is "the process by which God, working within history and human tradition, enables his spiritual creatures to achieve a higher level of consciousness."[9] The environmental crisis has generated and continues to generate a transformation of consciousness, an emerging awareness best described as an ecological shift in human self-definition.

The emerging ecological consciousness is shaped by the critical awareness of human relatedness to and dependency on the Earth's ecosphere and the intricate network of ecosystemic functions that support human existence and the existence of all life forms. This new way of thinking and doing is reflected in the growing interest in one's "ecological footprint" and the intentional adoption of sustainable practices that seek to reduce the human footprint now and for future generations. Theologically, this new awareness is characterized by the emergence of the various ecologies of grace to be discussed below.

Central to this awareness is ecological or creation spirituality, which seeks to cultivate an intimate relationship with human beings, Earth, and God. Ecological spirituality is often accompanied by a renewed sacramental consciousness that is mindful of Earth and the entire universe as a primary medium through which sacred reality is encountered. Recalling Ian Barbour's typology of the science-theology relationship in chapter 2, a "nature-centered spirituality" is an example of dialogue, and a "sacramental view of nature" is also an expression of a theology of nature that implies integration.[10]

The second way of interpreting the environmental crisis as a revelatory event is based on *the biblical view,* especially from ancient Israel's poets and sages, *that creation is the language of God.* It is the biblical view that creation using its own voice speaks the praises of God (see Ps. 148 in particular). The case of the environmental crisis, however, also involves revelatory "hearing" and bearing witness to the suffering of creation. An ecotheology of revelation incorporates the hearing of creation's suffering and seeks to unmask the intrinsic connection between the oppression of people and the oppression of creation. In this view, the work of ecojustice and the praxis of sustainability can be seen as a harbinger and a revelatory promise and ful-fillment in the renewal and restoration of creation. More will be said about this in the final chapter.

The third aspect of the environmental crisis as a revelatory event is to see it as *an example of divine instruction.* This idea is drawn from the Bible's Wisdom tradition (some examples are the books of Proverbs, Job, Ecclesiastes, Wisdom, and Sirach), a particular genre of biblical literature and teaching. In this literary-theological tradition, the Wisdom of God is personified as a feminine characteristic of God and is often referred to as Woman Wisdom (see Prov. 8). Woman Wisdom instructs the faithful seeker of wisdom in the ways of justice and righteousness. This view is based on the idea that creation, within which Woman Wisdom resides, is intelligible, and that through the study of and rational reflection on creation, Woman Wisdom reveals God and the way one should live in harmony with creation. This perspective is deeply embedded in ancient Israel's creation theology, which interpreted creation as a physical and moral order. In biblical Wisdom literature, Woman Wisdom maintains the physical and moral orderliness of creation.

More will be said about the significance of creation-Wisdom theology in the next chapter. For now it is important to recognize that an ecotheology of revelation must take into account the knowledge about creation provided by ecology and environmental science. While it would be a stretch to call it divine instruction, the science of ecology has certainly been instructional in the way we humans have lived in relation to the natural world, and it provides insight into the way we ought to live. To echo Haught, "Science can provide helpful assistance in our attempts to understand the circumstances within which the mystery of God is disclosed."[11]

The final characteristic of an ecotheological interpretation of the environmental crisis as a revelatory event is the fact that *it has challenged theology to reconfigure its understanding of God and God's action in the world.* The primary issues are God's immanence in and relatedness to the natural world. The reader is reminded that one of the central points of contact in the dialogue between theology and ecology is the category of relationship. The interrelatedness of the biophysical world, the domain of ecology, is, from a theological perspective, an extension of the interrelatedness between God and God's creation. The insights of ecology and the environmental crisis have created a shift in our understanding about God that has challenged theology to rethink and reexamine the immanence and relationality of God that embraces all existence. One of the key avenues in this ecotheological endeavor has been the retrieval and reappropriation of biblical creation-Wisdom theology. This and several examples of an ecotheology of God will be the subject of chapter 7.

Another aspect of revelation — related to the disclosure of God that has been the consequence of ecology and its companion sciences — is the notion that the entire universe is revelatory of God. The idea of God revealed in creation, what we in the modern world call the universe, is not new in Christian tradition and in fact extends back to the Bible itself. Unfortunately in Western Christianity, the revelatory character of creation has tended to take a back seat to the redemptive acts of God as revealed in such biblical events as the Exodus and the death and resurrection of Jesus.

Nevertheless, in the Roman Catholic tradition one can find references to the discovery of God in creation. In Thomas Aquinas, for example, we note the view that using human reason one can discover something about God's nature from observing creation. That idea was affirmed by the First Vatican Council (1869–1870), which declared that creation contains "natural manifestations" of God that can be known "through the light of human reason."[12] While the council did affirm that the experience of God through creation is a form of natural revelation, it gave primary status to "supernatural revelation." Supernatural revelation refers to God's self-disclosure in the biblical account particularly in the person of Jesus. This line of thinking reflects the distinction often made in Western theology between "natural" theology (rational reflection on the existence and experience of God through the observation of nature) and "revealed" theology (theological reflection on God's redemptive acts in history as revealed in the Bible). From a biblical as well as a modern perspective this distinction appears artificial and forced. For example, the Presbyterian Old Testament scholar James Barr (1924–2006) argued that it is nearly impossible to distinguish between natural and revealed theology in the Bible. He stated "that 'revelational' theology and 'natural' theology were irretrievably mixed up with one another."[13] In the Bible God is disclosed in both creation and redemption.

Bridging the Biblical World and Science

In the modern context, a theology of revelation must take into account the impact of science. One person who has made a significant contribution to bridging the biblical world and the world of scientific modernity is John Haught. His view is that "a theology based on revelation does not compete with science or conflict with it in any way. It is complementary to it, in the sense that it contributes something to the larger picture of reality that science cannot."[14] Haught's dialogue between theology and science draws from two sources. From *biblical theology,* Haught develops the notion of divine promise, a subtheme throughout the entire biblical narrative. From the *science of cosmology and evolution,* Haught develops the idea of emergence. Haught asserts that, especially in light of the environmental crisis, a theology of revelation must interpret the entire universe "as a gift of God's own being and selfhood."[15] He states, "The universe itself is, in a sense, an ongoing revelation. In its immensities of time and space, as well as in its love of endless diversity, it sacramentalizes the generosity, extravagance, and unpredictability of the creator known in biblical faith as the God of promise."[16]

Professor John Haught of Georgetown University is the author of numerous books and articles on the subject of science and theology. He is one of the leading voices within Christianity advocating genuine dialogue between science and theology. Speaking of a theology of nature, Haught says that "today a theology of nature may connect the divine promise to what science now refers to as emergence, the tendency of the universe to give rise occasionally and spontaneously to new forms of complexity, especially in the spheres of life and mind. When theology reflects on cosmic origins, the evolutionary thrust of life, and the emergent character of nature in general, the revelatory image that combines God's descent with God's promissory nature can frame natural phenomena in such a way as to discover a deeper meaning in natural processes than science alone can ever discover" (*Christianity and Science: Toward a Theology of Nature* [Maryknoll, N.Y: Orbis Books, 2007], 40–41).

Utilizing the insights of cosmology and evolution, Haught identifies the novel appearance of natural phenomena, such as life, as an example of the emergent character of natural processes. Linking the emergent character of the universe with the notion of God's promise, Haught maintains that "when theology reflects on cosmic origins, the evolutionary thrust of life, and the emergent character of nature in general, the revelatory image that combines God's descent with God's promissory nature can frame natural phenomena in such a way as to disclose a deeper meaning in natural processes than science alone can ever discover."[17]

In essence, what has occurred as a result of theology's attention to modern science is that the status of the natural world as a bona fide source of revelation has been raised to a new level and, consequently, treated with far more seriousness and value than in the past. This has challenged us to reconsider the taken-for-granted aspects of daily living, the air, water, and land that support and nurture our existence. Ecology has forced us to see these essential aspects of life in a new way and to realize that these characteristics of the natural world are in themselves revelatory of God. As Haught puts it,

> Revelation occurs not only in words but also in sacraments derived from nature. That is, natural phenomena, not just events in human history, participate in and thus point us toward the mystery of God. Water, light, food, soil, fertility, life, and human personality are indispensable to the experience of revelation. God is known not apart from nature but in and through it.[18]

The Environmental Crisis and the Meaning of Human Existence

In response to the environmental crisis, contemporary ecotheology also must reflect on the meaning of human existence. Traditionally referred to as *theological anthropology*, a theology of human existence attempts to define and assess the human condition by focusing on the theological categories of nature, grace, and sin. From an ecological standpoint it begins with the recognition that humanity — as Sittler put it — "is an ecological entity in relation."[19] In relation to revelation, grace is the faithful reception, experience, and interpretation of God's self-communication in our human existence.

Grace Defined

At this point it seems appropriate to ask, Why begin with grace? Doesn't sin predominate? Certainly if one were to examine and assess the specific environmental problems discussed in the previous chapters from a theological point of view, it would likely lead to the conclusion that humanity is living in a broken relationship with the natural world or, as Episcopalian theologian Sallie McFague puts it, we are "living a lie."[20] According to McFague, this phrase means that human beings are "living out of proper relations with God, self, and other beings."[21] Nevertheless, without deemphasizing the gravity and "sinfulness" of our environmental predicament, we begin with grace because chronologically and ontologically grace is first, what we will call *original grace*.

We must first briefly explore the contours of grace in the Bible. Simply put, God is gracious and the concept of grace reflects God's relationship with creation. In the Old Testament the transliterated Hebrew terms associated with grace are *hen, hanan,* and *hesed,* and in the New Testament the Greek term is *charis.* The root word in Hebrew for grace is *hnn,* from which is derived the noun *hen* and the verb *hanan. Hen* is usually translated as grace or favor, and *hanan* means to be gracious and/or to act graciously toward someone.

Both terms share three characteristics. First, *hen* and *hanan* reflect an inner quality, attitude, or disposition; second, they indicate the action or activity that flows from the inner quality; and third, they refer to the unmerited nature of the gift, favor, or action that has been granted. John Kselman states it this way:

> In both human-human relationships and human-divine relationships, *hen* (grace) in the OT involves a positive disposition of someone toward another....It is an undeserved gift or favor, which can be requested, which is freely and unilaterally given, not coerced, and which can be withheld.... This uncoerced and unilateral favor is more than a disposition of passive benevolence on the part of God. It is action that is requested, God's action in aiding the poor, delivering the oppressed and mortally ill.[22]

The third term, linguistically unrelated to *hen* and *hanan,* but perhaps the most significant, is *hesed.* Occurring well over two hundred times, particularly in the psalms, *hesed* belies easy translation. Usually taken to mean steadfast love or covenantal love, *hesed* is the key term in ancient Israel's covenantal understanding of itself and its relationship with God. An Old Testament text that exemplifies the meaning of *hesed* is found in Exodus 34:6–7, "The LORD, the LORD, a God merciful and gracious, slow to anger, and abounding in steadfast love and faithfulness, keeping steadfast love for thousands, forgiving iniquity and transgression and sin." As a synonymous term for grace, *hesed* points to God's unmerited and generous mercy and graciousness to persons in community. In ancient Israel, *hesed* was the model for Israel's reciprocal response to God and the basic principle for communal interaction. It was also the centerpiece of the prophet Hosea's critique of Israel — that Israel's covenantal relationship with God was seriously threatened by the people's lack of knowledge and steadfast love.

When compared with *hen* and *hanan, hesed* shares the basic qualities of inner disposition, activity, and relationality. Elizabeth Dreyer frames the connection this way: "*Hesed* is like *hen* and *hanan* in that it points to action as well as an attitude of kindness; it refers to what extends beyond strict obligation or duty; it suggests mutuality in relationship."[23] What is important to note in this brief excursion into the Old Testament's language of grace is that it is rooted in human-human and human-divine relationships and does, therefore, provide an obvious and important connection between a theology of grace and an ecology of grace. We will return to this key idea and experience of relationality shortly, but first a brief analysis of grace in the New Testament.

The New Testament demonstrates continuity with the Old Testament's understanding of grace, which is understandable, given the fact that the early Jesus movement was a Jewish phenomenon and that the person largely responsible for expanding the meaning of grace was Paul. Writing in Greek, however, the New Testament writers used the term *charis,* which is usually translated to mean the generous, unmerited, and gracious work of God. The primary difference between the Old and New Testament meanings of grace is the experience of salvation in Jesus Christ. This is particularly important for Paul as the death and resurrection of Jesus, central to Paul's experience, resulted in his expanded understanding of grace as the salvific work of God in Christ.

Central to Paul's understanding of grace is God and God's action. Reflecting on Paul's notion of grace, Elizabeth Dreyer writes that "for Paul grace is about God. Grace is not some entity or product of God."[24] She goes on to identify five aspects of Paul's theology of grace: (1) "Grace is God in God's creative graciousness," (2) "Grace is God in God's freedom," (3) "Grace is God in God's acceptance and embrace of a sinful and unworthy people," (4) "Grace is God in God's steadfast love and in God's generous gift of Jesus," and (5) "Grace is God in the dynamism of God, the active and effective power of God bringing aid to God's people."[25]

In the New Testament grace embodies the entire range of Christian existence, incorporating the experience of salvation in Christ and the way of living out that experience in community. One important aspect of this understanding is the experience of God's grace in creation. As St. Paul writes in his letter to the Romans, "Ever since the creation of the world his invisible nature, namely his eternal power and deity, has been clearly perceived in the things that have been made" (Rom. 1:20).

The language of grace in the Old and New Testaments describes what Dreyer has called "mutuality in relationship," and it points in the direction of Sittler's ecological notion of the "ontology of communion."[26] Building on Sittler's ideas, Canadian theologian Douglas John Hall makes a compelling argument that, when viewed through the lens of an ecological hermeneutic, the biblical tradition — what Hall calls the "tradition of Jerusalem" — reflects an "ontology of communion" and in fact allows us to reappropriate one of the basic insights of the Judeo-Christian tradition. Hall writes that "The 'ontology of communion' is a natural, and necessary, outcome of the biblical conception of God."[27] Hall proposes "a kind of theorem or axiom: the basic ontological category of the tradition of Jerusalem is not, as with Athens, that of 'being' as such, but *being with.* Or as an equation: Being=Being-With."[28] Hall goes on to state that "To claim the rudimentary ontology of the biblical tradition is being-with is to say that all being, from the Being who is the source and ground of all being to the smallest of created things, is being-in-relationship."[29]

What we have here, to borrow a phrase from Hans-Georg Gadamer, is a hermeneutical "fusion of horizons."[30] On the one hand we have an ancient source, the Bible, wherein the primary understanding of being is relational as being-with and, on the other hand, we have the modern contemporary insight of ecology, which defines and investigates the natural world as relationships in the biophysical environment.

What are the implications for an ecological definition of grace? Given the biblical "ontology of communion" and the insights of ecology, an ecotheology of grace means that the experiential milieu of grace in the Judeo-Christian tradition is the experience of being-with-God, the experience of being-with-humans, and the experience of being-with-the-natural-world. Bear in mind that this three-dimensional relationality is interdependent and interrelated.

This reflection on the biblical and ecological contours of grace suggests that *grace defined is God and God's gracious abiding presence and activity in and with creation*. Grace is life-giving, life-supporting, and life-renewing in the boundless expression of God's creative, generous, and liberative compassion for all beings and their biophysical environments. For human beings the primary milieu and experience of grace is the threefold relatedness with God, other human beings, and the natural world.

Original Grace

Before we were a species, God and God's grace was. In other words, human beings arrived relatively late in the approximately 14-billion-year trajectory of the universe. Therefore, an ecotheology of grace must return to the genesis of the universe, the beginnings of creation, or, from the standpoint of scientific cosmology, that primordial singularity commonly referred to as the "Big Bang." This cosmic event, an intriguing mystery for both science and theology, is the genesis of grace and the beginning of the universe. Theologian Thomas Berry has referred to it as the "primary sacred community."[31] This idea is well articulated by Dreyer when she declares that "my thesis is that the *primary* community of grace is the cosmos. All other expressions of community must be viewed and understood within this wider horizon."[32] Viewed theologically, the creation of the cosmos is God's first gift of grace, or, as Dreyer states it, "If grace is primarily the gift of Godself, creation is the resulting embodiment of that gift."[33]

From a general theological point of reference, creation — what we know as the physical universe — embodies God's grace and goodness. This is an ancient theological assertion extending back in time to the beautifully written mythic-poetic words of the Priestly authors' story of creation in the first chapter of Genesis. Is it possible, however, in dialogue with science, to be more specific in identifying key aspects of our unfolding universe that might provide a fuller interpretation and meaning of original grace?

An approach to answering this question can be based on the observations and insights of contemporary cosmologists who have made the assertion that very early in the creation of the universe — the rapid expansion of an unimaginable dense and hot singularity — a chain of cosmic events and developments unfolded in such a manner as to allow for the eventual emergence of life and, most importantly, self-conscious intelligent life. Cosmologist Stephen Hawking notes that the primordial stages of the cosmos "may have had a profound impact on the universe, perhaps even the properties of elementary particles and forces that were crucial for the development of biological life."[34] The key word in Hawking's statement is "crucial," reflecting what he has referred to as "the very finely adjusted properties of the early universe."[35]

While these crucial cosmological events are too numerous to identify here, the notion of original grace compels us to highlight some of the developments without which our earth would not exist. Consider for a moment the rate of expansion of the early universe. If it had not expanded at the rate it did, it would have collapsed. Stephen Hawking points out that "if the rate of expansion one second after the big bang had been smaller by even one part in a hundred thousand million million, the universe would have recollapsed before it ever reached its present size."[36]

Another crucial development is the emergence of the four fundamental forces of nature: *gravity, electromagnetism,* and *weak* and *strong nuclear forces.* In the furnace of the very nascent universe, the strong nuclear forces allowed for the binding of various subatomic particles (for example, "up" and "down" quarks) to form protons and neutrons; protons and neutrons to form nuclei, hydrogen atoms, then helium and other heavier elements like carbon and oxygen necessary for the emergence of biological life. Gravity is another example. The weakest of the four fundamental forces, we experience it and take it for granted every day but in spite of its weakness, gravity allowed for the evolution of the universe.[37]

John Haught provides an excellent summary of the crucial cosmic developments sketched above:

> If the force of attraction between protons, for example, had been just infinitesimally different from what it actually is, there could never have been hydrogen atoms (which require free protons). If there had been no hydrogen there would have been no galaxies and no stars to convert the hydrogen into the heavy elements essential to life. In other words, without a careful fine tuning at the beginning, there would never have been a life-bearing universe. From its birth, the physical constants and initial conditions have been such as eventually to allow for the origin and evolution of life and mind.[38]

The Anthropic Cosmological Principle

The line of reasoning at the core of our brief cosmological reflection has come to be known as the anthropic cosmological principle. The idea of the anthropic principle, a controversial notion in both science and theology, which emerged out of contemporary scientific cosmology, has been articulated in a range of ways. Hawking, for example, states that "the anthropic principle says that the universe has to be more or less as we see it, because if it were different, there wouldn't be anyone to observe it."[39] Joseph Silk, the Oxford astrophysicist, states that "the anthropic cosmological principle argues that the universe must have been constructed so as to have led to the development of intelligence."[40] Haught defines it this way: "The anthropic principle maintains that the cosmos, from its very opening moments, was set up in a way that allows for the eventual existence of persons with mind."[41] Simply put, the anthropic principle is grounded in crucial cosmological events, including those above, and the exact manner in which these cosmic events transpired produced intelligent life.

The controversial nature of the anthropic principle is accentuated in the different versions of the principle, ranging from a weak version (WAP), on the one hand, to a strong version (SAP), on the other. The weak version states the obvious — that *the structure of the universe is as we humans observe it because the universe produced an intelligent species capable of doing so.* In Hawking's words, "We see the universe the way it is because we exist."[42] Hawking claims that "although most scientists are reluctant to adopt a strong version of the anthropic principle, few people would quarrel with the utility of some weak anthropic arguments."[43] Hawking's position is that "the anthropic principle can be given precise formulation, and it seems to be essential when dealing with the origins of the universe."[44]

The strong version (SAP) goes further in its argument. First proposed by Australian physicist Brandon Carter, the SAP claims that *the crucial cosmic events during the initial stages of the universe and its concomitant development produced the inevitability of conscious life.* According to John Barrow and Frank Tipler,

> The early investigations of the constraints imposed on the constants of Nature by the requirement that our form of life exist produced some surprising results. It was found that there exist a number of unlikely coincidences between numbers of enormous magnitude that are, superficially, completely independent; moreover, these coincidences appear essential to the existence of carbon-based observers in the Universe.[45]

It is Barrow and Tipler's view that these rather amazing coincidences in the formation of the universe are what led Carter to prose the SAP: "The Universe must have those properties which allow life to develop within it at some stage in its history."[46]

There are other variants of the SAP. For example, Hawking's version of the SAP is "simple: if it [the universe] had been different we would not be here."[47] Haught describes the SAP as follows: "It holds that the physical character of the universe is the way it is *because* of mind. It is the natural world's impetus toward evolving into beings with minds that have shaped the fundamental features of the universe from the beginning."[48] Elaborating on the SAP, Haught claims,

> The eventual production of conscious beings, according to the SAP, is the simplest and most elegant explanation of why the universe began to expand at the rate that it did, why gravity has the force that it does, and why the ratio of electron mass to proton mass was fixed exactly the way it is. Its bent toward producing persons with minds best explains why the universe has so many stars and why it is so vast and old. A younger or smaller universe would not have produced us.[49]

Even though Haught cautions us not to "baptize" the SAP, he admits that it is "tempting, especially in the light of revelation by which we view the cosmos with the eyes of faith as well as science, to hold that the material dimension of our cosmos was shaped by the *promise* of life, consciousness, and faith from the time of its earliest formation."[50]

Cosmological Moments of Grace

The anthropic principle aside, the story of the universe as described above is incomplete. It continues with the creation of stars, galaxies, and supernovae, the stellar debris that produced our sun, a second- or third-generation star, and the heavier elements necessary for the formation of the solar system and the third planet from the sun. These cosmic events, what we have interpreted ecotheologically as signals of original grace, are identified by Thomas Berry (1914–2009) as "cosmological moments of grace."[51] Reflecting on the supernova that created the conditions for our solar system, Berry states, "This supernova event could be considered a sacrificial moment, a cosmological moment of grace that established the possibilities of the entire future of the solar system, Earth, and every form of life that would ever appear on Earth, including the spiritual dimension of the human mode of being."[52] Whether one interprets these cosmic events as the result of chance or teleological direction, one must remember that these crucial developments continued in the evolution of life on Earth.

As you take your next breath, think of the *origins of oxygen*. At its beginning the Earth was hot, with no atmosphere. In the cooling of time and the off-gassing of the planet's surface, approximately 4.1 billion years ago, a primitive atmosphere formed that contained gases such as hydrogen sulfide that are lethal. After several billion years of planetary perturbations, the removal of hydrogen sulfide occurred through the precipitation of iron sulfides, lightning discharges, and the appearance of simple primitive organisms capable of consuming a variety of resources, including hydrogen sulfide. Some primitive forms of bacteria began to photosynthesize, producing oxygen as a waste product. Ironically, as oxygen levels in the atmosphere increased, the atmosphere became poisonous to many early anaerobic bacteria. At this phase in the evolution of life a crucial event occurred — bacteria had to develop the metabolic means of using oxygen. Commenting on this key evolutionary transition, Berry notes,

> Earlier life forms that produced oxygen could not themselves live in contact with oxygen, for while living beings as we know them cannot do without oxygen in proper amounts, free oxygen was originally a terrible threat to every living form. . . .
>
> For a proper balance to be achieved and then stabilized a moment of grace had to occur, a moment when some living cell would invent a way of utilizing oxygen in the presence of sunlight to foster a new type of metabolic process. Photosynthesis was completed by respiration. At this moment under the threat of extinction, the living world as we know it began to flourish until it shaped Earth anew.[53]

In addition to the developments described by Berry, we might also consider the fact that land-based life forms would not have evolved on Earth without the formation of the *stratospheric ozone layer.*

Many other critical events in our evolutionary past can be identified as gracious moments in the unfolding of geological and biological time, but we turn now to the contemporary event of eating. *Eating food* is (as outlined in chapter 3) ecologically contextualized as the food chain, web, or pyramid composed of various trophic levels. It underscores the flow of energy and nutrients necessary for the survival of the vast majority of species that inhabit this Earth. Now think of a splendid salad, perhaps a pear arugula salad with candied walnuts, a little blue cheese, and light balsamic vinaigrette — delicious and good for you! While you are imaging this salad remember the very bottom of the food pyramid, the trophic level composed of primary producers, autotrophic photosynthesizing organisms — in other words, plants. As they utilize carbon dioxide and release oxygen, they not only link us with our evolutionary past but graciously remind us that in our contemporary human experience they continue to be key players in producing oxygen and regulating the planet's carbon cycle, a cycle that human activity has thrown into dangerous imbalance.

Additional ecological processes and cycles can be examined for the crucial role they play in supporting life. Consider the *nitrogen cycle,* something we rarely think about in our day-to-day living. The primary reservoir of nitrogen is N_2 gas in the atmosphere, and in that form it is essentially unavailable to us and other organisms. The vast majority of nitrogen is rendered accessible through nitrogen fixation and nitrification processes completely reliant on a sequence of particular microorganisms and their capacity to assimilate nitrogen gas and combine it with hydrogen and oxygen. When was the last time you thought of *Nitrobacter* and *Nitrococcus,* obscure and seemingly inconsequential bacteria? Without the oxides of nitrogen they produce as the nitrogen cycle goes from N_2 to ammonia and then onward, our ecosystem would not be able to exist. This and other ecological processes are what we interpret as the life-supporting aspects of grace.

The notion of original grace is the conscious and gracious recognition that the emergence of life and in particular the development of intelligent life is the result of a long process punctuated by critical stages and transitions that were absolutely essential and necessary. From the scientific study of *cosmogenesis,* which takes place in what is referred to by scientists as "deep time," we know that crucial events during the nascent stages of the universe created the possibility and eventuality of life's existence. From what we know of the 4.6 billion-year project we call Earth and the subsequent process of biological evolution, crucial geological and biological events occurring over time resulted in a species with the magnificent gift and capability to think back on itself and the immense journey that created it.

With the discoveries and insights of ecology and environmental science, we know that crucial biogeochemical cycles, along with an abundance of additional ecosystem services, sustain and support life on earth. The eco-theological idea of original grace interprets the entire range of crucial events as indications of God's life-giving and life-supporting activity in the unfolding of creation. The processes of cosmogenesis and evolution contain the signposts of God's gracious creativity that existed long before human beings made their appearance in cosmic time.

Our inquiry into original grace, the cosmic and biological origins of life, indicates that an ecotheological interpretation of grace means that human existence is relational, contingent, and dependent. It is because of our profound and conscious awareness of these conditions that we can accept them with gratitude and humility. In terms of human consciousness, we suggest that *grace is the epiphany of ecological consciousness: an awareness of this grace compels people to live life in their own time and place on earth with respect and gratitude for the past events and current processes that create, sustain, and support life.*

The profundity of ecological consciousness need not be what Dreyer calls "earth shattering experiences." She says:

> The profundity of grace can be experienced... in the simple sense of gratitude and praise evoked by the sight of the first shoot coming out of the ground each spring. Grace affects who we are as persons; it alters our consciousness; it influences and supports certain attitudes and flows outward into the way we live, into the choices we make and the actions we undertake.[54]

Finally, an ecological interpretation of grace points to our willingness and capacity to take stock of the damage human beings have caused to the biosphere, what we have called in chapters 4 and 5 the environmental signs of the times. In light of this capacity, ecological grace is the ability to lament and mourn the loss of vital habitat. In this regard one only needs to remember the mounting loss of biodiversity and the HIPPO acronym. Related to the diminution of ecosystems, ecological grace rejects denial and the refusal to admit that the human ecological footprint has become a serious threat to the support structures of our life, as well as the host of other species with which we share this planetary home. Moreover, ecological grace is the willingness and commitment to embrace a strategy of ethical action and respond to our current environmental condition.

Ecological Grace and the Praxis of Ethical Response

Earlier in this chapter, in our discussion of biblical notions of grace, we noted that one aspect of grace is the action and response that flows from one's inner attitude. *Grace,* therefore, in keeping with our ecotheological interpretation, also *includes the human ethical response to the environmental problems* we have already analyzed. One could argue that this is the most important characteristic of ecological grace. We call this the *praxis of ecological grace,* reminding the reader that praxis, discussed in chapter 2, refers to ethical engagement in the world. The experience of ecological grace, as the emergence of ecological consciousness, compels people to respond to the environmental crisis. Such a response is action grounded in the hope and the conviction that the ecological future is, to some degree, in human hands. The people who embrace this praxis are embodiments of God's grace. In her reflection on grace "In the Company of the Cosmos," Dreyer writes:

> Thankfully, a significant minority of the population has become aware of the effects of our destructive practices and is working with great dedication to save the earth. Such persons are a gift of grace to the cosmos and reflect in their actions the caring love of God that we call grace. We are challenged, as part of our life of grace, to join in their efforts.[55]

A useful template for investigating the ecological praxis of grace is the insightful and incisive analysis that Willis Jenkins provides in his text *The Ecologies of Grace.*[56] Essentially Jenkins's approach is a typology of what he considers to be the dominant ethical patterns and strategies that Christians have followed in their environmental discourse and ethical behavior. The reader is cautioned and reminded — based on our use of the science-theology typologies from chapter 2 — that the upside of a typology is its usefulness for analyzing ideal types and models, while the downside is that in actual discourse and action typologies often belie day-to-day human behavior. Nonetheless, Jenkins's investigation into the ecologies of grace is thorough and thought-provoking.

Jenkins's notion of the ecologies of grace is based on three theologies of grace scattered across the denominational spectrum of Christianity. He believes that Christian responses to the environmental crisis "seem contoured to their notions of relationship with God" and he seeks to show "how Christian environmental theologies reshape ways of living on the earth with patterns of living with God — how they inhabit distinct theologies of grace."[57] Using the metaphor of map making, Jenkins calls them ecologies of grace because they reflect "actual patterns of inhabitation" of Christian environmental ethical response.[58] In his view the three dominant patterns or ethical strategies are (1) the pursuit of ecojustice, (2) the call of stewardship, and (3) the practice of ecospirituality.

The Pursuit of Ecojustice

In his analysis the *pursuit of ecojustice reflects the theology of grace and salvation that tend to emphasize sanctification.* While he identifies the Roman Catholic tradition as his primary example, his actual investigation reveals that ecojustice is a rather ubiquitous ethical response that includes not only the Catholic tradition but also a number of mainline Protestant traditions such as Lutheran, Presbyterian, and Methodist. He argues that the pursuit of ecojustice emerged during the 1960s and 1970s as an outgrowth of Christian concern for social justice.

One of two key characteristics of the ecojustice strategy is the reappropriation of biblical creation theology and a renewed theology of creation. It follows then that the ecological praxis of ecojustice is the ethical work of renewing and maintaining the integrity of creation. The other key aspect of ecojustice is the emphasis on relationality: on the one hand with God, consistent with creation theology, and on the other hand, with the natural world. The gracefulness of persons who embody this approach is seen in their inclusive practice of justice for human beings and the well-being of Earth and all its inhabitants, as well as in their capacity to see the intrinsic connection between social and ecological justice.

The Call of Stewardship

Jenkins's second ecology of grace is the call of stewardship, which he links with the *theology of grace emphasizing redemption* and the evangelical Protestant tradition. He states that "stewardship emerged as a discrete theological discourse in the 1980s, supporting a public Christian environmentalism especially associated with evangelical Protestantism."[59] Like the ecojustice model, this ecological praxis of grace also draws upon biblical creation theology but in a more focused fashion. The strategy of stewardship reappropriates the role of human beings in creation based on the creation accounts in Genesis 1 and 2 and concludes that the human vocation in response to God's call is to be Earth-keepers. The point of emphasis in this Christian ecological praxis is on God's will and its obligatory mandate for humanity. Jenkins states, "The normative force for stewardship, therefore, comes not by nature's dignity but from the extrinsic command, by which human acts are claimed. Earth-keeping responsibilities derive from God's will, appear as a divine command and are performed for the sake of a loving God."[60]

Unlike the praxis of ecojustice, which is more reliant on the ecological integrity of the Earth, the approach of stewardship cares for the Earth because it arises from divine command. Grace is nevertheless at work in the strategy of stewardship because it is in and through grace that Christians freely respond to God's directive to care for the Earth (a gift of God's grace), and the work of stewardship is in itself an example of grace. Moreover, the stewardship approach tends to be more Christocentric, perceiving stewardship as an example of discipleship in Christ.

Of the three ecologies of grace, stewardship is perhaps the most controversial because its critics, particularly ecofeminists, rightly call attention to its monarchic biblical context and, consequently, its patriarchal and hierarchal overtones. In a nutshell, many consider the biblical notion of stewardship to be beyond rehabilitation. Nevertheless, the gracefulness of stewardship may lie in its practicality because the language of stewardship is widely used inside and outside Christianity. For example, the language of stewardship, a familiar term in many Protestant statements on the environment, has appeared in Roman Catholic documents with frequent regularity in the last twenty years, and it is commonly used in secular documents and organizations as well.[61] It is entirely possible that the grace of stewardship is grounded in its very practical potential for interdenominational dialogue as well as for dialogue and public discourse with many nonreligious people and secular organizations committed to environmental action.

The Practice of Ecospirituality

The third of Jenkins's ecologies of grace is the practice of ecospirituality. He believes that ecospirituality tends to reflect the theology of deification typically associated with Eastern Orthodox Christianity. The idea of deification might appear unfamiliar to many, but it has a long tradition in Orthodox theology. Basically, deification means that the human person or soul can be transformed and through the grace of God become Godlike. Orthodox theologian Edward Moore says that "deification (*theosis*) implies a state of being that was described, by the most gifted Church Fathers, as an endless, mystical yearning for divine fulfillment" and that it points to the theory that "the person, the soul, is intimately bound up with the inner working — or *eternally realized history* — of the cosmos, in so far as the soul co-operates with God in the maintenance of the cosmic order."[62] The cooperation with God in maintaining the cosmic order is the essence of ecospirituality.

Historically, ecological spirituality, more commonly known as creation spirituality, emerged during the 1970s but broke with the ecojustice and stewardship advocates in the late 1980s. While there are important distinctions among the various ethical strategies, creation spirituality does share an interest in creation theology with the other two approaches but with a cosmic twist. Unlike ecojustice and stewardship, Jenkins believes that

> creation spirituality refuses to begin from nature or human practice in prior isolation, and instead addresses their alienation within human personhood as the root of environmental problems. The common

creation story and the story of Jesus reveal the same sacred thing: human persons are a living cosmology, active manifestations of the world's communion.[63]

Central to the use of cosmology is the Christian notion of the cosmic Christ (see Col. 1:15–20) and an emphasis on creativity. According to Jenkins, "As the cosmic Christ restores human creativity into intimacy with the earth's, God's grace comes by way of the story of creation's grace."[64]

Additional characteristics of the praxis of creation spirituality are the experience of sacramentality and a theology of the Holy Spirit. In the practice of creation spirituality, the entire universe is sacramental, that is, the cosmos is imbued with the hidden presence of God, and the Spirit dwells in all things. Accordingly, in Jenkins's assessment, for the theologians of creation spirituality:

> The Spirit's active presence does not threaten but actualizes creation's own creativity. In the Spirit, then, we may glimpse how God brings creatures into communion in the divine life, and does so through the free agency of creation. In the work of the Spirit we find verbs of grace that usher creation into the divine life by enlivening creation's own verbs. In turn, pneumatological verbs guide how human creativity might mediate creation's participation in God, how creation might anticipate its humanization as glorifying grace.[65]

Creation spirituality is an important contribution to Christianity's ethical response to ecological disorder. Its gracefulness lies in its cultivation of an interior life of contemplation that seeks to experience God's sacred presence in creation, searching for ecological and spiritual wholeness. It is important to note, however, that while the three ecologies of grace have their special characteristics according to Jenkins's typology, their distinctions often blur in the actual practice and discourse of individual Christians and in denominational theologies of environmental responsibility. In other words the ecological praxis of grace, whether it is ecojustice, stewardship, or creation spirituality, need not be exclusive of the other strategies of Christian ethical praxis. They can and often do function in harmony, and they are complementary in the pursuit of ecological integrity. What is important to bear in mind is what links all three — the importance of creation theology, which has been an important outcome of theology's dialogue with ecology.

Ecological Sin

The theological flip side to grace is the reality of sin, and no ecotheology of human existence would be complete without an interpretation of sin from an ecological point of view. Theologically, sin is as old as the Bible and we begin to see its conceptual emergence in the mythic stories woven together by the Yahwist in Genesis 2–9. Known as the "J" author, the Yahwist begins with his version of creation and the primordial harmony of Adam and Eve in the Garden of Eden. Through human defiance and arrogance the primordial harmony is fractured, resulting in the threefold alienation between human beings and God, among humans, and between humans and Earth. Eventually creation unravels completely and returns to watery chaos, symbolized by Noah and the flood. The irony of this ancient story (it could date to 950 B.C.E.) is that Adam, the Earth creature who comes "out of the ground," is the very cause of the disorder in creation. In the ancient Israelite perspective the land literally suffers as a result of human sin (see Hos. 4:1–3). As James Nash puts it, "Sin literally defiles the land."[66]

Our contemporary experience may reveal an interesting parallel between our scientific worldview and this ancient mythic-theological interpretation of disorder. From an evolutionary viewpoint, the human species is the Earth become conscious of itself. Thomas Berry states it this way: "The human is by definition that being in whom the universe reflects on and celebrates itself in conscious self-awareness."[67] Even though our roots are cosmic in origin, biologically we evolved from the Earth and, ironically, we have become the primary cause of ecological disorder on the Earth. In other words, the catalogue of ecological sin(s) that we outlined in chapters 4 and 5 means that our present ecological crisis is anthropogenic — driven by human activity.

In the past the theology of sin was almost exclusively focused on sin as individual offenses (sins of commission and omission) against God and other human beings. In the 1960s and 1970s a new idea emerged that sin is also social in character. The concept of social sin recognized that destructive patterns of human behavior often become institutionalized. This notion was in direct relation to social realities like poverty, racism, and sexism and the Christian concern for social justice.

The notion of social sin has a great deal of merit in a theological interpretation of our current ecological predicament. Human beings not only engage in individual patterns of behavior that are ecologically destructive, but we also have created entire social, political, and economic institutions that produce ecological disorder. The ecological realities that we face have resulted in expanding the theological boundaries of our notion of sin. Nash has offered a particular example of ecological sin that is comprehensive. Nash defines ecological sin as:

The refusal to act in the image of God, as responsible representatives who value and love the host of interdependent creatures in their ecosystems, which the creator values and loves. It is injustice, the self-centered human inclination to defy God's covenant of justice by grasping more than our due (as individuals, corporate bodies, nations, and a species) and thereby depriving other individuals, corporate bodies, nations and species their due. It is breaking the bonds with God and our comrades in creation. It is acting like the owner of creation with absolute property rights. Ecological sin is expressed as the arrogant denial of the creaturely limitations imposed on human ingenuity and technology, a defiant disrespect or a deficient respect for the interdependent relationships of all creatures and their environments established in the covenant of creation, and an anthropocentric abuse of what God has made for frugal use.[68]

Nash's definition of ecological sin is an excellent example of the dialogue that has been going on between theology and ecology and the resulting ecotheological interpretation of key Christian doctrines such as sin and grace. The project of ecotheology is not, however, limited to providing an ecological interpretation of the major theological aspects of human existence. As we shall see in the next chapter, Christian theologians from across the denominational spectrum have been busy addressing other tenets of Christianity, including God and Jesus Christ. A significant aspect of some of these endeavors has been the utilization of biblical creation theology and wisdom theology and the ecological interpretation of God within the context of a renewed theology of creation.

Questions for Discussion

1. One of the most significant interdisciplinary connections between ecology and theology is the emphasis on relationship. How would you describe your current relationship with the natural world? What activities do you participate in that exemplify this relationship and how have these activities shaped your own sense of self and your current view of the natural world?

2. Based on your own religious tradition, what do you see as revelatory in our current environmental crisis? If you do not have a religious tradition in your background, what do you see as revealing truths about human beings in our current environmental crisis?

3. This chapter has implied that the current environmental crisis is an opportunity to gain wisdom about how to live. What wisdom do you see in the science of ecology and the discipline of theology that can help direct humanity as it moves into the future?

4. Using Jenkins's ecologies of grace (ecojustice, stewardship, and ecospirituality), identify the one that best reflects your current practice and future response to the ecological crisis.

Active Learning Exercises

◆ Using Jenkins's ecologies of grace (ecojustice, stewardship, and ecospirituality), identify and interpret one pertinent environmental event described in a newspaper, journal, or magazine article.

◆ Select one of the key terms from this chapter (revelation, grace, ecojustice, stewardship, etc.) and write your own version of what could be a well-referenced Wikipedia entry. Do not consult Wikipedia before doing this. Submit this as a three-page paper.

◆ Research a Christian denomination, parish, or congregation in your area engaged in environmental action. Analyze it based on Jenkins's ecologies of grace and format it as a PowerPoint presentation to be presented to your class. Alternatively, carry out the same assignment and create a YouTube video.

Recommended Readings

Berry, Thomas. *The Christian Future and the Fate of the Earth*. Ed. Mary Evelyn Tucker and John Grim. Maryknoll, N.Y.: Orbis Books, 2009.

———. *The Sacred Universe: Earth, Spirituality, and Religion in the Twenty-First Century*. Ed. Mary Evelyn Tucker. New York: Columbia University Press, 2009.

Dempsey, Carol J., and Mary Margaret Pazdan. *Earth, Wind and Fire: Biblical and Theological Perspectives on Creation*. Collegeville, Minn.: Liturgical Press, 2004.

Gatta, John. *Making Nature Sacred: Literature, Religion, and Environment in America from the Puritans to the Present*. New York: Oxford University Press, 2004.

Haught, John F. *Mystery and Promise: A Theology of Revelation*. Collegeville, Minn.: Liturgical Press, 1993.

Walker-Jones, Arthur. *The Green Psalter: Resources for an Ecological Spirituality*. Minneapolis: Fortress Press, 2009.

Chapter 7

The Ecology of God

Theological Reflections on Wisdom, God, and Jesus Christ

As humanity navigates the nascent stages of the twenty-first century, it is reasonable to conclude that we have been significantly influenced by ecology and environmental science. Never before in modern history have human beings become acutely aware of our dependency on the ecological systems and functions of the planet that support and maintain our existence and the existence of all life forms on Earth. We have called this awareness ecological grace.

The impact of the sciences and the subsequent ecological awareness drives home two compelling points that have shaped and continue to shape our contemporary theological self-understanding. First, experience and scientific evidence indicate that *we humans are deeply interrelated with and dependent on the complex interactions of our planet's ecosphere and the ongoing interactions of air, land, and water, and this interrelatedness is cosmic in scope.* Humanity, the byproduct of creative cosmic processes, is the one species — as far as we know — in which the cosmos has attained the capacity for critical self-reflectivity or, to use Teilhard de Chardin's words, humankind is "evolution becoming conscious of itself."[1]

Second, *we humans are aware that to some real degree we are the major player in the outcome of life's immense journey on this Earth.* For good or for ill we are in the driver's seat as the planet's most dominant species; what we decide to do today and tomorrow may likely determine the evolutionary outcome of our own and countless other species. If human beings caused the environmental crisis and if the extent of our ecological footprint has any silver lining, it is the recognition that we bear an enormous responsibility for what has transpired thus far and that we have a growing sense of moral obligation to protect the Earth's future. This is also an example of ecological grace, the realization that Christians must embrace a praxis of ecological responsibility. To borrow an idea from ecology, perhaps humanity is the planet's most important "keystone species." Australian theologian Denis Edwards frames the scenario this way:

> The common story of the universe suggests two basic principles for a contemporary anthropology: (1) the human person is profoundly and intrinsically interconnected with every other creature as a child of

142

the Earth and a child of the universe; (2) the human person has the particular dignity and responsibility which come from being one in whom the universe has come to self-awareness. These two principles emerge from the story that science tells.[2]

Edwards contends that the two basic principles from science can be supported theologically. We agree, and we would contend that these principles are deeply grounded in biblical theology. Edwards states that "theology supports the conviction that we are kin to all other creatures because it teaches that we share with them a common origin in God's creative action."[3] As we shall see shortly, the idea of a human kinship relationship with other life forms is consistent with biblical creation theology, particularly the Yahwist narrative in Genesis 2 in which humans, animals, and plants share a common source in the Earth and all come "out of the ground" (*ha adamah*, Gen. 2:7, 9, 19). In others words, we all are companions in creation and, as seen through a biblical lens, creation is profoundly relational.

Second, Edwards believes that theology "supports the particular dignity and responsibility of human beings because of its conviction that human beings are created in God's image. . . . "[4] This idea is also grounded in biblical creation theology, but in this case it was articulated by the Priestly author of the first chapter of Genesis (Gen. 1:26–28). The conviction that human beings are created in the image and likeness of God is an important source of theological reflection in an ecological age for two reasons. First, as noted in chapter 6, it is often interpreted as a source of Christian stewardship of creation; second, it is a valuation and validation of human dignity and the responsibility humans must exercise within creation.

These theological ideas and their linkage to ecology and scientific cosmology raise an important question: Should these experiences and insights — particularly the connections between theology and ecology — be construed as revelatory, that is, do they have something to do with God's self-disclosure at this moment in human history? It is our position that these insights do connect with God's self-disclosure, and one important way ecotheology has explored and developed the linkage between theology and ecology has been to reexamine and reappropriate biblical creation-Wisdom theology.

Ecology and the Wisdom of God

In the last chapter we introduced the body of biblical tradition and literature known as Wisdom literature, which includes the books of Job, Proverbs, Ecclesiastes, Song of Songs, Wisdom, and Sirach. The latter two books are apocryphal in the Protestant tradition but are deutero-canonical in Catholicism.[5] There are also a number of Wisdom psalms and, while there is not complete agreement among scholars, the following psalms are often identified as belonging to Wisdom: 1, 19, 32, 34, 37, 49, 73, 111, 112, 119, 127, 128, and 133.

This body of literature forms what biblical scholars often refer to as the sapiential tradition of ancient Israel, and until fairly recently it did not receive a great deal of attention in biblical scholarship. The reader will recall from the second chapter that many scholars held the view, promoted by Gerhard von Rad, that Wisdom literature and its underlying theology of creation was a later development in biblical history and was ancillary to Israel's theology of redemption. This perspective, known as *the salvation history approach to biblical interpretation,* held sway until the decade of the 1970s, when a new generation of biblical scholars began to persistently challenge the presuppositions of salvation history.

One scholar in particular, Claus Westermann, argued compellingly that the Old Testament contains two dominant theological perspectives, redemption and creation, both of which are necessary for an accurate and complete understanding of Old Testament theology. Since the 1970s a growing number of biblical scholars such as Leo Purdue, Kathleen O'Connor, and Terence Fretheim have devoted considerable time and energy to scrutinizing the Wisdom books, reminding us of Walter Brueggemann's claims that "the recovery of creation as the horizon of biblical theology encourages us to contribute to the resolution of the ecological crisis."[6]

Why would this be the case? There are several important aspects of Old Testament Wisdom theology that render it very significant for a contemporary ecotheology. First, the underlying theology of Wisdom literature is creation. In other words, nature and the elements of the natural world predominate in this body of reflection, and creation, and the way it functions, is a primary source of Wisdom. Second, Wisdom (*hokmah* in Hebrew) is personified as a feminine characteristic of God, and her attributes, while ancient in the biblical view, are surprisingly relevant for a contemporary ecotheology. For example, Wisdom is the divine way that the natural world is ordered, sustained, and made intelligible. The attribute of Woman Wisdom can provide a biblical foundation for the modern idea of ecological sustainability. Third, the creation-Wisdom writings of the Old Testament reveal an emphasis on relationality that affirms the connectivity between ecology and theology and their shared horizon for discourse and dialogue.

Attributes of Lady Wisdom

Commonly referred to as Woman or Lady Wisdom, Wisdom has an array of attributes. First and foremost, *Wisdom was created by God, but she existed from the beginning* and she is the vehicle through whom God created the universe. Consequently, as God's created co-creator, Woman Wisdom is a primary means of divine revelation. In Fretheim's view, "Wisdom's role with respect to human beings is mediatory and revelatory, that is, she mediates God's communication regarding God's will for life and well-being—which Wisdom has heard—to humankind."[7]

As God's first principle of creation and revelation, *Woman Wisdom is the ground of moral and cosmic order in the universe.* In Fretheim's words,

Woman Wisdom "was the necessary precondition for a well-constructed world," and she "is the 'glue' that holds everything in a stable and harmonious whole."[8] A unique feature of ancient Israel's creation-Wisdom theology is that creation — within which Wisdom resides — is a physical and moral order and that the wise person, through observation and study of the natural world, can come to know God and the correct way to live in the world. In other words, Wisdom renders creation intelligible and possesses an intimate awareness of how the world works, which, according to Fretheim, entails "knowledge of what today would be called 'scientific' because Wisdom knows the basic structures, components, patterns, and functions of reality."[9]

Perhaps it is fair to suggest that ecology and its knowledge of how the world works is a modern scientific extension of the way of Wisdom in creation and that observing the "wisdom" of Earth's functions might provide humanity with an ethical basis for living upon the Earth. This is precisely what Aldo Leopold (1887–1948) suggested in his famous work "The Land Ethic," which was a philosophical-ethical extrapolation from the modern science of ecology.[10]

Another attribute of Wisdom that allows for dialogue with ecology is that *she is essentially relational*. Fretheim suggests that Wisdom provides the "relational infrastructure" of creation because she is "dynamic, creative, developing, truly interactive, full of life, and genuinely relational with every other creature."[11] Wisdom is the ongoing process of interaction whereby she interacts with God, humanity, and nonhuman creation. The interrelatedness of Wisdom goes to the very core of creation, and it is the fundamental way the world works. As such, Wisdom is a significant biblical insight that appears to affirm a major insight of contemporary science. On the other hand, the primacy of relationality in modern science appears to affirm the biblical notion of the Wisdom of creation. From an ecotheological perspective this biblical-scientific hermeneutical dynamic is appropriate and necessary.

The final attribute of Woman Wisdom is that *she is present within creation and consequently a major way of understanding God's presence within the natural world*. In a poetic digression on God's mercy in creation, the book of Wisdom, identifying Wisdom as the Spirit of God, offers this beautiful depiction:

> For you love all things that exist,
> and detest none of the things that you have made,
> for you would not have made anything if you had hated it.
> How would anything have endured if you had not willed it?
> Or how would anything not called forth by you have been preserved?
> You spare all things, for they are yours, O Lord, you who love the
> living.
> For your immortal spirit is in all things. (Wisd. 11:24–12:1)

This tender and compassionate reflection on God in the book of Wisdom highlights the important characteristic of the *immanence of God and God's Wisdom within the natural world*. This attribute of Woman Wisdom is particularly relevant for ecotheology as it attempts to rethink the immanent presence of God, which an Earth–creation centered theology requires. As previously noted, the Western theological tradition of Christianity has tended to emphasize the transcendence of God at the expense of God's immanence, but the theological response to the ecological crisis, with its focus on Earth, has challenged theology to provide a more balanced understanding of God's presence, especially within creation.

The Wisdom tradition of ancient Israel provides us with a biblical foundation for adequately expressing the immanence of God. Some biblical scholars, such as James Crenshaw, suggest that the introduction of Woman Wisdom assisted the wisdom sages of ancient Israel in reconciling the tension between God's transcendence and immanence.[12] Leo Purdue, another contemporary scholar who has probed Wisdom literature, states that "God's immanence and compassionate humaneness are portrayed in expressions of divine care for the good creation and its mortal creatures. The God of the sages acts in justice and love to create, sustain, and bless all life."[13]

One of the key aspects of Woman Wisdom's relational immanence in creation is that she has a mediating function between God and God's creation. Fretheim reminds us:

> Wisdom belongs both in the world and with God.... Wisdom is both creature and divine. It is not simply a quality "immanent in creation" or an "attribute of the world"; it remains alongside God. Wisdom delighting with human beings carries the implication of divine immanence — direct presence and involvement in creation. The idea is that God not only created the world but, in and through the figure of Wisdom, chooses to dwell among the creatures in terms that are described as delightful.[14]

Fretheim's analysis of Wisdom literature is one part of his extensive treatment of the Old Testament's theology of God and God's relationship with the world. Several of his insights provide a basis for summarizing Israel's creation theology and for concluding this section on Wisdom and the ecology of God:

- The Old Testament's view of creation is that at its core it is a relational reality, and relationality is at the heart of God. As a relational being God interacts with God's creatures, and the relationship between God and creation is best described as interrelational. In describing the ecology of God and God's creation Fretheim writes that "the world of the Hebrew Bible is a spider web of a world. Interrelatedness is basic to this community of God's creatures.... In speaking very generally, God so relates to this interrelated world that every movement in the web affects God as well;

God will get caught up in these interconnections and work within them for the sake of the future of all creatures."[15]

♦ As the preceding quote indicates, the relationship between God and God's creation is also interdependent. While the Old Testament is very clear that all creatures are solely dependent on God for life, Fretheim reminds us that "God has freely chosen to establish an interdependent relationship with the creation. . . . Indeed, God has freely chosen to be dependent upon both human and nonhuman in the furtherance of God's purposes in the world."[16]

The interrelational and interdependent character of God's relationship with creation means that God and God's creatures have a shared responsibility in maintaining and sustaining the integrity of creation. This idea leads Fretheim to suggest that his analysis of creation theology implies what he calls "a mutuality of vocations," meaning that "both humans and nonhumans are called to a vocation on behalf of each other in the furtherance of God's purposes for the creation."[17]

♦ The biblical worldview holds that there is the future hope of salvation and, while the hope of salvation has been interpreted by humans in an overly anthropocentric manner, the Old Testament is clear that the future hope of a new creation includes the nonhuman world. Fretheim argues that "given the close interrelationship of human beings and environment, *only when the natural order has been healed will human salvation be fully realized.*"[18] He goes on to state, "God's salvation is not conceived in a narrowly human sense, as if only people will be affected by God's work. All nonhuman creatures will participate in a universal salvation, envisaged most fundamentally in the terms of the renewal of nature."[19] We will return to this important conclusion later in our discussion of the reign of God and the ecology of salvation.

♦ Finally, Fretheim's analysis of Old Testament creation theology leads him to declare that the biblical view of God's presence in creation must be "more strongly affirmed than it commonly has been."[20] He goes on to argue that "we need to find a clearer way between pantheism and *radical* transcendence. . . . The immanence/transcendence polarity is not adequate for talk about divine presence. The God who is present is *both* immanent and transcendent; both are appropriate words for a constant divine state of affairs."[21]

Our analysis of the environmental signs of the times and the eco-theological retrieval of biblical creation-Wisdom theology compels us to agree with Fretheim's observations. In the section that follows we will discuss three contemporary ecological models of God that seek to address Fretheim's concerns as well as the ecological disorder that all God's creatures face. While some of these models might appear "radical," they share the common goal of attempting to provide an alternative approach to the transcendence-immanence polarity in Western Christian theology and an ecologically relevant view of God and God's presence in the world.

Ecological Models of God: God in Process

Whitehead's Model

The first ecological model of God draws from Alfred North Whitehead's concept of God and the theological translation of Whitehead's philosophy in process theology. The reader will recall from chapters 1 and 2 that process philosophy and process theology were and continue to be attempts to produce a systematic philosophical-theological model of God and the universe consistent with new twentieth-century developments in biology and physics. Whitehead, who pioneered this philosophical paradigm, argued that process or creativity was the basic structure of all reality and that the entire universe — from the smallest subatomic particle to God — was composed of what he called "actual entities" or "occasions." Actual entities are conceptual (mental) and temporal (physical) "drops of experience" that move and become in an interrelated field of dynamic interaction. In Whitehead's metaphysics God is the essential and ultimate actual entity that integrates and unifies the entire field of existence and in doing so is intimately related to all things and creatures.

In Whitehead's system, like all actual entities, *God is dipolar,* that is, there are two sides to God's nature: what he called the primordial (mental) and consequent (physical) natures of God. Both are simultaneously transcendent and immanent. To use Thomas Hosinski's description, the *primordial side of God* is the "ultimate ground of order and value" in the universe, and it is often described as transcendent, eternal, and nontemporal.[22] God's primordial self is also immanent in the physical world because reality is the actualization of God's ordering potential and is, as Hosinski puts it, "immanent in each moment of experience in the universe."[23]

On the other hand, the *consequent side of God* is, in Hosinski's words, "the ground of meaning and unity."[24] The consequent nature of God is physical, temporal, and dynamic and can be understood as the actualization of God in the biophysical world — the universe itself — and the way God receives, grasps, and is impacted by physical reality. Through God's primordial and consequent sides, God is intimately related to the universe of all actual entities whereby they are taken up into God and unified and integrated within God's experience. This process understanding of God might be one solution to what Fretheim described as the inadequate transcendence-immanence polarity of interpreting the biblical experience of God.

Process theology might also be an adequate way to describe the interrelatedness and interdependence of God, an important aspect of the ecology of God and God's care for all creatures. Hosinski makes a good case for this:

Whitehead's philosophy of God offers a way of understanding God's presence to and care about every creature in the world. Furthermore, since every moment of experience affects God and lives everlastingly in God, we can come to see in a new way the transcendent value and worth of every creature. What is done to every creature and by every creature is done to God. This teaches us to find much deeper value and worth in our fellow-creatures than we might otherwise be prepared to discover in them.[25]

McDaniel's Model

One theologian who has attempted to translate process metaphysics and theology into an ecological model of God is Jay McDaniel, who believes that process theology provides a more adequate way of understanding God and God's relationship to the web of life. McDaniel argues that "in process theology 'the environment' is not simply an issue among issues but rather the context of all issues. It is the web of life on earth and more generally the vast, evolving universe."[26] In an effort to deal with the transcendence-immanence tension of classical theism (what McDaniel calls dualism), McDaniel, drawing from process theology, believes that the best way to describe God and God's relationship with creation is through the term *panentheism*. According to McDaniel, panentheism "implies an ecological way of thinking about God in which, even as God and creation are distinguished, *God is understood to be intimately connected to creation, and vice-versa.*"[27] Those who hold this view see panentheism as a more precise term for describing the transcendence-immanence of God in the biblical account and as an adequate way of mediating the extremes of pantheism and theism.

Theism	Panentheism	Pantheism
Transcendence	Immanence/Transcendence	Immanence
God apart from World	God in World/World in God	God is World

Often defined as meaning all-in-God and God-in-all, McDaniel describes panentheism this way:

Panentheism is properly distinguished from strict pantheism, which implies an absolute equation of God and creation, and also from strict dualism, which implies an absolute gulf between God and creation. Panentheism is the view that the creation and its processes are somehow "in" God even though God is "more than" creation. If God is the Sacred Whole, then that Whole is indeed more than the sum of its parts.[28]

There's no doubt that the term "panentheism" is controversial, particularly within very traditional sectors in Christianity where classical theism
holds sway. Nevertheless, a number of theologians in recent years (see chapter 1 on process theology) are convinced that panentheism is more adequate
for describing the total experience of God as expressed in the biblical narrative, and that it provides us with a more exact way of speaking about God's
immanence within creation without compromising God's transcendence. It
is interesting to note that in the New Testament Paul, as reported by Luke
in the Acts of the Apostles, addressed the Athenians about God, saying that
God is "not far from any one of us." To make his point, Paul quoted one
of their poets, declaring that "in him [God] we live and move and have our
being" (see Acts 17:22–31).

In what can be interpreted as a panentheistic way of defining our connection with God, Paul's description of God to the Athenians emphasizes
God's intimate relationship with us, noting that that intimacy is enhanced
or made possible because we are "in God." Following a panentheistic line
of reflection, McDaniel suggests that from a process theological perspective
God ought to be understood as the One-embracing-many, the One-within-
many, and the One-between-many. As the One-embracing-many, God is
the omnipresent universal consciousness who is immediately and instanta-
neously present to all things and beings in the universe. In other words, God
surrounds the universe and everything in it, which, according to McDaniel,
"means that the universe is in God, not unlike the way in which fish
are inside an ocean, or embryos are inside a womb, or clouds are inside
the sky."[29]

God as the One-embracing-many has significant implications for our
understanding of God, especially regarding what theology traditionally
refers to as theodicy — the problem of understanding God's goodness,
power, and will in relation to the existence of evil. In McDaniel's view,
"Just as embryos within the womb have creativity that is not reducible to
the mother and as fish in the seas have creativity not reducible to the ocean,
so things happen in the universe that are not reducible to God or God's
will."[30] This means that in the process scheme of things tragedy and suffering are not the result of God's will but are endemic to the way of the
universe. Nonetheless, because the universe is in God, God is affected by all
that occurs. To use Whitehead's words, "God is the great companion — the
fellow sufferer who understands."[31] This idea that God suffers is consistent
with Fretheim's analysis of God in the Old Testament, a God who through
his immanent presence experiences anguish and mourns with and for human
beings and the entire creation.[32]

God as the One-embracing-many also means that when we look upon
the universe and admire its beauty, richness, and diversity from the greatest
to the smallest of creatures, some of us experience a greater reality; a part of
what makes God "God." In McDaniel's view, this happens because God is
the "unity of the universe: the larger whole in which the universe unfolds."[33]

This embracing sacred presence is also the One-within-many and can be understood as the *ruah,* the Hebrew term for the breath and spirit of God, indwelling in all things and luring the universe forward in creative novelty.

In the process view the indwelling of God can be thought of as God's allure, God's enticing activity drawing all creatures and entities forward to realize their full potential. McDaniel says that the indwelling spirit of God is "within each creature as its innermost lure" and that God "lures the universe into the self-creation of new forms of order relative to what is possible in the situation at hand. Evolution is an ongoing process, not yet finished, that is prompted but not coerced by the indwelling spirit of God into newness."[34]

Lastly, God is the One-between-many that emphasizes the relationality of God and God's creation. For McDaniel God not only encircles and indwells but is also "between all living beings, inasmuch as living beings dwell in mutually enhancing relations."[35] In his discussion of God as the One-between-many, McDaniel raises an interesting question about predator-prey relationships, a key idea in ecology regarding ecosystem and population dynamics. He asks, "If God is a lure toward wholeness within each living being, whose side is God on as the fox chases the rabbit?" McDaniel's answer is provocative:

> The process view is that God is on the side of each: luring the fox to find the rabbit, since it is the only way the fox can survive given his or her genetic dispositions, and luring the rabbit to escape the fox, given that it is the only way for the rabbit to survive too. This can mean either that God is deeply pained by the relationship, precisely because it is not mutually enhancing since one individual must be frustrated; or it can mean, as many environmentally minded thinkers might prefer, that God is in the relationship itself, as a necessary way that life has to unfold on earth.[36]

Readers may not find McDaniel's answer completely satisfying, but the main point is that the interrelatedness occurring in the natural world is "in God" and reflects an essential characteristic of God from a process-ecological interpretation of God's action in the world. Moreover, the fundamental role of interrelatedness and interdependency in creation is indispensable for the evolutionary advance of species and it reflects the ultimate principle of creativity underlying all reality. However, the primacy of creativity in process thought raises a significant theological problem for typical theologies of God.

McDaniel, and other process thinkers faithful to Whitehead's metaphysics, understands creativity as the ultimate principle in the universe, which may imply that creativity is greater than God. McDaniel says that "Creativity is the ultimate reality; God is the ultimate actuality."[37] McDaniel describes creativity as "pure activity, beyond good and evil" that seems to suggest that God is a byproduct of something more fundamental and supreme.[38] If this is the case, what does that assertion mean for the central Christian claim that God is creator?

It is Hosinski's observation that the process view of creativity and its relation to God may need to be revised for a Christian context because it seems to compromise the belief that God is ultimate and the creator of all things and, therefore, may not be "compatible with the implications of Christian experience and faith."[39] Nevertheless, in spite of this serious theological conundrum, the process attempt to produce an ecologically relevant view of God and God's relationship to creation is insightful and provocative and not unlike the next ecological model of God.

McFague's Model

Sallie McFague's ecological model of God bears a striking similarity to McDaniel's process interpretation of ecology. In fact, it is interesting to note that McDaniel refers to and endorses McFague's approach in her book *Body of God* and, conversely, McFague acknowledges her indebtedness to process theology and the work of Teilhard de Chardin. McFague's approach, however, is distinctive because she works out of an ecofeminist and liberationist perspective with a style that is intentionally metaphorical.

Her ecology of God, like that of most of the theologians named in this text, is also shaped by dual poles of commitment. On one hand, McFague's theology is influenced by and a response to modern scientific cosmology, evolution, and the ecological devastation that has occurred on Earth. On the other hand, her theology is influenced by her Christian commitment to the biblical vision of God. It is her view, consistent with the core theme here, that *an ecological model of God must account for relationality and interdependence and provide an appropriate understanding of God's relationship with and within creation*. McFague's approach also addresses the Christological and eschatological implications for an ecological model of God. The first task is to briefly discuss her method and her use of the body metaphor.

Reflecting on her own life as a woman and a theologian, McFague notes the experience of embodiment is the "common thread" of her experience. She states, "That common thread is the body in all its cognate forms and associations: embodiment, incarnation, flesh, matter, death, life, sex, temptation, nature, creation, energy, and so on...."[40] The body is therefore an all encompassing metaphor for the full range of our human experience; beginning with our own embodied existence it can be applied to the smallest atomic particle as well as to the cosmos. McFague describes the body paradigm this way:

> The use of the model of body as a way of interpreting everything that is, from an atom to the entire universe, stretches the notion in both directions: neither an atom nor the universe is a body, strictly speaking.... Yet we do speak of any solid bit of matter, large or

small, any material thing as a "body," and from what we are learning about evolutionary, ecological interrelatedness and interdependence, it is appropriate to do so: the atoms in *our* bodies were formed in the "bodies" of the early stars. "Body" does not, therefore, necessarily mean a living body, although that is its primary meaning; moreover, the lines between nonliving and living in evolution as well as the interconnectedness in ecosystems support the use of the model as a broad interpretive lens.[41]

For McFague *the body is the hermeneutical nexus (the key for interpreting) for her analysis of the universe as the body of God.* The idea seems very similar to the process interpretation of God's consequent nature, the physicality of which is actualized in the universe. McFague, however, does not pursue that line of reflection. Rather, she utilizes the image of body as the point of departure in her ecological theology to create an organic model of speaking about God and God's relationship to the universe. She cautions us to remember that in speaking of the universe as God's body, that it is metaphorical theological reflection wherein we are "extrapolating from our own experience, what is familiar to us, in order to speak of what we cannot experience or know directly."[42] McFague makes the point that "we are not describing God as having a body or being embodied; we are suggesting that what is bedrock for the universe — matter, that of which everything is made — might be, perhaps ought to be, applied to God as well."[43] This approach becomes the keystone principle in her discussion of an organic paradigm of God.

Why the model of an organic body? Bodies are obviously organic, but the organic essence of our bodies is deeply rooted in and the byproduct of an immense evolutionary journey and the "deep time" of cosmogenesis. Influenced by scientific cosmology, McFague identifies unity-diversity and interrelatedness-interdependence as key characteristics in the unfolding story of the creation of the physical universe, which she describes as a story of embodiment. She notes that "the distinctive aspect of the common creation story pertinent to the formation of an organic model of reality is the particular way both unity and differentiation are understood. It is a form of unity based on a common beginning and history, but one that has resulted in highly complex networks of interrelationships and interdependencies among all life-forms and supporting systems on this planet."[44]

In addition to the scientific view of the universe, McFague's other reason for promoting an organic-body paradigm for God is her incarnational theology. In other words another primary reason for favoring an organic-body model for reality is the centrality of Jesus Christ and the Christian claim that he is the embodiment of God — the incarnation of God in human flesh. Taken together, the scientific and theological interpretation of reality form the foundation of McFague's organic paradigm, which she summarizes as follows:

The organic model we are suggesting pictures reality as composed of multitudes of embodied beings who presently inhabit a planet that has evolved over billions of years through a process of dynamic change marked by law and novelty into an intricate, diverse, complex, multileveled reality, all radically interrelated and interdependent. The organic whole that began from an initial big bang and eventuated into the present universe is distinguished by a form of unity and diversity radical beyond all imagining.... All of us, living and nonliving, are one phenomenon stretching over billions of years and forms of matter — including our own. The universe is a body;... it is matter bodied forth seemingly infinitely, diversely, endlessly, yet internally one.[45]

The organic paradigm becomes McFague's primary metaphor in discussing the universe as God's body, and it is an intriguing way of describing God's relationship with creation. In developing her model, McFague opts for the analogy that God is to the universe as the spirit is to the body. Her approach is, therefore, in technical theological language *pneumatological* and *incarnational,* which simply means that for McFague God is Spirit, and God as Spirit is incarnate or embodied in the universe. While obviously linked to the Christian tradition's view of God as Holy Spirit, McFague's understanding of spirit is primordially grounded in the ancient Hebrew view of the *ruah* of God, that is, the breath, wind, or spirit of God that moved upon the face of the waters in the Priestly creation story of Genesis 1:2. Her rationale is straightforward: "Spirit, as wind, breath, life is the most basic and most inclusive way to express centered embodiment," and consequently she proposes "that we think of God metaphorically as the spirit that is the breath, the life, of the universe that comes from God and could be seen as the body of God."[46]

McFague is convinced that her *paradigm of God as Spirit embodied in the universe* has a number of advantages. First, she believes that it is amenable to the scientific view of an evolving universe and planet. The emphasis on Spirit identifies God's presence and action within the cosmic process of creation; in fact, God as embodied Spirit is the creative evolutionary impulse underlying the universe that is responsible for the plurality, richness, and diversity of life.

Her theological interest here is to deemphasize the idea of God as the ordering and controlling "Mind" behind the universe and to highlight the activity of God as the universe's "source and empowerment, the breath that enlivens and energizes it. The spirit perspective takes seriously the fecundity, diversity, range, and complexity of life and of life-supporting systems."[47] McFague states that "a spirit theology focuses attention ... on the rich variety of living forms that have been and are *now* present on our planet. The breath of God enlivening each and every entity in the body of the universe turns our attention to a theology of nature, a theology concerned with the relationship of God and our living breathing planet."[48]

Ecofeminist theologian Sallie McFague, whose ecotheology reflects a deep commitment to liberation and justice, believes that, in light of environmental problems like global warming and climate change, ecological literacy and commitment to sustainability must be inherent to any Christian theology of human existence. She declares that "ecological literacy is *basic* survival knowledge," and with typical insight she observes, "If we were to accept ecological unity as the working interpretation for our dealings with each other and with our world, we would have two responses: *appreciation and care*. We would see ourselves as part of the web of life, an incredibly vast, complex, subtle, beautiful web that would both amaze us and call forth concern. We would feel awe about and care for our planet." If we did this humanity would be "recentered as God's partners, the ones who can help work for a just and sustainable planet" (*A New Climate for Theology: God, the World and Global Warming* [Minneapolis: Fortress Press, 2008], 53, 59).

Herein lies another advantage of McFague's model of God: *it emphasizes God's immanence and relatedness to the created world*, a consistent feature of ecological models of God. She wants to emphasize the connectivity between God and universe and that this "connection is one of *relationship* at the deepest possible level."[49] At the same time, McFague's paradigm accentuates divine activity within the universe and leads her to argue that her metaphorical image of God as embodied Spirit is best understood as a panentheistic model, another parallel to McDaniel's process theology.

McFague takes great care to note that her model is not pantheistic but that it "radicalizes both divine immanence (God is the breath of each and every creature) and divine transcendence (God is the energy empowering the entire universe)."[50] She states:

> Pantheism says that God is embodied, necessarily and totally; traditional theism claims that God is disembodied, necessarily and totally; panentheism suggests that God is embodied but not necessarily or totally. Rather God is sacramentally embodied: God is mediated, expressed, in and through embodiment, but not necessarily or totally.[51]

The epitome of God's embodiment in the universe is, in McFague's ecotheology, Jesus Christ, the longstanding theological claim of Christianity that *God is incarnate in Jesus of Nazareth* — "and the Word became flesh and dwelt among us" (John 1:14). This Christ event gives further shape and meaning to the image of the universe as the Body of God — what McFague calls the "Christic paradigm."

Several important implications from a liberationist perspective underscore McFague's reflection on the Christic paradigm as it influences our understanding of the universe as the Body of God. First, the Christic paradigm is *inclusive* of all creation. She states that "within a Christic framework, the body of God encompasses all of creation in a particular salvific direction, toward the liberating, healing, and fulfillment of all bodies."[52] Second, the Christic paradigm means that *God is compassionate and is in solidarity with those who suffer.* She adds that by radicalizing "love for the vulnerable and the oppressed, the embodied God identifies with all suffering bodies."[53]

This idea recalls Fretheim's Old Testament theology of God's suffering and the process notion that God is the "fellow sufferer who understands." On this point, the Christic paradigm means that God's compassionate concern embraces those who have been excluded — the poor, marginalized, and oppressed — as well as the nonhuman world. McFague claims that "the distinctiveness of Christian embodiment is its focus on oppressed, vulnerable, suffering bodies, those who are in pain due to the indifference or greed of the more powerful. In an ecological age, this ought to include oppressed nonhuman animals and the earth itself."[54]

The third and final feature of the Christic paradigm is that, while it is shaped by the historically particular — the death and resurrection of Jesus of Nazareth — it is also *cosmic* in scope. This interpretation of the Christic paradigm is what theologians have called the Cosmic Christ. A hallmark characteristic of Teilhard's Christology, the notion of the Cosmic Christ arises out of the New Testament, particularly the Letter to the Colossians (see Col. 1:15–20). There are four key aspects to the meaning of the Cosmic Christ: (1) all creation was created through and for Christ, (2) all creation holds together in Christ, (3) in Christ the fullness of God dwells, and (4) through the blood of his cross Christ reconciles all things in creation — not just human beings.

The implications are significant for McFague's notion of the Christic paradigm and all ecotheologies, which in her words mean that "the cosmic Christ suggests that the cosmos is moving toward salvation and that this salvation is taking place *in* creation."[55] McFague writes:

> The entire fifteen-billion-year history of the universe and the billions of galaxies are, from a Christian perspective, from this concrete, partial, particular setting, seen to be the cosmic Christ, the body of God in the Christic paradigm. Thus the direction or hope of creation, all of it, is nothing less than what I understand that paradigm to be for myself and other human beings: the liberating, healing, inclusive love of God.[56]

The place and role of creation in the Christian vision of salvation is an extremely important aspect of ecotheology, especially in its effort to decenter the overly anthropocentric interpretation that the biblical view of salvation typically receives. As McFague's ecotheology indicates, the notion of the Cosmic Christ provides a fruitful avenue to pursue in our attempt to ground an understanding of salvation that is consistent with both the biblical tradition and ecology. We will return to the idea of the ecology of salvation, its eschatological context and ethical implications in the final section of this chapter, but first we turn to one additional ecological model of God — a view from "down under."

Edwards's Model

Consistent with the preceding ecological models of God in this chapter, the approach of Australian theologian Denis Edwards is a comparable attempt to craft an ecotheology of God that is shaped by his attentiveness to science — ecology and cosmology — and one that is also deeply rooted in the Western Christian theological tradition. The connection between the two sides of the equation — a consistent theme in ecotheology — is the principle of relationality. Consequently, one of Edwards's primary assumptions, which he shares with McDaniel and McFague, is the primacy of relationship. He states that "reality is *ontologically* relational. The very *being* of things in our universe is relational being."[57] But while there is a singularity of purpose in developing their ecotheologies, and obvious similarities and parallels with McDaniel and McFague, Edwards's work has its own distinctive mark. His approach is decidedly Trinitarian, revealing an emphasis on God as Creator Spirit, Jesus as the incarnate Wisdom of God, and the relationship of mutual love that binds God within God's self and the created universe, which for Edwards is the creative self-expression of God.

Akin to McFague's pneumatological theology of God, Edwards describes *God as the Creator Spirit,* grounding the idea biblically in the Hebrew word *ruah* and the Greek word *pneuma.* As the Creator Spirit, the Breath of God is the "giver of life" who is the immanent presence and power in the universe, the generative energy and creative force that propels the evolutionary advance of creation. Edwards says that the Creator Spirit "is the energizing power of continual creation who breathes life into the emergence of bacteria, eukaryotes, multicellular creatures, land animals, plants, hominids, and modern humans."[58] As this quote suggests, the main scientific idea underlying Edwards's understanding of God as Creator Spirit is the reality of evolutionary emergence. For Edwards, the *Creator Spirit is the fundamental creative force or energy in the universe* that science identifies as the evolutionary process. He says:

> I think it is faithful to the biblical and theological tradition to see the Creator Spirit, always in the communion of the Trinity, as the immanent presence of God who empowers the process of self-transcendence and the emergence of a life-bearing universe. At the deepest level, beyond the level of scientific explanation, the life-giving Spirit of God enables creatures to become. This Creator Spirit is the immanent divine power of evolutionary emergence.[59]

A crucial point of emergence in the evolutionary advance into novelty is, for Edwards, Jesus Christ, who is the quintessential expression of divine power in the universe; according to Edwards, that divine power revealed in the Christ-event is a "power-in-love," a "relational power."[60] Edwards believes that "if divine power is redefined in the Christ-event as involving respect for and vulnerability before the integrity of creaturely freedom and creaturely processes, then this suggests that it may be appropriate to think of the Creator Spirit as freely respecting not only the integrity of human beings but also the integrity of natural processes."[61]

Simply put, Edwards holds Jesus of Nazareth up as the definitive revelation of God's activity — not only in human history but in the universe — as a countervailing form of power, a compassionate, transformative love working within creation to liberate, renew, and restore. As the "power-in-love," the Creator Spirit is present within creation as the "loving companion" to all creatures and, like the process ecology of God, the Spirit is the one "who enters the pain of the world, who suffers with suffering creation."[62] Moreover, as the "power-in-love" the Creator Spirit is the essence of relationship itself, and it binds and embraces all things in love. For Edwards, the Creator Spirit is the "unspeakable nearness of God" discerned in "the experience of mountains, deserts, forests, and seas, in the sense of being deeply connected with a place, and in moments of real encounter with trees, flowers, birds, and animals."[63] The primacy of relationship in Edwards's ecotheology is most fully developed in his Trinitarian understanding of God as "Persons-in-Mutual-Relationship."

As noted above, the unique feature of Edwards's approach is its Trinitarian nature; to develop this ecotheology of God, he revisits the Trinitarian theology of the great Franciscan theologian St. Bonaventure (1221–1274).

Edwards believes that there are several reasons why Bonaventure's theology is pertinent as a theological foundation. First, he observes that Bonaventure's Trinitarian theology arises out of what theologians call the "economy of salvation." The *economy of salvation* — and what is often referred to as the *economic Trinity* — basically refers to God's work or *God's business of redemption* and to the human experience of God's salvation in history. This idea is in large part shaped by the biblical narrative, the apex of which in Christianity is God's redemptive work in Jesus Christ.

Second, Bonaventure is relevant because his Trinitarian approach is consistent with Wisdom Christology, which, we shall shortly see, is another distinct contribution of Edwards to ecotheology.

Third, Bonaventure's theology is significant because in Edwards's appraisal Bonaventure's approach to God is "dynamic and processive." According to Edwards, Bonaventure views creation as "the free self-expression of an ecstatic and fecund God. And this ecstasy and fecundity are located at the heart of the dynamic reality of the Trinity."[64] This observation leads Edwards to claim that Bonaventure's theology is a form of process theology — although not the type reflected by Whitehead. Consequently, Edwards is convinced that Bonaventure's dynamic understanding of God "is congruent with a worldview of emergence, with Big Bang cosmology and its understanding of the expanding universe, and with the evolutionary history of life on Earth."[65]

Fourth, Edwards maintains that Bonaventure's theology of God has merit because it has the potential for seeing the entire created order — that is, the universe — as being redeemed in God. Edwards, however, issues an important caveat — Bonaventure's theology of God and the place of creation in salvation will suffice only after being "radically corrected" by a more biblical perspective. Edwards believes this is so because Bonaventure's theology was predominantly anthropocentric and shaped by the philosophy of Neoplatonism, a philosophy that is not ecologically useful.[66] His analysis of Bonaventure's theology is extremely important because it raises the huge question of the role of creation in the grand scheme of salvation — an issue that we will address in the final section of this chapter.

The fifth reason Edwards offers is his view that Bonaventure's theology has "profound ecological consequences." In Bonaventure's theology of God, every creature in creation is a direct expression of God reflecting "God's dynamic Trinitarian presence."[67] Edwards states that for Bonaventure "every creature in its form, proportion, and beauty reflects the Word and Wisdom of God, the divine Exemplar. Every creature is a revelatory word written in the great book of creation. Every species, every ecosystem, the whole biosphere, every grain of sand and every galaxy, is a self-expression of the eternal Art of divine Wisdom."[68] Edwards concludes his assessment of Bonaventure's view of God by acknowledging that it is not pantheistic but is a type of panentheism, an understanding of God and God's relationship with creation that is shared by McDaniel and McFague.

Using Bonaventure, for the most part, as his theological platform, Edwards proceeds to provide six proposals for an ecologically relevant Trinitarian theology.

1. The triune God of Christianity should be viewed as "Persons-in-Mutual-Relationship" who is/are unified in a "communion of love." Creation, the self-expression of God, should been seen as the "Trinity's free, loving relationship with a world of creatures."[69]

2. To see the Trinity as "Persons-in-Mutual-Relationship" is to understand that relationality is the underlying ultimate reality of existence. In Edwards's words, "Ultimate reality is understood as Persons-in-Dynamic-Communion."[70] He goes on to say that "if we view relationships as the primary reality, then this means that we can begin to see all creation, the universe itself, the biosphere on Earth, individual ecosystems, a living tree, a cell, or a proton, as fundamentally relational and part of a network of interrelationships."[71]

3. The Trinity comprises a "God of dynamic, ecstatic, and fecund self-communication."[72] From this perspective creation is the prolific and abundant manifestation of God's revelation and is, therefore, sacramental, because the natural world and everything in it "is a mode and a sign of divine presence."[73]

4. A view of God as the Trinity of "Persons-in-Mutual-Communion" has implications for a theology of human existence. It means that human beings are not essentially solitary individuals but "persons-in-relationship, as persons who are both self-possessed and self-giving in communion."[74] This definition of humanity is in keeping with human ecology, which emphasizes and studies human relationships, especially the interrelatedness between the human social-institutional world and the biophysical environment.

5. Edwards's fifth proposal is that while creation is the work of the entire Trinity, special emphasis should be given to the Creator Spirit who is immanently present in creation and is the relational creative power of creation itself. According to Edwards, "This Holy Spirit, breathing through creation, is that which connects created things in God, the web of unity, the basis of the community of creatures."[75] Because of the indwelling of the Creator Spirit, creation is primarily a communion of subjects and not an arrangement of isolated objects.

6. Edward's final thesis is that God's Trinitarian relationship with creation is defined by the "vulnerability and liberating power of love."[76] According to Edwards, God's "love respects both the freedom of human beings and the integrity of natural processes."[77] The main theological issues here — and a thorny one at that — is the problem of evil (known as theodicy) and God's relationship to and participation in creation's suffering. Drawing on Anglican theologian John Polkinghorne and his argument that God's

love respects human freedom and the integrity of natural processes, which includes what is often referred to as "natural evil," Edwards declares that "if God freely creates in such a way as to be committed to the integrity of the processes of the universe, then God is not free to override these processes" and, consequently, because of God's self-imposed limitation God cannot prevent all suffering.[78] Edwards concludes, "It seems to me that this is the only line of thought on suffering which is congruent with what is revealed about God's compassion in the cross of Jesus. Here God is revealed as suffering with a suffering world in order to bring healing and liberation."[79] Edwards's position on this is reminiscent of McDaniel's approach and the approach of other process theologians who understand God as the "fellow sufferer who understands."

A key point in Edwards's ecotheology — and one of its distinctive features — is that by drawing on biblical creation-Wisdom theology, he identifies the Spirit with the Wisdom of God, and this becomes the basis for his ecological Christology. Readers will recall that the use of biblical Wisdom literature is one approach some theologians have utilized to construct an ecotheology that is biblically grounded and ecologically relevant. As God's primary agent of creation, Woman Wisdom is immanently present within the natural world, where she orders and sustains creation and instructs human beings in the way to live righteously. Wisdom theology also finds its way into the New Testament; scattered throughout its pages, it is often used in reference to Jesus of Nazareth.

Edwards's "Christic Paradigm," to use McFague's language, is Jesus the Wisdom of God, in which he reappropriates one of the earliest Christian attempts to interpret and define Jesus Christ. In the Pauline letters and the Gospel of John, early Christian theologians described Jesus as the incarnate Wisdom, Spirit, and Word of God. Central to Edwards's reconstruction of Wisdom Christology is the great Christological hymn that appears in Paul's Letter to the Colossians in 1:15–20, which was briefly discussed above.[80] Because of the passage's significance to Edwards, the full text is given here:

> He is the image of the invisible God, the first-born of all creation;
> for in him all things in heaven and on earth were created,
> things visible and invisible,
> whether thrones or dominions or rulers or powers —
> all things have been created through him and for him.
> He himself is before all things, and in him all things hold together.
> He is the head of the body, the church.
> He is the beginning, the first-born from the dead,
> so that he might come to have first place in everything.
> For in him all the fullness of God was pleased to dwell,
> and through him God was pleased to reconcile himself all things,
> by making peace through the blood of the cross.

The significance of this passage for Edwards is that it links creation and the redemption of creation in Christ. The movement of the passage begins with creation — in and through Jesus — using Wisdom as the template for Christ. Just as the universe was created in and through Wisdom, so it is with Jesus; like Wisdom, Jesus is the unifying personality who binds, orders, and sustains all things in existence. The hymn's movement of Jesus the Wisdom of God at the beginning of creation, in whom the universe is bound together, comes to completion with the novel theological claim that all creation is redeemed through Jesus' crucifixion, thus giving the death and resurrection of Jesus cosmic and universal significance. Edwards rightly asserts that "Colossians will not allow us to contain our theology of redemption with the narrower ... orbit of human sin and forgiveness. It must involve other creatures. . . . The Colossians hymn insists that the whole universe is caught up in the Christ event."[81]

The cosmological and ecological implications of the Christological hymn in Colossians are wide-ranging for Edwards, but perhaps the most important point he makes is that the material universe is not irrelevant in the cosmic scheme of God's redemptive activity, ultimately revealed in the Christ event. It is through the life, death, and resurrection of Jesus that the entire universe is transformed, that is, creation will experience the future hope of redemption and salvation. This view overtly challenges the overly anthropocentric interpretation that the Christ event typically receives. Edwards declares:

> The material universe ... is neither simply a stage on which human beings play out their relationship with God nor a kind of launching pad for a more spiritual state of existence, a launching pad which will later become unnecessary. The material universe itself will be transformed in the power of the risen Christ. The resurrection promise embraces not just human beings but the whole creation.[82]

Eschatological and Ethical Implications

The future hope of redemption and salvation falls under the theological category known as eschatology. Coming from the Greek word *eschaton*, literally meaning "end time," *eschatology is typically concerned with the future longings and deepest hopes of the human heart often associated with the hope of life after death* — in a word, *salvation*. McFague offers a succinct description of eschatology when she writes, "Eschatology can mean many things. Often in the Christian tradition it has been concerned with death and the afterlife, with 'last things' such as judgment, hell and heaven, the second coming. But it can also mean the breaking in of new possibilities, of hope for a new creation."[83] The idea of a new creation, which is deeply embedded in the biblical narrative, will serve as the centerpiece for this final section.

Australian theologian Denis Edwards is one of the leading ecotheologians in the Roman Catholic tradition. He believes that the environmental movement is one of several indicators that the Spirit of God is at work in our contemporary world. He says, "As the sense of the global crisis deepens, there is a growing movement of people committed to finding an alternative way forward, an ecological movement. It is made up of people from diverse backgrounds — farmers, artists, scientists, trade unionists, business leaders, school children, and politicians, among many others. They are connected in a common love for the Earth and its creatures. I am convinced that this movement, along with the interrelated movements committed to justice for the poor of the Earth and to the full equality of women, represents a central way in which the Spirit of God is at work in our world today" (*Ecology at the Heart of Faith: The Change of Heart That Leads to a New Way of Living on Earth* [Maryknoll, N.Y.: Orbis Books, 2006], 2).

Eschatology began to surface in biblical history with the great prophets of ancient Israel during the eighth and seventh centuries B.C.E. During this extremely difficult time, which culminated in the destruction of the first temple, prophets such as Isaiah and Jeremiah began to project the hope of God's redemptive activity into the future. That future hope of redemption was expressed in a range of images and symbols, including such ideas as the expectation of a messiah; a new covenant; a new exodus; the coming of Elijah, the eschatological prophet; and ultimately the kingdom, or reign, of God.

Within this mix of salvific images — and what is central to our discussion here — is that the prophetic hope of eschatological redemption is intrinsically connected with creation. In other words, the redemption of humanity occurs within the redemption of all creation and is perhaps best articulated in the book of Isaiah: "For I am about to create new heavens and a new earth" (Isa. 65:17). This eschatological vision of a new heaven and a new earth captures the "hope of a new creation." In her analysis of the biblical prophets' view of redemption, Carol Dempsey states that "the redemption of humankind is linked to the natural world, and the natural world's experience of transformation and new creation often happens in the process of humanity's being redeemed from its sinfulness, liberated from its oppressive situations...and that God's plan for salvation is one of cosmic redemption secured by promises that are divine and eschatological."[84]

The eschatological hope of future redemption does not end with the Old Testament prophets. On the contrary, it becomes a thematic thread that weaves its way through the entire biblical narrative and is expressed in the New Testament in Jesus' proclamation of the reign of God. In spite of the dearth of knowledge we have about the historical Jesus, most contemporary New Testament scholars are confident that the reign of God was central to Jesus' historical proclamation and ministry.

Characterizing him as a "wisdom teacher," Edwards says that Jesus "is one in whom the Wisdom tradition is made radical by the anticipatory presence of God's Reign. The wisdom Jesus preaches is the wisdom of God, which challenges traditional human wisdom, shattering conventional worldviews and opening out onto the world of the Reign of God."[85] Unfortunately Jesus did not leave us a treatise on what exactly he meant by the reign of God. Moreover, he often spoke about God's reign in parables, according to the Gospels of Matthew, Mark, and Luke, and his message was often perceived as enigmatic, challenging theologians with the task of deciphering its meaning.[86]

Nevertheless, regardless of the long history of scholarly debate and discussion regarding Jesus' proclamation of God's reign, several comments are necessary. First and foremost, the *kingdom of God is a symbol,* but a multivalent one, meaning that the reign of God cannot be easily reduced to a singular item. Second, while its meaning is often expressed in multiple ways, it is ultimately a *symbol for God's eschatological salvation,* and the emergence of that eschatological salvation in history is identified in the New Testament with Jesus' death and resurrection. Arguably, the New Testament communities of faith — the early church — interpreted Jesus of Nazareth as the embodiment of the kingdom of God. In other words, the reign of God, God's redemptive activity, is revealed in Jesus' life, ministry, and ultimately in his crucifixion and resurrection.

Third, the reign of God offers salvation to all humanity. While it is comprehensive and inclusive, it is clear, based on the Gospel's description of Jesus' life, that the kingdom includes a special option of care and concern for the poor and oppressed. Edwards notes this by stating that "the practice of the Reign of God, Wisdom's practice, is made manifest in the praxis of a radically inclusive love, which involves priority for the poor and outcast."[87]

Fourth, while the reign of God is offered to humankind, it embraces the natural world, meaning that Jesus' eschatological symbol of salvation points to the renewal, restoration, and transformation of all creation.

Referring to Jesus' teaching of God's *basileia* (*basileia,* Greek for kingdom, reign, or empire), theologian Tatha Wiley says that "the symbol of *basileia* expressed hopes for national liberation as well as the transformation of the whole creation by God's intervention."[88] Elaborating on this idea, Wiley writes:

> The *basileia* includes all creation. For the biblical writers the whole created order, including the social order, is the fruit of divine freedom, creativity, and decision. God deems that it is good through a divine *value* judgment. Jesus' vision of God's *basileia* frames his own "theology" of creation.... It is a theology of *creation* because Jesus affirms the basic tenet of biblical creation faith: the earth is God's (Ps. 24:1).[89]

This last point—that the *reign of God refers to the renewal and restoration of all creation — inclusive of the human and natural world* — is very likely one of the most important contributions of ecotheology. Utilizing an ecological hermeneutic and interpreting the biblical narrative through the lens of our ecological crisis has allowed biblical scholars and theologians concerned for our common environmental future to reappropriate the ecological motif of God's design for redemption.

As previously noted, the common theological language used to describe the redemptive activity of God in *human* history has been the "economy of salvation." Readers will remember that Edwards's ecotheology of the Trinity is based on the "economic" Trinity, reflecting the history of salvation as it is played out in the Bible. Because eschatological redemption incorporates the hope of a new creation, we suggest that it is more appropriate to refer to God's redemptive activity as *the ecology of salvation.*

There are several reasons for our perspective. First, the primary focus of God's economy of salvation has been human history; in others words, the theological emphasis has been on the historical economy of salvation as experienced by human beings, reflecting an exclusively anthropocentric interpretation of God's redemptive activity. But while humankind does have a unique role and vocation within creation, the ecological models of God described above hold the common view that God is interrelated with all creation and that relationality is best articulated by ecology.

Second, based on our analysis of the symbol of the reign of God, *human history is not the exclusive domain of God's redemption.* From the perspective of biblical Wisdom-creation theology and contemporary ecological models of God, creation participates directly in God's salvific design. Consequently, the eschatological horizon of salvation embedded in the symbol of the reign of God is the renewal and restoration of creation, and naming this the ecology of salvation is more inclusive and more theologically accurate.

The third and final reason has to do with the language of "economy" itself. It is no secret that global economies, as they are currently structured, are ethically and ecologically problematic for human and nonhuman creation. From a social justice standpoint, economies can and often do exploit and oppress human beings for the purpose of greed and profit. Furthermore, as we have argued in this text, economies such as that in the United States are driven by an addiction to overconsumption. Thus, from an ecological perspective our global economies are notoriously unsustainable and a major reason for global ecological devastation. It is our view that the two issues — *social and ecological justice — are systemically linked and must be addressed as a whole.* We maintain that theologians — and ecologists for that matter — should consider the ecology of salvation as the new paradigm for the future. This, of course, raises a crucial question: How does humankind participate in God's ecology of salvation, or, phrased differently, what is our vocation in relation to the future vision of God's reign?

Earlier, as we pointed out, Terence Fretheim, in his insightful analysis of God's relationship to the world in the Old Testament, argues that the Old Testament reveals a relational theology of creation. He concludes his analysis with some reflections on the ethical implications of his work for the human and nonhuman world. He states, "Thus I speak of a mutuality of vocations; both humans and nonhumans are called to a vocation on behalf of each other in the furtherance of God's purpose for the creation."[90] He explores several options of naming what he calls *"an interdependent mutuality of vocations,"* including stewardship, partnership, and servanthood.[91] But he reminds us that, whatever option is embraced, "it is important to remember a key foundation point: the 'co-creatureliness' of human and nonhuman, each of which without distinction, is 'good,' has inherent value, is a focus for moral concern, and stands in a unique relationship with God."[92]

In similar fashion, Sallie McFague says that *"in the vision of the new creation, we human beings have a special vocation."*[93] Elaborating, she writes:

> Our knowledge of the common creation story and where we fit into it means that we are responsible for taking evolution to its next step, one in which we will consciously bond with other human beings and other life-forms in ways that will create a sustainable, wholesome existence for the rich variety of beings on our planet.[94]

In Denis Edwards's perspective, Jesus, the Wisdom of God, and his proclamation and practice of God's reign mean that we humans must rethink our way of living on this planet because "This Wisdom demands not just new ways of thinking, but an ortho-praxis in the light of God's coming Reign."[95] In the Christian context, orthopraxis, meaning correct ethical practice, is the ethical response of faithful persons to and on behalf of the future coming of God's reign. This refers to the ethical implications Edwards envisions for the ecology of God, and it involves a number of important characteristics.

These ethical characteristics include the intrinsic value of all creatures, a special option for the poor of the earth, a reverence for all life-forms, ethical concern for ecosystems and their biological communities, a sense of companionship with our comrades in creation, and the practice of ecological sustainability.[96] He argues that *"A Christian praxis which respects the intrinsic value of all creatures involves a commitment to an ecologically sustainable economic and political system and to a lifestyle congruent with sustainability.*"[97] While we endorse the insights of Fretheim and McFague, as well as the full range of Edwards' ethical characteristics for Christian ecological praxis, on the basis of the analysis here we maintain that the ethical praxis of sustainability best frames the nature of the human vocation within God's ecology of salvation.

Questions for Discussion

1. One of the major aspects of ecotheology — or any theology for that matter — is to return to the Bible for insight and direction when faced with contemporary issues. What merit (or lack thereof) do you see in this approach for drawing upon an ancient source for our current environmental problems? Does the Bible really have anything worthwhile to say about our ecological predicament?

2. A major strategy for a number of ecotheologians has been to affirm and utilize the Wisdom literary and theological traditions from the Old Testament (also used by New Testament authors to describe Jesus). What "wisdom" do you see in this, and why do you think these theologians have pursued this line of reasoning? What characteristics of Wisdom appear to you as both ancient and modern?

3. Discuss the pros and cons of the ecological models of God proposed by McDaniel, McFague, and Edwards. With your own image of God as a point of reference, what ideas about God in their positions appear novel, intriguing, and/or objectionable to you and why?

4. This chapter introduced the biblical and theological idea of eschatology, which literally means the study of the "end time" and embodies the biblical hope for the future. How would you describe your own eschatology — not what you think will happen but what you hope will happen — for the future of humanity and the planet? What specific actions will you embrace that will assist in realizing your future vision?

Active Learning Exercises

◆ Chose a specific Christian denomination or other religious tradition (preferably your own if you have one) and research what official statements this religious community has made regarding the environmental crisis. Once the research is complete, create a student-led forum for your class to present and discuss the various statements.

◆ Design a one-day learning "field experience" for you and a group of students to engage in some form of ecological restoration in your local community (for example, invasive plant removal, tree planting, stream/riparian recovery). A local environmental group, campus office, or public agency can assist in this). Create a digital "poster" or video of this event and present it to your class. (This could make a great extra-credit opportunity.)

Recommended Readings

Dempsey, Carol J., and Russell A. Butkus, eds. *All Creation Is Groaning: An Interdisciplinary Vision for Life in a Sacred Universe.* Collegeville, Minn.: Liturgical Press, 1999.

Edwards, Denis. *Ecology at the Heart of Faith.* Maryknoll, N.Y.: Orbis Books, 2007.

Fowler, Robert Booth. *The Greening of Protestant Thought.* Chapel Hill: University of North Carolina Press, 1995.

Johnson, Elizabeth A. *Women, Earth, and Creator Spirit.* Mahwah, N.J.: Paulist Press, 1993.

McDaniel, Jay B. *With Roots and Wings: Christianity in an Age of Ecology and Dialogue.* Maryknoll, N.Y.: Orbis Books, 1995.

McFague, Sallie. *A New Climate for Theology: God, the World, and Global Warming.* Minneapolis: Fortress Press, 2008.

Miller, Richard W., ed. *God, Creation, and Climate Change: A Catholic Response to the Environmental Crisis.* Maryknoll, N.Y.: Orbis Books, 2010.

Rasmussen, Larry L. *Earth Community, Earth Ethics.* Maryknoll, N.Y.: Orbis Books, 1996.

Rolston, Holmes. "Ecology and the Bible." *Interpretation: A Journal of Bible and Theology* 50, no. 1 (January 1996): 16–26.

8

Sustainability for a Small Planet

Theological and Scientific Reflections

Sustainability has many definitions, with many organizations, movies, and books now dedicated to it, but as yet there is no universally agreed-upon meaning. To some, a sustainable future harkens back to an Eden-like existence with people living in what are essentially garden communities that meet their needs for food, fiber, and water on a local level. To others, a sustainable future has more of the flavor of a 1950s science-fiction book cover, with gleaming towers that produce their own energy from wind and sunlight, connected by electric monorails that transport people without polluting the atmosphere. Sustainability can also be understood as a future of appropriate employment for the billions still in poverty — or for gradually reducing human population levels.

This complicated set of possible "sustainabilities" forms a real barrier to proposing a comprehensive definition and, perhaps most importantly, it challenges us with this question: How do we actually implement a vision of sustainability to reverse ecological decline and move toward a society that we can admire and that can exist over the long term? This final chapter focuses on sustainability. It is a limited attempt to answer the preceding question — limited because the actual practice of sustainability is a much bigger and broader challenge than issues in the realm of theology or science. Nevertheless, we must address the future well-being of human communities, biological communities, and the supportive ecosystems in which they reside. This is why we now turn to exploring the meaning and practice of sustainability and our shared commitment to it through this interdisciplinary conversation between theology and environmental science.

A Theological Perspective

Some preliminary observations are necessary, the most important of which is that theology and science do not share the same point of departure in their respective approaches to the meaning of sustainability. *Ecology* begins with the empirical realization that the natural world is self-sustaining, that is, the natural world contains internal processes such as biogeochemical cycles, nutrient cycles, solar energy, and so forth that maintain and sustain ecosystems. *Theology*, on the other hand, begins with the faith assumption that the natural world — creation — is not self-sustaining but is sustained by the ongoing presence of God. This biblical perspective also means that creation is not finished and that, similar to evolution, creation continues into the future, where it will be renewed and restored in the form of "a new heaven and a new earth."

These different starting points are not mutually exclusive. From a theological point of view, the ecological insights that nature is sustained by physical processes can be interpreted as specific indications of God's action in the universe. Beyond that, however, lies a more important issue: the place and role of humanity in the creative evolutionary process.

From the theological side of the equation, human beings have a vocation within creation. The biblical view is that humanity participates with God in sustaining the creation through the practice of justice and righteousness. Recall that in biblical creation-Wisdom theology creation has a God-given physical and moral order, and consequently human beings have an ethical responsibility to sustain the integrity of creation. In light of the environmental crisis, our position is that the practice of justice and righteousness in our contemporary world must include the ethical practice — the *orthopraxis* — of sustainability.

From a scientific view, human beings have become the dominant species on this planet and are the primary culprit in causing ecological deterioration. If ecological decline is going to be reversed, if damaged ecosystems are going to be restored, and if the well-being of human and biological communities and the ecosystems upon which they depend is going to be sustained, then humanity must implement an environmental ethic oriented toward sustainability. In other words, from both scientific and theological viewpoints, human beings and their interrelatedness within the natural world are the key agents in the pursuit of a sustainable planet. If life — creation — is going to be maintained and sustained into the future, human beings will play a vital role.

What Is Sustainability?

The last chapter concluded with two critical insights from the ecotheology of Denis Edwards. First, the centrality of the proclamation and practice of the reign of God for Jesus, the Wisdom of God, requires his followers to embrace "an orthopraxis in the light of God's coming Reign." Second, this orthopraxis must include a "commitment to an ecologically sustainable economic and political system and to a lifestyle congruent with sustainability." Because the reign of God, the primary symbol of salvation in the life, death, and resurrection of Jesus, means the restoration and renewal of all creation, the Christian ethical praxis of sustainability ought to be grounded in and motivated by this ultimate horizon of Christian faith: the future hope of God's redemption. In light of this claim, the ethical practice of sustainability is the praxis of hopeful anticipation (to some degree all Christian ethics is anticipatory of God's reign). It is the praxis of anticipatory hope that the future of Earth, the transformation of creation that is in God's salvific design, requires our participation.

Sustainability, therefore, defined theologically, means that it is the ethical praxis of hopeful anticipation in the future restoration and renewal of creation, and it requires the practice of ecological and social justice to restore, sustain, and maintain the integrity of creation.

The reader may recall that in connection with the discussion of ecological grace, we addressed Willis Jenkins's thesis that the Christian ethical response to the environmental crisis takes three dominant forms — ecojustice, stewardship, and ecospirituality. Using Jenkins's method of analysis, the theological contours of this book would likely fall within the category of ecojustice. While we would not dispute that, we would remind readers that ethical typologies are rarely "pure" in the real world of Christian practice; we maintain that the ethical responses of ecojustice, stewardship, and ecospirituality are not mutually exclusive. In other words, the option of stewardship — if properly understood — must include the practice of ecological and social justice and that practice is in itself spirituality.

While the ethical responses of ecojustice, stewardship, and ecospirituality reflect varying theologies of salvation and grace, as well as underlying motivations, the ethical metapurpose of all three ought to be the praxis of sustainability. In a Christian context sustainability cannot be reduced to mere discourse. Christians must "walk the talk": sustainability can result only from a strategic and applied ethic. First, *strategic* because it requires both planning and implementation. This is particularly true for larger organizations (businesses, universities, parishes, and so on) where strategic planning is a function of carrying out the institutional mission or organizational culture. Second, sustainability is also an *applied ethic* at all levels — personal and institutional — because it requires making conscious choices that impact day-to-day living. This is how we interpret Edwards's point that Christian orthopraxis must include "a lifestyle congruent with sustainability."

Regardless of the specific definition of sustainability one adopts, the following outline of key social and economic points must correspond with any vision for a sustainable future:

- *Restraint in consumption.* A sustainable society will necessarily be one in which excessive consumption is considered a personal failing rather than a sign of success. Frugality, once a well recognized virtue, need not be synonymous with an unpleasant life. In fact, much of recent experience suggests that a life based on ever-increasing consumption rather than human relationships becomes an ultimately unsatisfying life.

- *Efficiency in resource utilization.* Many of our technologies could be improved significantly, with design priority being given to energy and material efficiency rather than cheapness in production. Over the long run, more efficient and better-made products will cost less, provide longer service, and require less of our finite resources. This means a move away from designing objects so that they become dated or worn out as quickly as possible, moving away from the culture of disposable objects to one of long-term use and reuse.

+ *Option for the poor and authentic development.* A sustainable society must provide long-lasting, sufficient, and meaningful employment that does not degrade the world around it. Having billions of people left in poverty is not sustainable; billions of people left behind while a small fraction of the human race accumulates more wealth will eventually destabilize any social structure in which the poor lack access to the necessities of life. Real and lasting sustainability must include release from the sort of grinding poverty that makes chopping down the last tree, catching the last fish, or defecating near a river also used for drinking water the only alternative open to people. Sustainability is about long-term thought.

+ *Personal liberation and social-institutional transformation.* Sustainability, of necessity, is about doing things differently, giving up past individual and social practices that led to environmental deterioration and neglect. Liberation from our patterns of consumptive thinking and living should be a relief, as we move from a world in which we objectify both resources and ourselves toward a life in which relationship and connection are recognized as primary. Sustainability involves personal liberation from consumerism as a dominant ideal. Because social institutions are by their very nature institutionalized patterns of human behavior, as human behavior changes so will institutions. That change is already occurring at many levels, from individual recycling to universities reducing their carbon footprint to energy providers investing in renewable sources of energy and people choosing to purchase those renewable forms of energy.

Continuing with our dialogue on sustainability we move now from theological and ethical considerations to a scientific analysis of sustainability and a historical reflection on where we have been as a global community to where we must arrive if sustainability is to be achieved.

Scientific and Historical Considerations[1]

In chapter 3 we proposed an *ecological definition of sustainability* that emphasized the following points: (1) ecosystem energy flows and nutrient cycles are stable or fluctuating within a normal range of variability; (2) species diversity and population levels of organisms are not reduced; (3) habitat diversity and connectivity of natural habitats are sufficient to allow organisms to flourish; (4) toxic materials are not accumulating in the soil, air, or water, and; (5) overall nondeterioration of the biotic and abiotic elements of ecosystems is the hallmark of ecological sustainability.

While these are basic ecological principles that must be observed, the reality is that many ecosystems have been altered and damaged by human activity. Consequently, sustainability must involve *ecological restoration*—an actual branch of ecology that emerged in the 1980s. Ecological restoration, as defined by the Society for Ecological Restoration International, is "an intentional activity that initiates or accelerates the recovery of an ecosystem with respect to its health, integrity and sustainability."[2] This necessity is in keeping with our basic understanding of sustainability—that it must address the well-being of biological communities and the ecosystems in which they reside. Nonetheless, as essential as ecological restoration is to achieving sustainability, the entire landscape of sustainability is incomplete without addressing human communities and their social and economic systems. That brings us to what is arguably the most commonly noted definition of sustainability—the one proposed in 1987 by *Our Common Future*.

The Brundtland Commission Report

In 1983 the United Nations appointed Gro Harlem Brundtland, formerly the prime minister of Norway, to lead the World Commission on Environment and Development (WCED) in writing its report, begun in 1984 and released in March 1987, commonly known as either the *Brundtland Report* or *Our Common Future*. The report was designed to be the first major attempt to integrate discussions of environmental concerns with issues of economic development and to discern what sustainability would look like. The mission of the WCED is noteworthy:

> to propose long-term environmental strategies for achieving sustainable development by the year 2000 and beyond; to recommend ways concern for the environment may be translated into greater co-operation among developing countries and between countries at different stages of economic and social development and lead to the achievement of common and mutually supportive objectives that take account of the interrelationships between people, resources, environment, and development; to consider ways and means by which the international community can deal more effectively with environment concerns; and to help define shared perceptions of long-term environmental issues and the appropriate efforts needed to deal successfully with the problems of protecting and enhancing the environment, a long-term agenda for action during the coming decades, and aspirational goals for the world community.[3]

The *Brundtland Report* described patterns of economic activity that essentially represented the present generation stealing from future ones. Point 25 of the report overview states:

> Many present efforts to guard and maintain human progress, to meet human needs, and to realize human ambitions are simply unsustainable—in both the rich and poor nations. They draw too heavily, too quickly, on already overdrawn environmental resource accounts to be affordable far into the future without bankrupting those accounts.

AMERICAN VISIONS OF SUSTAINABILITY

Moving toward sustainability is a process of reclaiming a hopeful long-term vision for our society, not a dramatic move away from our origins. Some voices from our past:

Theodore Roosevelt, writing in 1916

The "greatest good for the greatest number" applies to the number within the womb of time, compared to which those now alive form but an insignificant fraction. Our duty to the whole, including the unborn generations, bids us restrain an unprincipled present-day minority from wasting the heritage of these unborn generations. The movement for the conservation of wildlife and the larger movement for the conservation of all our natural resources are essentially democratic in spirit, purpose, and method.[4]

Robert Kennedy, in a speech at the University of Kansas in 1968

Too much and for too long, we seem to have surrendered personal excellence and community values in the mere accumulation of material things. Our Gross National Product, now, is over $800 billion dollars a year, but that Gross National Product — if we judge the United States of America by that — that Gross National Product counts air pollution and cigarette advertising, and ambulances to clear our highways of carnage. It counts special locks for our doors and the jails for the people who break them. It counts the destruction of the redwood and the loss of our natural wonder in chaotic sprawl.... Yet the Gross National Product does not allow for the health of our children, the quality of their education, or the joy of their play. It does not include the beauty of our poetry or the strength of our marriages, the intelligence of our public debate or the integrity of our public officials. It measures neither our wit nor our courage, neither our wisdom nor our learning, neither our compassion nor our devotion to our country. It measures everything, in short, except that which makes life worthwhile.[5]

The great American author Edward Abbey may have described the problem most succinctly, over thirty years ago: Growth for the sake of growth is the ideology of the cancer cell.[6]

They may show profit on the balance sheets of our generation, but our children will inherit the losses. We borrow environmental capital from future generations with no intention or prospect of repaying. They may damn us for our spendthrift ways, but they can never collect on our debt to them. We act as we do because we can get away with it: future generations do not vote; they have no political or financial power; they cannot challenge our decisions.[7]

A brief summary of this statement has now become the most typical definition of sustainability: *meeting the needs of the current generation without compromising the ability of future generations to meet their needs.* The report went on to describe additional elements of a sustainable future, including assurance that the poor get their fair share of resources, the establishment of political systems that ensure citizen participation in decision making, the adoption of more modest levels of consumption by the affluent, a harmony between rates of population growth and the productive capacity of the ecosystem, and avoiding exploitation of local resources that will have wider effects (such as floods caused by deforestation, industrial development whose pollution ruins fisheries, excessive irrigation that drives ecologically connected marginal land into desert and produces environmental refugees, and so forth).[8]

While these points sound surprisingly contemporary, the insight of the commission into threats to sustainability that reside in political structures seems prescient. Under the heading of "The Institutional Gaps" the report mentions the barriers to sustainability posed by slow government responses and an unwillingness to embrace change, the fragmentary responsibility and narrow mandates of responsible government agencies (a phrase we have elsewhere called "the bureaucratic conundrum"),[9] a diminution in confidence in international cooperation just as it is most needed, a false sense of security provided by the existence of national environmental agencies, and the use of narrow decision structures by government economic ministries or sectors and international aid agencies.

Under the heading of "The Policy Directions," the *Brundtland Report* made policy proposals two decades ago that the international community and national governments have not yet had the political will to implement. These proposals, among others too numerous to list fully, include:

+ strengthen social, cultural, and economic structures designed to help people cope with a rapidly changing world

+ limit extreme rates of population increase so that the global population stabilizes in the range of 6 billion persons

+ exhibit sensitivity to indigenous peoples and recognize their traditional rights,

- adopt agricultural policies that encourage conservation of fertile soil and assist farmers in developing countries with modern agricultural tools to improve their productivity and protect their land

- pay attention to global food distribution systems to improve food security and reduce hunger

- protect species diversity and threatened ecosystems and develop a network of protected areas around the world

- redesign energy strategies to provide for increased energy use by developing nations, and increased energy efficiencies globally, without relying on increased fossil fuel use that leads to global climate change and acid precipitation

- develop renewable energy resources and develop new industrial processes that produce more with less use of energy and raw materials

- have industrialized nations and transnational corporations assist newly industrializing nations to prevent inappropriate industrial development that would produce a legacy of pollution

- tighten controls on new toxic industrial chemicals and wastes and on their export and dumping

- develop explicit strategies worldwide so that growing cities provide basic facilities and services needed for human life and to prevent the development of sprawling slums or "informal settlements" (whose primitive facilities leave them rife with disease) around the edges of growing cities

- decentralize funds and personnel and political power for urban planning and ensure that the urban poor are given a role in the future plans for cities[10]

It is difficult to imagine how many fewer critical issues we would face today if even some of the *Brundtland Commission*'s policy directions had been adopted. These were written before China developed a robust economy and became a giant terrain of smokestacks and environmental toxicity (with India and Indonesia now not far behind), before the barrios of the world had grown to epic scales, before childhood respiratory diseases and autism and pediatric cancers soared in an increasingly toxic environment, before climate change reached its present critical level that many experts fear is near a tipping point. As perhaps the weakening of international cooperation in the 1980s doomed these policy directions even as they were written, it is informative to see what the *Brundtland Commission* said about international cooperation and institutional reform.

International Cooperation

The vision of international cooperation described in the report calls for (among other things) an assurance of ecosystem sustainability and an equitable basis for exchange for developing nations; debt service reduction for nations that draw on their natural resources in a nonrenewable way to satisfy debt payments; respect for environmental concerns on the part of multinational corporations as they negotiate with developing nations; international fisheries agreements that prevent overexploitation of fish stocks as well as conventions to prevent ocean dumping of wastes; money spent on poverty reduction instead of armaments, including nuclear weapons; increasing the roles and capacities of environmental protection and resource management agencies; a greatly improved capacity to assess and report on global environmental risks; and investment in activities like pollution control, agricultural conservation, and renewable energy by multinational agencies, including the World Bank.[11]

By now it should be clear that the U.N. report commissioned in 1983 described what a sustainable world would look like, the problems we faced in achieving sustainability, and avenues along which the international community could and should move forward. Compared to the scale of the challenge, the global community did virtually nothing. Seventeen years after the *Brundtland Commission* was given its charge, the secretary general of the United Nations called for the beginning of a process of global discernment now commonly called the Millennium Ecosystem Assessment. Thousands of experts around the world were involved in writing a series of technical chapters as well as synthetic documents, and these are readily available to anyone with an interest in examining the details of the statements and recommendations.[12]

We will briefly turn to one of the Millennium Ecosystem Assessment documents dated 2005. The report entitled *Ecosystems and Human Well-being: Synthesis* lists three major problems now visible in our management of the global ecosystem:

> First, approximately 60 percent (15 out of 24) of the ecosystem services examined during the Millennium Ecosystem Assessment are being degraded or used unsustainably, including fresh water, capture fisheries, air and water purification, and the regulation of regional and local climate, natural hazards, and pests....
>
> Second, there is established but incomplete evidence that changes being made in ecosystems are increasing the likelihood of nonlinear changes in ecosystems (including accelerating, abrupt, and potentially irreversible changes) that have important consequences for human well-being. Examples of such changes include disease emergence, abrupt alterations in water quality, the creation of "dead zones" in coastal waters, the collapse of fisheries, and shifts in regional climate....

Third, the harmful effects of the degradation of ecosystem services (the persistent decrease in the capacity of an ecosystem to deliver services) are being borne disproportionately by the poor, are contributing to growing inequalities and disparities across groups of people, and are sometimes the principle factor causing poverty and social conflict.[13]

Had we implemented the recommendations of the *Brundtland Commission* with vigor, the Millennium Ecosystem Assessment would perhaps have sounded very different in tone. The honest truth is that, despite the efforts of a huge number of people in nonprofit organizations and agencies worldwide,[14] as a society we barely tried. Some visionaries in the business world worked to improve manufacturing and commerce, government pronouncements that sounded comforting were made, public and private funds were expended, but the ecosystemic slide of the planet accelerated.

A careful review of efforts toward sustainability in light of the reports already mentioned, as well as other documents, was published by David Runnalls in 2008.[15] He reviewed the history of major documents about sustainability and then went on to assess progress in four major areas. His conclusions are sobering and worth examining:

Private-Sector Steps toward Sustainability

Much progress is to be found in the more enlightened parts of the private sector. . . . The emergence of the Business Council for Sustainable Development (now the World Business Council for Sustainable Development, WBCSD) . . . moved industry from the periphery to the center of the sustainable development debate. WBCSD represents more than 200 CEOs from some of the world's largest companies. . . .

These initiatives still involve relatively few companies. Furthermore, they are often associated with a senior executive or CEO. When that person passes from the scene, it is often difficult to maintain the momentum. The programs are all voluntary, and experience with a number of voluntary initiatives shows that they are often too easy to flaunt or abuse. . . .

And these are large corporations with substantial intellectual and financial resources; the majority of jobs worldwide are provided by small and medium-sized enterprises for which these concepts are foreign.[16]

National Policies and Institutions

Both the *Brundtland Report* and the commitment to sustainable development have been taken far more seriously in Europe than in the rest of the world, and even there the record has been spotty. . . .

Integrating environment and economic decision making has proven to be a tough task. . . .

Even in the case of those most committed to sustainable development — Germany and the Nordic countries, for example — it would be difficult to isolate social policies that owe their origins primarily to a desire to complete the sustainable development triad of economic growth and equity, natural resource conservation, and social development, rather than for other policy or political reasons.[17]

Change within Aid Agencies

Environmental guidelines are now well established in these organizations.... Environmental impact assessments are routinely required for large projects....

It can be difficult to reconcile the need to dispense large amounts of money quickly and efficiently while building in the appropriate safeguards. This difficulty can be compounded in an era where the emphasis has been on recipient-driven foreign assistance. If sustainable development is low on the priority list of the recipient, it can be difficult for even the most proper donor to insist on another priority.[18]

International Regimes for Sustainable Development

To complete our tale of gloom, we need only turn to the subject of international governance of the environment. The good news is that we have been very active in the creation of international regimes for environmental protection....

The bad news is that most of these agreements are supported by small secretariats with inadequate budgets.... And none have effective compliance regimes. They also are cursed by a lack of accountability. Although these are legal agreements, most governments seem willing to sign up to a whole series of commitments with little intent of honoring the majority of them.[19]

Runnalls concludes that, despite all the apparent activity, we are in fact making little headway in moving our society toward environmental sustainability. He concludes that some of the most persuasive voices asking for societal transformation are "falling on deaf ears" and that there is a great need for leadership, including in the United States, that actually moves ahead quickly while there is time, instead of continuing to talk about the issues and convening commissions. We have spent much of the time we had in 1983, and spent it on little concrete progress and many words.

Also published in 2008 was a review of progress made since the *Brundtland Commission Report* on management of common-pool resources such as fisheries and forest resources.[20] The article by Elinor Ostrom describes both successes and failures in management, documenting a decline in global fish stocks and failures of the Economic Exclusion Zones as many nations actually increased their national fishing fleets once the zones were in place. Included in her evaluation is the cod debacle of the Canadian Department of

Fisheries and Oceans but also the successful management of Maine lobster stocks. The examples described in Ostrom's report are well worth reading, as they describe turtle egg management, timber overharvesting, and other causes of decades-long declines in ecosystemic productivity.

The report also emphasizes several observations of note, including the observation that there are no cure-all approaches in the absence of local and regional knowledge. Human-resource systems require a level of adaptive governance capable of collecting vital information, and dealing with conflict and rule compliance rather than more rules. Ostrom describes processes by which progress in the management of common-pool resources might be made, even though two decades of opportunities have been lost.

The preceding reflections on the distance between our public discourse and our individual and communal actions over the course of the last quarter century and more contain one clear lesson: *talking and planning for change has done little beyond providing a social analgesic for the perception that things are going wrong.* Every year that passes makes the transition to a sustainable society more difficult, as we have fewer natural resources to work with, more contamination to clean up, and ever-reducing biodiversity to restore. We need to begin to make the changes that have been waiting for us for over a human generation. What are the personal, public, and global steps we need to take to achieve a sustainable society and how can we develop a sense of urgency and momentum?

Steps to Sustainability

First, on the international level, *we need a climate treaty* that will prevent atmospheric carbon dioxide from tripling beyond its preindustrial level. A good case that this is feasible has been made by a partnership between members of the academic community, the oil industry, and the automobile industry that proposes that existing technologies implemented with sufficient seriousness of purpose and vigor can already achieve this goal.[21]

The future for carbon mitigation could be even more positive, given the international emphasis on and funding for research into alternative energy technologies including tidal and wave power, ocean thermal energy conversion (which produces electricity from the temperature difference between warm surface waters and cold deep waters in tropical seas), photovoltaic energy, reverse electrodialysis and pressure-retarded osmosis power (which are two ways to harvest power from the difference in salt concentration between ocean water and river water at a river's mouth), enhanced geothermal systems that harvest the heat beneath the Earth's surface for power, and fusion power (the power inherent in our own sun). The perfection of cellulosic ethanol production that makes ethanol by fermenting plants such as corn stalks or grasses into alcohol might eventually make the term "agricultural waste" an oxymoron. These approaches are already being worked on, but an acceleration of the research could pay huge dividends both literally and conceptually.

Second, the *rules of the World Trade Organization (WTO) need to be changed*. Although the language establishing the WTO actually contains a provision that could lead to environmental sensitivity, in fact it has not done so. The WTO charter says:

> Relations in the field of trade and economic endeavor should be conducted with a view to raising standards of living, ensuring full employment and a large and steadily growing volume of real income and effective demand, and expanding the production of and trade in goods and services, while allowing for the optimal use of the world's resources in accordance with the objective of sustainable development, seeking both to protect and preserve the environment and to enhance the means for doing so in a manner consistent with their respective needs and concerns at different levels of economic development.[22]

In practice, the WTO has consistently ruled against environmentally oriented trade options. Most Americans have not known that the WTO has the power to rule against provisions of the U.S. Clean Air Act, which specifies how clean gasoline must be made, because it discriminates against foreign refiners. Also generally unknown is the fact that the WTO ruled to forbid member states to link trade issues with environmental issues or even those of human rights and child labor. Similarly, the WTO has the power to override the sovereignty of member states when environmental regulations are judged to impede free trade.[23]

Recently there have been some initial signs of movement in a positive direction to protect the environment on the part of the WTO; while they should be applauded, they should also be interpreted as only early steps. Recognizing economic pressure being exerted by consumers who want to be able to choose between environmentally friendly products so that they can spend their resources in ways that reflect their values, the WTO convened a session in 2010 to explore carbon-intensity labeling.[24]

In a broader sense, corporations need to adopt transparent labeling practices that specify the intensity of carbon release, water consumption, release of various toxins, and so on so that consumers have the needed information to make purchasing decisions and corporate visions for environmental and social responsibility can be carried out. Purchasing decisions based on a combination of price, quality, and environmental impact will be possible only if corporations become widely engaged and if the WTO becomes at least a neutral force in the global environmental arena.

At present there has also been minor WTO movement in terms of controlling the environmental impact of agricultural exports, but in general the WTO has historically served as the "police" of free trade, promoting unimpeded trade regardless of its environmental impact or the desires of importing nations that want to assure that imported goods have been manufactured as sustainably as possible. Note that the WTO is not part of the United Nations, that it therefore need not comply with U.N. mandates, and that it acts with great influence although it is neither an elected body nor a congress of nationally elected officials. This type of structure embodies a sort of nonrepresentative power that our own nation has a history of rejecting.

Third, *the public policy-making power of corporations needs to be reduced* to a reasonable level. Corporations were invented and operate to increase shareholder value, and their vision of the common good, therefore, is often limited to their shareholders (or their executives, ignoring their shareholders). Corporations have all too frequently been happy to externalize costs in the form of pollution and resource depletion. For sustainability, policy decisions must look further ahead than the next quarterly report or executive bonus toward decisions that are more appropriate from the perspective of future generations. Corporations fulfill an important and appropriate role when they allow shareholders to invest with a limited risk in commercial ventures that provide the goods, services, and jobs necessary for and beneficial to our society. However, the short-sighted scale of corporate visions and their limited goals make them a poor choice for having enormous influence over public policy decisions that affect generations of future populations in all corners of the world. Even a rudimentary view of the history of corporate behavior indicates that corporations need to live within the rules of human societies and not shape them, if both the corporations and societies are to prosper over time.

Fourth, *we need to consume less energy and water-intensive foods and beverages* (for example, avoiding large portions of grain-fed beef) and cultivate the enjoyment of appropriate local and seasonal foods in our diet. Eating a less meat-heavy diet could increase our potential for biofuel production, without adding to agricultural water demands or reducing the grains and legumes available for human consumption.[25] With the average item on an American plate now traveling anywhere from twelve hundred miles to fifteen hundred miles to reach our tables, the fossil fuel cost of agriculture has become ever higher. We need to develop a preference for local food that is well informed and reasonable.

In prioritizing dietary decisions, however, it is important to realize that the production phase of the modern agricultural system accounts for on average 83 percent of techniques that gas emissions by the agricultural system,[26] while long-distance transportation of food accounts for only 11 percent of emissions, and retail delivery only 4 percent. Transporting food in ships over longer distances sometimes has a lower environmental impact than shorter transport distances by trucks. In addition, foods of various types are more suitable to certain climates than others, and no benefit can be derived by insisting on local food production that requires energy-intensive techniques that replace simpler agricultural practices elsewhere. For example, producing cheese, lamb, or apples in New Zealand and shipping them to Great Britain for consumption actually has a lower carbon footprint than producing and storing the food domestically.[27] While these facts are not a reason to abandon agriculture in Great Britain, they constitute a valuable warning about oversimplification in complex decision making. Similarly, the higher carbon emission cost of trucking as compared to shipping means that for American oenophiles on the East Coast, it is actually more environmentally sensitive to drink wine from Bordeaux that arrived by ship than wine trucked from the Napa Valley.[28]

In these cases, food miles were not a good proxy for a commodity's environmental footprint, but in other instances food miles will prove to be a useful metric. Food miles are especially reliable if two sources utilizing the same form of transportation are being compared. Additionally, the issue of exporting virtual water in the form of commodities must always be considered. There are times when a tradeoff exists between the export of water embodied in food from more arid regions to more temperate regions and the reduction of carbon emissions due to transportation. In this case, as with other tradeoffs, careful thought must be given to the two scenarios, since no metric presently exists that allows us to produce a decision that takes all of the different environmental concerns into account.

Fifth, *recycling needs to be strongly encouraged,* both on a household and an industrial scale. We do not live on an infinite planet and ever-increasing resource utilization is not possible. However, if recycling is significantly increased, economic development can be separated from the need for ever-increasing resource use. The human economy should more closely resemble the natural biogeochemical cycles in which materials cycle endlessly and are therefore never depleted. Some industries have been able to dramatically increase their profitability by increasing their recycling and diminishing their use of natural resources, and many more could do so.[29] Recycling needs to include the promotion of animal and human wastes as sources of biofuel production (such as using bacterial fermentation to produce methane), which would remove a large amount of potentially toxic material from the waste stream and turn it into one of the needed future fuels.

Sixth, *freshwater resources must be protected,* and prevented from becoming a petroleum-like commodity available globally to the highest bidder, rather than belonging to communities that have always had access to that water. Fresh water is needed for drinking, bathing, agriculture, and industrial processes of many types. Water supplies are limited and becoming highly contaminated in many areas of the world. While we can imagine alternative futures with energy sources other than fossil fuels, there is no alternative to water consumption for either humans or our crop plants and animals. Water and air are equally vital, and we must view the prospect of water becoming a privately held commodity exactly as we would view the prospect of that happening to the air we breathe.

As the twenty-first century progresses, freshwater availability is threatened by the actions of multinational corporations working continually to obtain ownership of what they correctly perceive to be an increasingly limited resource. It is also threatened by the release of industrial effluents and municipal sewage, in some places by excessive water withdrawals for irrigation associated with aquifer depletions that turn agriculture into a form of "water mining," and the loss of glaciers and ice fields that have served as important sources of drinking water and summer river flows.

The sustainability-related aspects of this topic are too complex to deal with here at length but a U.N. thematic report titled *Coping with Water Scarcity* gives a brief account of some of the major issues involved,[30] and various organizations, including Food and Water Watch,[31] maintain substantial online libraries addressing various aspects of freshwater supply, contamination, scarcity, and privatization. Suffice it to say, we must begin to recognize that fresh water is a limited and precious public good and treat it as such.

The issue of a virtual water trade alluded to above is a significant concern for the future of freshwater supplies in some locations. Whenever irrigation-intensive crops are grown in one region and shipped in vast quantities to another region, an unrecognized trade in virtual water is taking place. Such trade can have significant environmental costs for the exporting nation if it begins to ship overseas the freshwater resources needed to maintain the stability of its ecosystem. Comprehensive coverage of this topic, which embodies environmental science, economics, and social justice issues, merits an entire book, and an excellent resource is Maude Barlow's *Blue Covenant*.[32]

Closely associated with the issue of protecting freshwater supplies is the vital concern of reducing soil erosion and the loss of fertile agricultural lands to desertification or urban sprawl. We have paved over or abused beyond use large areas of fertile soil, and we must recognize the irreplaceable nature of that component of the biosphere. Planning for community growth, giving preferential treatment to farmland preservation, and growing crops in a way that does not deplete freshwater resources are all important attributes for any serious effort to preserve agricultural soils and the surface or subsurface waters on which they depend.

Seventh, *we need* to use all of the components of our educational institutions *to develop a vocabulary, manner of analysis, and thought that is consistent with processes that can lead us to a sustainable future.* From K–12, to higher education, to MBA courses and in-service educational opportunities, we need to make space in curricula and content for systems of thought that can elevate the frequency and quality of discussions about ways to obtain a sustainable future. One such system of thought originated by Karl-Henrik Robèrt and developed by the Natural Step Network has articulated four system conditions that can be used to guide decision making. This method of attaining sustainability is a good example of an applied strategy that has been successfully used by a number of corporations and organizations.[33] The system conditions are related to pollution caused by natural materials as they become concentrated, pollution caused by materials that have been synthesized, loss of biologically productive areas, and equity in resource distribution. They are based upon an understanding that

A SHORT LIST OF EFFECTIVE ACTIONS AMERICANS CAN TAKE TO REDUCE THEIR ENERGY CONSUMPTION

(Actions providing roughly 2 percent improvement or more were selected from a longer list in Gardner and Stern (2008).[34]

Carpool to work (saves up to 4.2 percent of annual household energy use on average)

Tune up your car with air filter changes (saves up to 3.9 percent of annual household energy use on average)

Drive without sudden starts and stops (saves up to 3.2 percent of annual household energy use on average)

Combine errand trips to drive half as many miles (saves up to 2.7 percent of annual household energy use on average)

Cut highway speed from 70 to 60 mph (saves up to 2.4 percent of annual household energy use on average)

Replace old light bulbs with compact fluorescents (saves up to 4.0 percent of annual household energy use on average)

Set heating at 68 degrees F during the day and 65 degrees at night; set air conditioning at 78 degrees F (saves up to 3.4 percent of annual household energy use on average)

Buy a more fuel efficient car (30.7 mpg epa average composite value) (saves up to 13.5 percent of annual household energy use on average)

Caulk and weather-strip your home (saves up to 2.5 percent of annual household energy use on average)

Install and/or upgrade attic insulation and venting (saves up to 7.0 percent of annual household energy use on average)

Install a high efficiency furnace (92 percent +) (saves up to 2.9 percent of annual household energy use on average)

Install a more efficient air conditioner: Seasonal Energy Efficient Ratio (SEER 13) or Energy Efficient Ratio (EER 12) (saves up to 2.2 percent of annual household energy use on average)

Install a more efficient energy star refrigerator/freezer (saves up to 1.9 percent of annual household energy use on average)

Karl-Henrik Robèrt is one of Sweden's leading cancer scientists. In 1989, Dr. Robèrt initiated an environmental movement called The Natural Step (TNS). In recent years, he has returned to his passion of scientific research through Real Change, an international initiative linking university research specializations with real-world application using the Natural Step Framework. Dr. Robèrt holds a Ph.D. in medicine from Karolinska Institute and has served on the faculties of many of Sweden's most prestigious hospitals and universities.

all life is supported by natural processes such as photosynthesis and the biogeochemical cycles, processes essential to maintaining the ecosystem. The four "Natural Step System Conditions" are:

1. In a sustainable society, nature is not subject to systematically increasing concentrations of substances extracted from the Earth's crust (e.g., heavy metals, fossil fuels).

2. In a sustainable society, nature is not subject to systematically increasing concentrations of substances produced by society (e.g., synthetic organic pesticides; industrial chemicals).

3. In a sustainable society, nature is not subject to systematic deterioration of nature and natural processes (e.g., forests, estuarine ecosystems, etc.).

4. In a sustainable society people are not subject to conditions that systematically undermine their capacity to meet their needs.[35]

A two-day workshop at the University of Portland to rearticulate the fourth System Condition[36] from the perspective of Catholic social teaching produced an alternative version: "In present and future societies that are just and sustainable, all persons — especially the most vulnerable — deserve, and have a right to, the basic social and ecological conditions necessary for life and dignity. This cannot be separated from the care and defense of all

BACK TO THE FUTURE

Sustainable development is about planning for a feasible future. A sustainable society can be created only if its economy doesn't erode the social and ecological fabric on which that society is based. This is a challenge that puts great demands on strategic leadership.

Many heads of organizations believe sustainability is all about values, and the voters as well as the market would be prepared to vote for, and pay more for, only services that take the environment and social responsibility into account. This would have a positive effect on the "brand," so investing in sustainability is directly proportional to profits. But it is just one aspect of the challenge. While values are essential, strategic sustainability planning demands increased competence from our leaders.

Today's global society is moving into a "funnel" of declining opportunities to sustain prosperity — and civilization itself. Our habitat is exposed to ever higher concentrations of waste, smaller areas of ecosystems, and shrinking biodiversity. At the same time, there are fewer cultures where people are truly connected, and the more individually focused our cultures become, the less enthusiastic we will be about working together to create a sustainable society. This does provide the leadership of our time with an opportunity of Churchillian dimensions: to come up with visions on sustainability, stick to them, and learn how to communicate measures and investments that are socially, financially, and politically acceptable.

Most organizations are very much part of the "unsustainability" problem. Soon there may be not six, but nine billion people laying claims to the biosphere's remaining resources. It will inevitably lead to increased financial risk for each individual organization; to rising costs for natural resources, waste management, insurance, and taxation. And to flawed investments. This can be avoided. Systematic innovation and design to provide services without contributing to the sustainability problem mean less risk of the financial consequences of social and environmental impacts.

At TNS we coach top management in business and policy around the world to imagine rigorously defined principles of a sustainable future and plan systematically to arrive at this image of success. This is "Backcasting from principles" (as opposed to "Forecasting from trends"). Our framework works in a strategic way. It identifies investments that stand a good chance of giving not only social, financial, and political returns, but also laying the foundations for future investments; in other words, how to link short-term actions with longer-term goals from a sustainability perspective.

A corporate vision should contain much more than sustainability. But only if that vision is based entirely on sustainable principles is any transition likely to succeed — not only socially and ecologically, but also financially.

— Karl-Henrik Robèrt

of creation." Other religious traditions could also rearticulate this system condition to adapt it to their own language and religious tradition.

Other valuable approaches to define sustainability include Frederick Steiner's units of human ecology (habitat, community, landscape, region [bioregion or ecoregion], nation-state, and planet)[37] and William McDonough and Michael Braungart's version of the "triple bottom line" of ecology, economy, and equity.[38]

Eighth, *the ongoing loss of global biodiversity must be halted before it is too late.* The Convention on Biodiversity, signed by global leaders in 2002, which pledged to achieve a significant decrease in the rate of biodiversity loss by 2010, has failed. A recent analysis of the consequences of the convention published by a large group of the world's leading experts found that there has been virtually no decrease between 2002 and 2010 in the loss of wildlife, their extinction risk, or the loss of habitats. Moreover, since the adoption of the convention in 2002, indicators of a worsening situation such as resource consumption, invasive species, nitrogen pollution, climate change, and excessive exploitation of resources have actually accelerated.[39] The 2002 convention and its subsequent failure to produce actions point out the great danger inherent in "green-washing." If we all agree to make positive changes in our actions and then go home feeling good about the agreement, but do nothing to live up to its goals, things will continue to deteriorate instead of improve.

Ninth, *we must act to save the oceans before conditions worsen.* This distinct problem integrates challenges related to climate change, biodiversity loss, and threats to sustainable economies. Ocean acidification due to excess CO_2 emissions with CO_2 dissolving in the ocean as carbonic acid threatens to produce a world ocean that is depleted in aragonite (a crucial form of dissolved carbonates), beginning with southern ocean surface waters by around 2050. By 2100 the oceans may be too acidic (and hence aragonite depleted) in all regions for the survival of corals, clams, oysters, mussels, coccolithophores and other phytoplankton with calcareous outer structures, crabs, lobsters, snails, calcareous tube worms, pteropods, starfish, sand dollars, and other marine organisms with calcium carbonate skeletons.[40] This will indirectly threaten a great number of other marine organisms, most obviously coral reef fishes that cannot survive without their habitat.

Coral reef fish constitute not only a huge percentage of the available protein for people in subsistence-based economies who live nearby but also represent a significant portion of the global biodiversity of fish. In many areas, destructive fishing practices such as bottom trawling have the same effect as clear-cutting forests in order to harvest the deer in them; what is removed is not only the animals but also the ecosystems.[41]

More benign fishing practices also become destructive when the number of fishing vessels exceeds the reproductive capacity of fish populations, and various estimates of the global fishing fleet today indicate that currently in operation are three to four times the number of boats that our oceans can sustainably support. In the long run, there will be many more fish for people to catch and eat if we moderate our harvest now and extend the life of the fisheries, rather than harvesting to excess for a much shorter period of time. This is often not so much a matter of regulation but enforcement, in light of the fact that unenforced fishing regulations are a rampant global phenomenon. Often governmental subsidies encourage what would otherwise be economically impossible overfishing to continue,[42] and such subsidies, which have a deleterious impact on both the world's oceans and ultimately on the fishing industry, should be discontinued. Alternative plans with no long-term ecological damage are needed to assist people dependent on fishing.

Additionally, the establishment and protection of a network of marine reserves where fish and other organisms can safely reproduce and that would provide a source from which populations could spread and reestablish themselves is a critical element in saving the oceans. Such preserves have often proven very effective when properly located and protected from encroachment.[43]

Finally, in order to protect our oceans, we need to stop spilling millions of barrels of petroleum into the ocean. Oil pollution has devastating ecological effects that linger for decades.[44] This is so self-evident that there is no need to dwell on it, but it is clear that moderating our demand for fossil fuels will not only reduce CO_2 emissions but also reduce the need for offshore oil production in increasingly deep and hostile environments. When offshore drilling is unavoidable the safety standards for petroleum exploration, extraction, and transportation must be substantially improved. The 2010 oil disaster in the Gulf of Mexico reinforces our observation that current dependency on fossil fuels, oil in particular, is not sustainable.

Tenth, *we must reconceptualize our approach to anthropogenic environmental toxins* in a way that protects children and other vulnerable populations. As already discussed at length, present laws in the United States are weak and insufficient in their breadth of coverage. However, there are signs in both the United States and the European Union that lawmakers are moving toward regulatory processes that will be more protective of our most dependent citizens. Legislation requiring the testing of all industrial chemicals has already been adopted in the EU (a 2006 law for the "registration, evaluation and authorization of chemicals," known as REACH),[45] and the Safe Chemicals Act of 2010 (Lautenberg Bill) was debated by the U.S. Congress, due in part to a Government Accountability Office report in 2009 that named the Toxic Substances Control Act a "high-risk" priority. The Lautenberg Bill was read twice and sent to committee by the 111th Congress, and it is to be hoped that the 112th Congress will see it reintroduced, give it rapid attention, and pass it into law. More precaution and accountability for chemical use is clearly needed if we are going to prevent harm to highly vulnerable members of our society.

TOXIC SUBSTANCES AND SUSTAINABILITY

An innovative approach toward sustainability exists in the Toxics Use Reduction Institute (TURI) at the University of Massachusetts campus at Lowell. The widespread distribution of environmental toxins is a clear threat to a sustainable future, as their impact ranges from the pediatric health effects detailed in chapter 5 to the ongoing decline of orcas in Puget Sound. (These whales have the highest PCB levels ever measured in marine mammals).

Testing and potentially banning chemicals that are candidates for toxicity is a laborious procedure that involves animal tests, epidemiological investigations, legal actions, counteractions, and counter-counter actions — a process that can take years for even the most potentially dangerous material. TURI has moved to a new paradigm that combines environmental and commercial sustainability. TURI researchers don't work only to determine the toxicity of chemicals; rather, they also work to find nontoxic replacements for chemicals currently fulfilling industrial roles. The TURI model is based on a 1989 Massachusetts law requiring firms using toxic materials to develop plans to reduce their use, and on an inclusive vision of sustainability able to move forward, encouraging interactions between businesses and academe, rather than inevitably stalling in lengthy litigation. For more information see *www.turi.org/*.

Eleventh, *we need to give the highest international priority to investments in renewable energy sources that can dramatically reduce CO_2 release*. We have made some progress. According to the National Academies of Science,[46] the United States already produces more electricity from geothermal sources than any other nation in the world, and the amount of electricity generated with wind power in 2008 was five times that generated in 2002, with this sector continuing to grow quickly. Much remains to be done with emerging technologies such as advanced biofuels and supercritical or ultra-supercritical coal power plants, although in both of these cases the potential exists for an unfortunate tradeoff with greatly increased water use. Other emerging technologies might have less or no tradeoff with water resources, and perhaps we have not yet imagined what the best power source or sources will be for the future.

Equally important is reducing consumption and the waste of power. People in the United States must discontinue our profligate ways in energy use and realize that many other countries with very acceptable standards of living use far less energy per capita than we do. The keywords here might be social innovation and personal conservation in consumption, in the arena of various forms of power. This combination of *innovation* and *conservation* could be usefully generalized to all of our uses of natural resources.

Twelfth, we must make use of backcasting, a process in which a desirable future is envisioned in detail, and then steps to achieve it are identified in order to promote movement toward that future. Incremental improvements to deal with a variety of small problems, which is how we typically deal with complicated situations, are not likely to add up to a substantially different future, since this type of process includes no endpoint toward which to work.

The implementation of backcasting, guided by rules like the four Natural Step System Conditions, could provide a process for developing an endpoint for our society to move toward.[47] From a theological view the Natural Step Process is an attractive strategy for achieving sustainability because the fourth system condition allows — even requires — ethical application in matters related to social justice. In utilizing the Natural Step Process or another backcasting technique, it is important to remember that broadly based stakeholder participation is necessary for the results to be recognized as a valuable outcome.[48]

Conclusion

Carrying out the twelve points outlined above appears daunting. In reality it is because it amounts to a global revolution in the way humanity currently lives on Earth. Bear in mind, however, that humanity did not arrive at its current environmental predicament overnight, and we will not emerge from it overnight. However, we must acknowledge in hopeful anticipation that sustainability is a possibility supported by the fact that many — perhaps millions of people worldwide — have already set a course in the direction of a sustainable future.

One way of approaching the daunting issues that need to be addressed is to follow the much overused yet warranted phrase "think globally, act locally." This phrase, coined by René Dubos (1901–1982) in 1972, suggests that global environmental problems, which can often be overwhelming, are best confronted and solved in and through one's local ecological, social, and economic context.

Perhaps a perspective from human ecologist Frederick Steiner, briefly noted above, might help. Taking an ecological approach to human communities and organization, Steiner believes that there is a range of human interaction that occurs within components or levels of human ecology that begins with local habitat and proceeds to community, landscape, region (bioregion or ecoregion), nation-state, and planet.[49] What this suggests is that human actions — unsustainable or sustainable — begin with the most basic and local form of human habitation and proceed outward in ever-expanding but interrelated circles of human activity, ultimately incorporating the entire planet. From a visual perspective, Steiner's levels of human ecology can be represented in the following manner:

CONCENTRIC CIRCLES OF HUMAN ECOLOGY

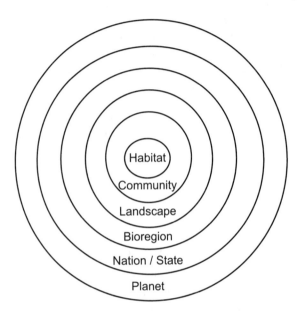

This visualized representation of Steiner's perspective teaches us that ecological processes function at every level of human interaction and that what we do at home — our local habitat — will impact the entire plant in some way. Therefore, think globally but act locally. Because sustainability is an applied ethic — the ortho-praxis of hopeful anticipation for a sustainable future — some practical suggestions on where to begin are provided on page 194 below.

One person who has charted a course toward sustainability is Paul Hawken. In his book *Blessed Unrest*, Hawken describes in detail what he calls the "largest social movement in history," which is taking place among people all over the planet.[50] In a summarized form, given in a commencement address at the University of Portland in 2009, Hawken said:

There is invisible writing on the back of the diploma you will receive, and in case you didn't bring lemon juice to decode it, I can tell you what it says: YOU ARE BRILLIANT, AND THE EARTH IS HIRING. The earth couldn't afford to send any recruiters or limos to your school. It sent you rain, sunsets, ripe cherries, night-blooming jasmine, and that unbelievably cute person you are dating. Take the hint. And here's the deal: Forget that this task of planet-saving is not possible in the time required. Don't be put off by people who know what is not possible. Do what needs to be done, and check to see if it was impossible only after you are done.

When asked if I am pessimistic or optimistic about the future, my answer is always the same: If you look at the science about what is happening on Earth and aren't pessimistic, you don't understand the data. But if you meet the people who are working to restore this Earth and the lives of the poor, and you aren't optimistic, you haven't got a pulse. What I see everywhere in the world are ordinary people willing to confront despair, power, and incalculable odds in order to restore some semblance of grace, justice, and beauty to this world. The poet Adrienne Rich wrote, "So much has been destroyed I have cast my lot with those who, age after age, perversely, with no extraordinary power, reconstitute the world." There could be no better description. *Humanity is coalescing.* It is reconstituting the world, and the action is taking place in schoolrooms, farms, jungles, villages, campuses, companies, refugee camps, deserts, fisheries, and slums.[51]

Such coalescing of humanity will need to be a true coalition. Citizens will need to moderate their consumption and free themselves from destructive habits that impoverish future generations. The business community will need to follow its visionary leaders such as Paul Hawken, Ray Anderson of Interface, Inc., and others, and move to achieve the promise of the World Business Council for Sustainable Development. Without the business community as a committed and active partner, the move to achieve a sustainable society will fail. NGOs will need to continue to do the work they have been doing and indeed step forward to do more. All faith communities will need to come together to provide an ethical, moral, and influential voice and, most importantly, walk the talk of hopeful anticipation. Governments will need to find ways to empower those who dream of a better future, rather than those who pander to polls for the next election cycle.

If humanity cannot manage to achieve this, then we will continue on our present downward path, unmoved by voices of warning from generations in the past and careless of voices belonging to an impoverished future. It is our view that the hoped-for future that we believe most people desire is in our hands now and that faith, with a good dose of scientific knowledge, will allow us to realize a sustainable future.

ACTIONS WITH A POSITIVE IMPACT
ON ECOLOGICAL FOOTPRINTS

Eat less meat, or at least eat less grain-fed beef

Conserve water with efficient faucets and appliances and short showers

Plant native vegetation that doesn't need watering; don't use lawn herbicides

Purchase local and organic foods; start a vegetable garden

Install solar panels on your home for hot water or electricity or both

Don't use disposable paper and plastic goods

Install energy-efficient double or triple glazed windows

Enjoy hiking, swimming, fishing, and climbing as low-energy outdoor pursuits

Unplug electronics when not in use

Ride a bus, train, or bicycle; reduce air travel when possible

When air or car travel is necessary, purchase carbon offsets

Avoid overpackaged products; buy in bulk when possible

Host a vegetarian potluck or local food party; find people having fun doing this

Support a local environmental group making a difference near your home

Compost, recycle, reduce

Questions for Discussion

1. Do you know of examples of "green-washing" with products or services that are represented as having environmental benefits that they actually lack? If so, should steps be taken to counter this in a free society?

2. How can the United States display leadership on global environmental issues without sacrificing its economic vitality?

3. How can we interpret the simultaneous growth of awareness about the environmental crisis and of consumption of natural resources?

4. If hydraulic fracturing to extract natural gas supplies simultaneously imperils groundwater and also provides a fossil fuel resource much cleaner than coal, should it be allowed to continue? If so, should it be altered in some way?

5. What five actions could you take personally to make your life more environmentally sustainable?

6. What actions for sustainability has your school, church, or city endorsed and implemented?

Active Learning Exercises

- There are several online resources that will let you approximate the impact your lifestyle has on the planet. Your assignment is to calculate your ecological footprint using any two of the programs listed below. Using your real lifestyle choices, then print out only the conclusion page for each program. Experiment with the programs, and see what would happen if you drove less often, ate less meat, used public transit, and so on. Then write a two-page reflection on your ecological footprint and what you might and might not be able to do to reduce it.

    www.myfootprint.org/

    www.bestfootforward.com/footprintlife.htm

    http://survey.happyplanetindex.org/

    www.footprintnetwork.org/en/index.php/GFN/page/calculators/

- Look up the local sustainability initiatives on your campus or in your town or city. These are generally featured in some fashion on university and municipal websites and often appear as press announcements in the local media. For institutions of higher education, you might get some help from the NWF Campus Ecology website (*www.nwf.org/On-Campus.aspx*) or the Association for the Advancement of Sustainability in Higher Education website (*www.aashe.org/*). Write a two-page reflection on what is being done and what you think ought to be happening in order to move the milieu you live in toward a sustainable future.

- Vegetarian diets consume fewer environmental resources in general than carnivorous diets, because of the amount of grain used to feed most livestock, the amount of water required in their rearing and processing, and the extensive water pollution and waste disposal problems associated with the operation of concentrated animal feed operations (CAFOs). Although free-range meats do exist in the marketplace, they are by far the minority product available. Adopt a vegetarian diet for three days, log what you eat, and record any difficulties you encounter. Make sure that you visit a restaurant at least once during this period. Write a two-page reflection on your brief period of vegetarianism and turn it in along with your food log. If you are already a vegetarian, try doing the same thing for three days with a vegan diet, which can consume even fewer resources, since dairy cattle, sheep, and goats require animal feed and water in significant quantities. If you are already a vegan, write a two-page reflection on why you adopted this diet.

Recommended Readings

DeGunther, Rik. *Alternative Energy for Dummies*. Hoboken, N.J.: Wiley Publishing, 2009.

McDonough, William, and Michael Braungart. *Cradle to Cradle: Remaking the Way We Make Things*. New York: North Point Press, 2002.

Robèrt, Karl-Henrik. *The Natural Step Story: Seeding a Quiet Revolution*. Gabriola Island, B.C.: New Society Publishers, 2002.

Weasel, Lisa H. *Food Fray: Inside the Controversy over Genetically Modified Food*. New York: AMACON Books, 2009.

Notes

Introduction

1. National Commission of the BP Deepwater Horizon Oil Spill and Offshore Drilling, *Deepwater: The Gulf Oil Disaster and the Future of Offshore Drilling* (2011), available at *www.oilspillcommission.gov/*.

2. "Morel e-mailed BP drilling engineer Brett Cocales to question the need for additional centralizers.... Cocales responded that the team would 'probably be fine' even without the additional centralizers and that 'Guide is right on the risk/reward equation'" (National Commission of the BP Deepwater Horizon Oil Spill and Offshore Drilling, *Deepwater*, 97).

3. "BP wanted to use these materials as spacer in order to avoid having to dispose of them onshore as hazardous waste pursuant to the Resource and Conservation Recovery Act, exploiting an exception that allows companies to dump water-based 'drilling fluids' overboard.... At BP's direction, M-I SWACO combined the materials to create an unusually large volume of spacer that had never previously been used by anyone on the rig or by BP as a spacer, nor been thoroughly tested for that purpose" (National Commission of the BP Deepwater Horizon Oil Spill and Offshore Drilling, *Deepwater*, 106).

4. "Documents identified after the blowout reveal that Halliburton personnel had also conducted another foam stability test earlier in February. The earlier test had been conducted under slightly different conditions than the later one and had failed more severely" (National Commission of the BP Deepwater Horizon Oil Spill and Offshore Drilling, *Deepwater*, 101).

5. Ibid., 125.

6. Ibid., vii.

7. Patriarch Bartholomew I, Address at the Environmental Symposium, Saint Barbara Greek Orthodox Church, Santa Barbara, California, November 8, 1997, available online at *www.ec-patr.org/docdisplay.php?lang=en&id=461&tla=en*.

Chapter 1: Environmental Science and Theology in Dialogue

1. E. O. Wilson, *The Creation: An Appeal to Save Life on Earth* (New York: W. W. Norton and Company, 2006), 4–5.

2. See the original document hosted on the Forum for Religion and Ecology website at *http://fore.research.yale.edu/publications/statements/preserve.html*.

3. *www.ecd.bnl.gov/steve/jointappeal.html*.

4. Jane Goodall et al., *Hope for the Animals and Their World* (New York: Grand Central Publishing, 2009), 348–49.

5. *www.rsesymposia.org/*.

6. *www.aess.info/*.

7. *http://ieaonline.org/*.

8. *www.aarweb.org/*.

9. *www.ctsa-online.org/*.

10. *www.collegetheology.org/.*

11. *www.wiserearth.org/.*

12. *www.wiserearth.org/issues#248.*

13. Aldo Leopold, *A Sand County Almanac with Essays on Conservation from Round River* (New York: Oxford University Press, 1966), 231–32.

14. Ibid., 238.

15. Ibid., 224–25.

16. Will Deming, *Rethinking Religion: A Concise Introduction* (New York: Oxford University Press, 2005), 120–21.

17. Stephen B. Bevans, *Models of Contextual Theology* (Maryknoll, N.Y.: Orbis Books, 2002), 1.

18. Daniel D. Chiras, *Environmental Science: Creating a Sustainable Future,* 6th ed. (Sudbury, Mass.: Jones and Bartlett Publishers, 2001), 173.

19. Bevans, *Models of Contextual Theology,* 1.

20. Pope John XXIII, *Pacem en Terris* (1963), no. 126. Pope John XXIII did not use this phrase in a biblical apocalyptic sense (see Matt. 16:3) but rather as an indication of new and significant developments in human experience.

21. Abraham Malherbe, *Paul and the Popular Philosophers* (Minneapolis: Fortress Press, 1989), 68.

22. Edward B. Pusey, trans., *Confessions of Saint Augustine* (New York: Collier Books, 1972), 112.

23. *Gaudium et Spes,* no. 2, in *The Documents of Vatican II,* ed. Walter M. Abbott (New York: Guild Press, 1966), 200.

24. *Praxis,* a Greek word, can be traced back to the philosophy of Aristotle where in general it referred to knowledge arising out of activity, but specifically it meant ethical practice. Used frequently in contemporary theology, it refers to ethical engagement in a social context.

25. The relationship between liberation theology and the Vatican has been anything but smooth. In 1984 the Congregation for the Doctrine of Faith directed by Cardinal Joseph Ratzinger (now Pope Benedict XVI) issued the "Instruction on Certain Aspects of the 'Theology of Liberation,' " a document highly critical of liberation theology. Shortly thereafter, in 1985, the same congregation silenced Leonardo Boff for a period of a year and more recently, in March 2007, the Congregation censured Jon Sobrino.

26. Leonardo Boff and Clodovis Boff, *Introducing Liberation Theology* (Maryknoll, N.Y.: Orbis Books, 1992), 1.

27. Dean William Ferm, *Third World Liberation Theologies: An Introductory Survey* (Maryknoll, N.Y.: Orbis Books, 1988), 12.

28. John Paul II, Encyclical Letter *Sollicitudo Rei Socialis,* no. 42 (December 30, 1987); *Ecclesia in Asia,* no. 34 (November 6, 1999).

29. Boff and Boff, *Introducing Liberation Theology,* 28.

30. Gustavo Gutiérrez, *A Theology of Liberation* (Maryknoll, N.Y.: Orbis Books, 1973), 6–13.

31. Walter Altmann, "Liberation Theology Is Alive and Well," is available online from the World Council of Churches (2009) at *www.oikoumene.org/en/news/news-management/eng/a/article/1634/liberation-theology-is-al.html.* Also see James H. Cone, "The Content of Theology," in *A Black Theology of Liberation: Twentieth Anniversary Edition* (Maryknoll, N.Y.: Orbis Books, 1990), 1–20.

32. Rosemary Radford Ruether, "The Emergence of Christian Feminist Theology," in *The Cambridge Companion to Feminist Theology*, ed. Susan Frank Parsons (Cambridge: Cambridge University Press, 2002), 3.

33. Anne M. Clifford, *Introducing Feminist Theology* (Maryknoll, N.Y.: Orbis Books, 2001), 33.

34. Ibid., 35.

35. Ibid.

36. Ibid., 34.

37. Alfred North Whitehead, *Process and Reality: An Essay in Cosmology*, ed. David Ray Griffin and Donald W. Sherburne (New York: Free Press, 1978), 18.

38. Thomas E. Hosinski, *Stubborn Fact and Creative Advance: An Introduction to the Metaphysics of Alfred North Whitehead* (Lanham, Md.: Rowman and Littlefield, 1993), 21.

39. Ibid., 155–56.

40. Ibid.

41. John B. Cobb Jr., *A Christian Natural Theology: Based on the Thought of Alfred North Whitehead* (Philadelphia: Westminster Press, 1962), 271.

42. John B. Cobb Jr., *God and the World* (Philadelphia: Westminster Press, 1976), 72.

43. John B. Cobb Jr., *Is It Too Late? A Theology of Ecology* (Philadelphia: Westminster Press, 1972), 112.

44. Ibid., 125.

45. Ibid.

46. Pierre Teilhard de Chardin, *How I Believe*, trans. Rene Hague (New York: Harper and Row, 1969), 3; W. Henry Kenney, S.J., *A Path through Teilhard's Phenomenon* (Dayton, Ohio: Pflaum Press, 1970), 51.

47. For an interesting discussion of this concept, see Kenney, *A Path through Teilhard's Phenomenon*, 87–89.

48. Teilhard's writings were suppressed by Catholic Church censors and were not published until after his death.

49. John F. Haught, *Christianity and Science: Toward a Theology of Nature* (Maryknoll, N.Y.: Orbis Books, 2007), 69.

50. Roderick Frazier Nash, *The Rights of Nature: A History of Environmental Ethics* (Madison: University of Wisconsin Press, 1989), 98.

51. Philip N. Joranson, "The Faith-Man-Nature Group and a Religious Environmental Ethic," *Zygon* 12, no. 2 (June 1977): 175–79.

52. Richard A. Baer, Jr., "Land Misuse: A Theological Concern," *Christian Century*, October 12, 1966, 1239–41; "Conservation: An Arena for the Church's Action," *Christian Century*, January 8, 1969, 40–43.

53. H. Paul Santmire, *Brother Earth: Nature, God, and Ecology in Time of Crisis* (New York: T. Nelson, 1970), 151, 185–86.

54. H. Paul Santmire, *The Travail of Nature: The Ambiguous Ecological Promise of Christian Theology* (Minneapolis: Fortress Press, 1985), 9.

55. Ibid.

56. H. Paul Santmire, *Nature Reborn: The Ecological and Cosmic Promise of Christian Theology* (Minneapolis: Fortress Press, 2000), 6.

57. Ibid., 9.

58. Ibid.

59. Julie Thompson Klein, *Interdisciplinarity* (Detroit: Wayne State University Press, 1990), 19.

60. Ibid., 20.

61. Ibid., 21.

62. Ibid., 11.

63. Ibid., 1.

64. Ibid., 4.

65. Ibid., 11.

66. Boyer Commission on Educating Undergraduates in the Research University, *Reinventing Undergraduate Education: A Blueprint for America's Research Universities* (1998), 23.

67. Eastern Mennonite Mission Statement, available at *www.emu.edu/president/mission/*.

68. Doug Graber Neufeld, "The Word via the World: How Does Faithful Teaching and Science Make Visible the Relationship between the Created World and the Incarnated Word of God? Crossing Borders between Science, Faith and Society," Mennonite University Faculty Conference keynote address (Harrisonburg, Va.: Eastern Mennonite University, 2008), 1.

69. Ibid., 3–5.

70. Ibid., 15.

71. John Paul II, *Ex Corde Ecclesiae* (August 15, 1990), nos. 15, 32.

72. Ibid., no. 16.

73. Ibid., no. 20.

74. Ibid., no. 19.

Chapter 2: The Relationship between Science and Theology

1. Lynn White Jr., "The Historical Roots of Our Ecologic Crisis," *Science* 155 (1967): 1203–7.

2. Ibid., 1206–7.

3. For a thorough and well-balanced analysis of White's thesis on Christianity and the environmental crisis see the chapter titled "The Ecological Complaint against Christianity," in James A. Nash, *Loving Nature: Ecological Integrity and Christian Responsibility* (Nashville: Abingdon Press, 1991), 68–92.

4. For a compelling historical analysis from an ecofeminist perspective on the role of science in the destruction of nature see Carolyn Merchant, *The Death of Nature: Women, Ecology and the Scientific Revolution* (San Francisco: Harper and Row, 1980).

5. See, for example, Charles L. Redman, *Human Impacts on Ancient Environments* (Tucson: University of Arizona Press, 1991), and Clive Pointing, *A Green History of the World: The Environment and the Collapse of Great Civilizations* (New York: St. Martin's Press, 1992).

6. White, "The Historical Roots of Our Ecologic Crisis," 1205.

7. H. H. Schmid, "Creation, Righteous, and Salvation: 'Creation Theology' as the Broad Horizon of Biblical Theology," in *Creation in the Old Testament*, ed. Bernard Anderson (Philadelphia: Fortress Press, 1984), 102–17.

8. Walter Brueggemann, "The Loss and Recovery of Creation in Old Testament Theology," *Theology Today* 53, no. 2 (July 1996): 177–90.

9. White, "The Historical Roots of Our Ecologic Crisis," 1205.

10. For a general description of the quest for salvation in the world's religions see Lawrence S. Cunningham and John Kelsay, *The Sacred Quest: An Introduction to the Study of Religion* (Upper Saddle River, N.J.: Pearson Prentice Hall, 2006), 142–58.

11. A deontological ethic is one that is grounded in the sense of moral obligation and duty. In the field of environmental ethics the person who has articulated this approach is Holmes Rolston III. In Rolston's view values generate duty to the natural world. See Holmes Rolston III, *Environmental Ethics: Duties to and Values in the Natural World* (Philadelphia: Temple University Press, 1988).

12. Ian G. Barbour, *Religion and Science: Historical and Contemporary Issues* (San Francisco: Harper Collins, 1997), 77–105.

13. John F. Haught, *Science and Religion: From Conflict to Conversation* (Mahwah, N.J.: Paulist Press, 1995), 9–26.

14. Ibid., 9.

15. Barbour, *Religion and Science*, 78.

16. For more information on *Edwards v. Aguillard* and similar legal cases see the website of the National Center for Science Education at *http://ncse.com*.

17. The conflictual issue regarding intelligent design is not what it attempts to do regarding God and the natural world but rather that the contemporary adherents of intelligent design have tried to argue that it is scientific in nature and, consequently, should be taught alongside evolution in schools. It is therefore another example of what Haught calls a conflation.

18. Barbour, *Religion and Science*, 84.

19. Ibid.

20. Haught, *Science and Religion*, 15.

21. Ibid., 13.

22. Barbour, *Religion and Science*, 90.

23. In science the precautionary principle means acting under the guidance of caution or prudence when faced with uncertain knowledge; it is often articulated as "do no harm."

24. Jerry Ravetz, "The Post-normal Science of Precaution," *Futures* 36 (2004): 347–57; Dennis Bray and Hans von Storch, "Climate Science: An Empirical Example of Postnormal Science," *Bulletin of the American Meteorological Association* 80 (1999): 439–55.

25. Barbour, *Religion and Science*, 93.

26. New England transcendentalism was a literary and philosophical movement that was a liberal offshoot of the Unitarian Church in the Boston area around 1830–50. Inspired in large part by Ralph Waldo Emerson's essay called *Nature*, the transcendentalists, including Henry David Thoreau, believed that nature was a primary arena through which God could be experienced directly. John Muir, the founder of the Sierra Club and major promoter of Yosemite as a national park, was much influenced by Emerson, whom he called the "Sage of Concord." In Muir we see a unique combination of a scientific naturalist and a mystic, and his writings called for a dialogue, if not an integration, of science and religious experience.

27. Haught, *Science and Religion*, 17.

28. Ibid., 18.

29. Joint Appeal by Religion and Science for the Environment, "Declaration of the Mission to Washington," Washington, D.C., May 12, 1992, available at *www.ecd.bnl.gov/steve/jointappeal.html*, accessed May 21, 2009.

30. Ibid.

31. Ibid.

32. Barbour, *Religion and Science*, 98.

33. Ibid., 98–99.

34. Ibid.

35. *Zygon: Journal of Religion and Science, www.Zygonjournal.org/peacocke .html.*

36. Barbour, *Religion and Science*, 101.

37. Ibid., 102.

38. Ibid., 102–3.

39. For a good example see John B. Cobb Jr. and David Ray Griffin, *Process Theology: An Introduction* (Philadelphia: Westminster Press, 1976).

40. Barbour, *Religion and Science*, 104.

41. Haught, *Science and Religion*, 22.

42. Ibid., 23.

43. Ibid.

44. For the most recent example of this collaboration see Kolmes and Butkus, "Got Wild Salmon? A Scientific and Ethical Analysis of Salmon Recovery in the Pacific Northwest and California," in *Salmon 2100: The Future of Wild Pacific Salmon,* ed. Robert T. Lackey, Denise H. Lach, and Sally L. Duncan (Bethesda, Md.: American Fisheries Society, 2006), 333–61.

45. Stephen B. Bevans, *Models of Contextual Theology* (Maryknoll, N.Y.: Orbis Books, 2002), 65.

46. Ibid., 63–64.

47. Juan Luis Segundo, *The Liberation of Theology* (Maryknoll, N.Y.: Orbis Books, 1976), 7–39.

48. Joe Holland and Peter Henriot, S.J., *Social Analysis: Linking Faith and Justice* (Maryknoll, N.Y.: Orbis Books, 1983), 8.

49. *www.un.org/events/tenstories/06/story.asp?storyID=800.*

50. *The Columbia River Watershed: Caring for Creation and the Common Good,* An International Pastoral Letter by the Catholic Bishops of the Region (January 8, 2001). For complete text see *www.columbiariver.org,* accessed May 21, 2009.

51. W. Nehlsen et al., "Pacific Salmon at the Crossroads: Stocks at Risk from California, Oregon, Idaho, and Washington," *Fisheries* 16, no. 2 (1991): 4–21.

52. One run was already listed under the ESA.

53. Holland and Henriot, *Social Analysis,* 8.

54. See Kolmes and Butkus, "Got Wild Salmon?"

55. A nongovernmental organization, commonly referred to as an NGO, is a legal organization created by people that functions independently of a government and, consequently, has no governmental status. The typical purpose of an NGO is to further the social, political, or environmental interest of the organization and the people who support it.

56. E. O. Wilson, *The Creation: An Appeal to Save Life on Earth* (New York: W. W. Norton, 2006), 75–76.

57. P. McElhany et al., *Viable Salmonid Populations and the Recovery of Evolutionarily Significant Units,* U.S. Department of Commerce, NOAA Tech. Memo. NMFS-NWFSC-42 (2000), 156. Most NOAA technical memorandums NMFS-NWFSC are available online at *www.nwfsc.noaa.gov,* accessed 5/21/09.

58. Daniel D. Heath et al., "Rapid Evolution of Egg Size in Captive Salmon," *Science* 299 (2003): 1738.

59. "An Outline for Salmon Recovery Plans," State of Washington Department of Fish and Wildlife (2003): 30, available at *www.sharedsalmonstrategy.org/files/salmon_recovery_plan_model_dec03.pdf*.

60. *The Columbia River Watershed: Caring for Creation and the Common Good*, 12.

61. Ibid.

Chapter 3: Ecological Foundations for Environmental Science

1. *www.arcworld.org/faiths.asp?pageID=121*.

2. Presbyterian Church U.S.A., *Restoring Creation for Ecology and Justice*, 1990.

3. *www.arcworld.org/faiths.asp?pageID=121*.

4. John Paul II, Encyclical Letter *Centesimus Annus* (On the Hundredth Anniversary of *Rerum Novarum*), May 1, 1991.

5. Robert C. Stauffer, "Haeckel, Darwin, and Ecology," *Quarterly Review of Biology* 32 (1957): 141.

6. Joseph Grinnell, "The Niche-Relationships of the California Thrasher," *The Auk* 34 (1917): 433.

7. A. G. Tansley, "The Use and Abuse of Vegetational Concepts and Terms," *Ecology* 16 (1935): 299.

8. Eugene P. Odum, "The Strategy of Ecosystem Development," *Science* 164 (1969): 262–70.

9. Ibid., 267.

10. G. E. Hutchinson, "Homage to Santa Rosalia, or Why Are There So Many Kinds of Animals?" *American Naturalist* 93 (1959): 149.

11. Ibid., 150.

12. Rachel Carson, *Silent Spring* (New York: Houghton Mifflin, 1962), 7–8.

13. Alain Demers et al., "Risk and Aggressiveness of Breast Cancer in Relation to Plasma Organochlorine Concentrations," *Cancer Epidemiology Biomarkers and Prevention* 9 (2000): 161–66; B. A. Cohn et al., "DDT and Breast Cancer in Young Women: New Data on the Significance of Age at Exposure," *Environmental Health Perspectives* 115 (2007): 1406–14; Annette Pernille Høyer et al., "Repeated Measurements of Organochlorine Exposure and Breast Cancer Risk (Denmark)," *Cancer Causes and Control* 11 (2000): 17–184; S. M. Snedeker, "Pesticides and Breast Cancer Risk: A Review of DDT, DDE, and Dieldrin," *Environmental Health Perspectives* 109 (2001): 35–71.

14. Murray Bookchin, *The Ecology of Freedom: The Emergence and Dissolution of Hierarchy* (Oakland: AK Press, 2005).

15. Richard J. Borden, "A Brief History of SHE: Reflections on the Founding and First Twenty-five Years of the Society for Human Ecology," *Human Ecology Review* 15, no. 1 (2008): 95–108.

16. Frederick Steiner, *Human Ecology: Following Nature's Lead* (Washington, D.C.: Island Press, 2002).

17. Ibid., 24.

18. Committee on Watershed Management et al., *New Srategies for America's Watersheds* (Washington, D.C.: National Academies Press, 1999), 1.

19. Steven A. Kolmes, Comment on "Use of U.S. Croplands for Biofuels Increases Greenhouse Gases through Emissions from Land-Use Change," *Science Magazine,* comment posted on March 25, 2008, *www.sciencemag.org/cgi/eletters/319/5867/ 1238#top,* accessed May 21, 2009.

20. H. Steinfeld et al., "Livestock's Long Shadow: Environmental Issues and Options" (report originated by Agriculture and Consumer Protection Department of the Food and Agriculture Organization of the United Nations, 2006), *www.fao.org/docrep/010/a0701e/a0701e00.htm,* accessed May 21, 2009.

21. Doris Janzen Longacre, *Living More with Less* (Waterloo, Ontario: Herald Press, 1980); Doris Janzen Longacre, *More-with-Less Cookbook (World Community Cookbook),* 25th ann. ed. (Waterloo, Ontario: Herald Press, 2000).

22. Ibid., 1.

23. David Hulse et al., eds., *Willamette River Basin Planning Atlas: Trajectories of Environmental and Ecological Change* (Corvallis: Oregon State University Press, 2002), 18.

24. University of Kansas, "Habitat Destruction May Wipe Out Monarch Butterfly Migration," *Science Daily,* April 5, 2008, *www.sciencedaily.com/releases/2008/04/ 080401230705.htm,* accessed May 21, 2009; Lincoln P. Brower et al., "Quantitative Changes in Forest Quality in a Principal Overwintering Area of the Monarch Butterfly in Mexico, 1971–1999," *Conservation Biology* 16 (2002): 346–59.

25. Russell Butkus and Steven Kolmes, "Ecology and the Common Good: Sustainability and Catholic Social Teaching," *Journal of Catholic Social Thought* 4 (2007): 403–26.

26. Daniel Pauly, "Anecdotes and the Shifting Baseline Syndrome of Fisheries," *Trends in Ecology and Evolution* 10 (1995): 430.

27. Peter H. Kahn Jr. and Stephen R. Kellert, eds., *Children and Nature: Psychological, Sociocultural, and Evolutionary Investigations* (Cambridge, Mass.: MIT Press, 2002), 106.

28. Mathis Wackernagel and William Rees, *Our Ecological Footprint: Reducing Human Impact on the Earth* (Gabriola Island, B.C.: New Society Publishers, 1996), 7–12.

Chapter 4: The Impact of People on Ecological Processes

1. Intergovernmental Panel on Climate Change (hereafter IPCC), "Synthesis Report" and "Summary for Policymakers," *Fourth Assessment Report: Climate Change 2007, www.ipcc.ch/pdf/assessment-report/ar4/syr/ar4_syr_spm.pdf* (accessed December 3, 2007).

2. Stratigraphy Commission of the Geological Society of London, "Are We Now Living in the Anthropocene?"*GAS Today* 18, no. 2 (2008): 4–8.

3. One part per million represents one molecule out of a million total molecules. For a good mental picture, the most commonly used analogy is that it is like one car in bumper-to-bumper traffic between Cleveland and San Francisco, or to use another type of mental image it would be the same proportion as a little over a half a second taken out of a week.

4. J. Hansen et al., "Climate Impact of Increasing Atmospheric Carbon Dioxide," *Science* 213, no. 4511 (August 1981): 957–66.

5. *www.columbia.edu/~jeh1/2008/TwentyYearsLater_20080623.pdf.*

6. J. Hansen et al., "Global Climate Changes as Forecast by Goddard Institute for Space Studies Three-Dimensional Model," *Journal of Geophysical Research* 93 (D8) (1988): 9341–64.

7. *www.columbia.edu/~jeh1/2008/TwentyYearsLater_20080623.pdf.*

8. IPCC, *Fourth Assessment Report.*

9. Ibid.

10. In mathematical terms these are called "positive feedback loops," referring to the increasing (positive) rate of change over time; however, because that terminology tends to be confusing due to the common connotations of the word "positive," we will refer to self-accelerating destructive processes as "destructive feedback loops."

11. IPCC, "Summary for Policy Makers," *Fourth Assessment Report.*

12. S. A. Kolmes, "The Social Feedback Loop," *Environment* 50 (2008): 57–58.

13. IPCC, *Fourth Assessment Report.*

14. N. Myers, "Environmental Refugees: A Growing Phenomenon of the 21st Century," *Philosophical Transactions of the Royal Society of London* B 357 (2002): 609–13.

15. IPCC, *Fourth Assessment Report.*

16. IPCC, *The Physical Science Basis*, in *Fourth Assessment Report*; P. Shaobing Peng et al., "Rice Yields Decline with Higher Night Temperature from Global Warming," *Proceedings of the National Academy of Sciences (USA)* 101, no. 27 (2004): 9971–75.

17. Contribution of Working Group III to the Fourth Assessment Report of the Intergovernmental Panel on Climate Change, 2007; *www.ipcc.ch/publications _and_data/ar4/wg3/en/contents.html* (accessed December 10, 2010).

18. In mathematical terms these would be called "negative feedback loops," referring to the decreasing (negative) rate of change over time, but once again the common connotations of the word "negative" have caused us to refer to these sorts of processes as "constructive feedback loops."

19. U.S. Conference of Catholic Bishops, *Global Climate Change: A Plea for Dialogue, Prudence, and the Common Good* (Washington, D.C.: USCCB, 2001), 5.

20. Ibid., 12.

21. Ibid.

22. *www.usccb.org/comm/archives/2007/07-029.shtml.*

23. J. Ball, *Global Warming and the Risen Lord: Christian Discipleship and Climate Change* (Washington, D.C.: Evangelical Environmental Network, 2010).

24. *www.creationcare.org/index.php* (accessed December 13, 2010).

25. *www.lausanne.org/ctcommitment#_ftn24.*

26. Available online at *www.creationcare.org/media.php?what=21&c_id=&file= &page=4* (accessed December 13, 2010).

27. *http://ecusa.anglican.org/78703_86656_ENG_HTM.htm* (accessed December 13, 2010).

28. Naomi Oreskes and Erik M. Conway, *Merchants of Doubt* (New York: Bloomsbury Press, 2010), 169–215.

29. Ibid., 5–6.

30. Ibid., 5–7.

31. *http://royalsociety.org/displaypagedoc.asp?id=23780.*

32. W. R. L. Anderegg, J. W. Prall, J. Harold, and S. Schneider, "Expert Credibility in Climate Change," *Proceedings of the National Academy of Sciences* (June 21, 2010), doi: 10.1073/pnas.1003187107.

33. J. E. Lovelock, "Atmospheric Fluorine Compounds as Indicators of Air Movements," *Nature* 230 (1971): 379.

34. Mario Molina and F. S. Rowland, "Stratospheric Sink for Chlorofluoromethanes: Chlorine Atom-Catalysed Destruction of Ozone," *Nature* 249 (1974): 810.

35. F. S. Rowland and M. J. Molina, "Chlorofluoromethanes in the Environment," *Review of Geophysics and Space Physics* 13 (1977): 1–35.

36. Rob Gutro, "NASA and NOAA Announce Ozone Hole Is a Double Record Breaker," 2006, NASA News Feature available online at *www.nasa.gov/vision/earth/lookingatearth/ozone_record.html*.

37. F. Sherwood Rowland, Nobel Prize Address, 1995.

38. National Academy of Sciences, "The Ozone Depletion Phenomenon, 2003," available at online *www.beyonddiscovery.org/content/view.txt.asp?a=73*; U.S. Climate Change Science Program, "Trends in Emissions of Ozone-Depleting Substances, Ozone Layer Recovery, and Implications for Ultraviolet Radiation Exposure, Synthesis and Assessment Product," 2, 4 (2008), available online at *http://downloads.climatescience.gov/sap/sap2-4/sap2-4-final-all.pdf*.

39. Brian K. Paulson, "Las Vegas Faces Water Challenges," *Environmental Practice* (2008), 175.

40. Environmental News Service, "Lake Mead Could Dry Up by 2021" (2008), available at *www.ens-newswire.com/ens/feb2008/2008-02-12-095.asp*.

41. Wenonah Hauter, "Food & Water Watch" (2006), *www.foodandwaterwatch.org/*.

42. John Scanlon, Angela Cassar, and Noémi Nemes, "Water as a Human Right" (Washington, D.C.: International Union for Conservation of Nature, 2004).

43. United Nations, UN-Water Thematic Initiatives Program, *Coping with Water Scarcity* (2006).

44. Archbishop Renato R. Martino, "Water, an Essential Element for Life," Note prepared by the Pontifical Council for Justice and Peace, as a contribution of the Holy See to the Third World Water Forum in 2003.

45. William E. Rees, "Ecological Footprints and Appropriated Carrying Capacity: What Urban Economics Leaves Out," *Environment and Urbanisation* 4 (1992): 121–30, available at *http://eau.sagepub.com/cgi/content/abstract/4/2/121*.

46. Mathis Wackernagel and William E. Rees, *Our Ecological Footprint: Reducing Human Impact on the Earth* (Gabriola Island, B.C.: New Society Publishers, 1996).

47. Johanna Yarrow, *How to Reduce Your Carbon Footprint: 365 Simple Ways to Save Energy, Resources, and Money* (San Francisco: Chronicle Books, 2008).

48. Anja Kollmuss and Benjamin Bowell, "Voluntary Offsets for Air-Travel Carbon Emissions, Evaluations and Recommendations of Voluntary Offset Companies," Tufts Climate Initiative, 2006, available at *www.tufts.edu/tie/carbonoffsets/index.htm*.

49. World Water Council, "E-Conference Synthesis: Virtual Water Trade–Conscious Choices," World Water Council (Marseilles, 2004), online at *www.worldwatercouncil.org/fileadmin/wwc/Programs/Virtual_Water/virtual_water_final_synthesis.pdf*.

50. D. Zimmer and D. Renault, "Virtual Water in Food Production and Global Trade: Review of Methodological Issues and Preliminary Results," in *Virtual Water Trade: Proceedings of the International Expert Meeting on Virtual Water Trade,*

Value of Water, ed. A. Y. Hoekstra, Research Report Series no. 12 (Delft, The Netherlands, 2003).

51. D. Renault and W. W. Wallender, "Nutritional Water Productivity and Diets: From 'Crop per drop' towards 'Nutrition per drop,'" *Agricultural Water Management* 45 (2000): 275–96.

52. *www.waterfootprint.org/index.php?page=files/home.*

53. A. K. Chapagain and A. Y. Hoekstra, "The Water Footprint of Coffee and Tea Consumption in the Netherlands," *Ecological Economics* 64 (2007): 109–18.

54. Millennium Ecosystem Report, *Ecosystems and Human Well Being: Current State and Trends Assessment* (Washington, D.C.: Island Press, 2005), esp. 79; available at *www.millenniumassessment.org/en/Condition.aspx#download.*

55. Ibid.

56. Jeremy B. C. Jackson, "Ecological Extinction and Evolution in the Brave New Ocean," *PNAS* 105, supp. 1 (2008): 11458–65.

57. The World Commission on Forests and Sustainable Development, *Summary Report, Our Forests Our Future, World Commission on Forests and Sustainable Development* (Winnipeg, 1999), 6, available at *www.iisd.org/pdf/wcfsdsummary.pdf.*

58. Edward O. Wilson, *The Creation: An Appeal to Save Life on Earth* (New York: W. W. Norton, 2006), 75.

59. Original text available at *www.hubbertpeak.com/hubbert/Bibliography.htm.*

60. M. King Hubbert, *A Report to the Committee on Natural Resources of the National Academy of Sciences,* National Research Council Publication 1000-D (Washington, D.C.: National Academy of Sciences–National Research Council, 1962), original text available at *www.hubbertpeak.com/hubbert/Bibliography.htm.*

61. Walter Sullivan, "A Catholic Bishop Speaks Out against Mountaintop Removal," *Catholic Virginian* (January 2004), at *www.appvoices.org/index.php?/site/voice_stories/a_catholic_bishop_speaks_out_against_mountaintop_removal/issue/29.*

62. *www.coalcandothat.com/index.php.*

63. Barbara Freese et al., "Coal Power in a Warming World: A Sensible Transition to Cleaner Energy Options" (Cambridge, Mass.: Union of Concerned Scientists, 2008), available at *www.ucsusa.org/assets/documents/clean_energy/Coal-power-in-a-warming-world.pdf.*

64. *www.princeton.edu/~cmi/.*

65. *www.princeton.edu/~cmi/news/CMIinBrief.pdf.*

66. *www.nrel.gov/otec/what.html; www.alternative-energy-news.info/technology/hydro/tidal-power/; http://cleantechnica.com/2008/11/13/will-nuclear-fusion-solve-the-energy-crisis/;* David Biello, "Deep Geothermal: The Untapped Energy Source," *Environment* (2008): 360, available at *http://e360.yale.edu/content/feature.msp?id=2077.*

67. *www.hydrogen.gov/.*

Chapter 5: The Environmental Signs of the Times

1. Cerebrus was the three-headed dog of Greek and Roman mythology that guarded the gates of Hades.

2. Rachel Carson, *Silent Spring* (New York: Houghton Mifflin, 1962).

3. Eckardt C. Beck, "The Love Canal Tragedy," *EPA Journal* (January 1979), available at *www.epa.gov/history/topics/lovecanal/01.htm.*

4. Aimin Chen et al., "IQ and Blood Lead from 2 to 7 Years of Age: Are the Effects in Older Children the Residual of High Blood Lead Concentrations in 2-Year-Olds?" *Environmental Health Perspectives* 113 (2005): 597–601; Paul J. Lioy, Natalie C. G. Freeman, and James R. Millette, "Dust: A Metric for Use in Residential and Building Exposure Assessment and Source Characterization," *Environmental Health Perspectives* 110 (2002): 969–83; Nancy J. Simcox et al., "Pesticides in Household Dust and Soil: Exposure Pathways for Children of Agricultural Families," *Environmental Health Perspectives* 103 (1995): 1126–34; Steven G. Gilbert, "Ethical, Legal, and Social Issues: Our Children's Future," *Neurotoxicology* 26 (2005): 521–30.

5. E. M. Faustman et al., "Mechanisms Underlying Children's Susceptibility to Environmental Toxicants," *Environmental Health Perspectives* 108, Supp. 1 (2000): 13–21; D. Rice and S. Barone Jr., "Critical Periods of Vulnerability for the Developing Nervous System: Evidence from Humans and Animal Models," *Environmental Health Perspectives* 108 Supp. 3 (2000): 511–33.

6. Jane Houlihan et al., *BodyBurden: The Pollution in Newborns* (Washington, D.C.: Environmental Working Group, 2005), 13; see online at *www.ewg.org/reports/bodyburden2/*.

7. Philippe Grandjean et al., "The Faroes Statement: Human Health Effects of Developmental Exposure to Chemicals in Our Environment," *Basic and Clinical Pharmacology and Toxicology* 102 (2008): 73–75.

8. Houlihan et al., *BodyBurden*, 1.

9. Ibid., 7.

10. Ibid., 7–8.

11. Ibid., 27.

12. Andreas Kortenkamp, "Ten Years of Mixing Cocktails: A Review of Combination Effects of Endocrine-disrupting Chemicals," *Environmental Health Perspectives* 115 (2007): 98–105; Andreas Kortenkamp et al., "Low-level Exposure to Multiple Chemicals: Reason for Human Health Concerns?" *Environmental Health Perspectives* 115 (2007): 106–14.

13. K. M. Cecil et al., "Decreased Brain Volume in Adults with Childhood Lead Exposure," *Public Library of Science Medicine* 5, no. 5 (2008): e112; available at *http://www.plosmedicine.org/article/info:doi/10.1371/journal.pmed.0050114*.

14. Joseph M. Braun et al., "Association of Environmental Toxicants and Conduct Disorder in US Children: NHANES 2001–2004," *Environmental Health Perspectives* 116 (2008): 956–62; J. P. Wright et al., "Association of Prenatal and Childhood Blood Lead Concentrations with Criminal Arrests in Early Adulthood," *Public Library of Science Medicine* 5, no. 5 (2008): e101; available at 10.1371/journal.pmed.0050101.

15. Bruce P. Lanphear et al., "Low-Level Environmental Lead Exposure and Children's Intellectual Function: An International Pooled Analysis," *Environmental Health Perspectives* 113 (2005): 894–99.

16. Lourdes Schnaas et al., "Reduced Intellectual Development in Children with Prenatal Lead Exposure," *Environmental Health Perspectives* 114 (2006): 791–97; Howard Hu et al., "Fetal Lead Exposure at Each Stage of Pregnancy as a Predictor of Infant Mental Development," *Environmental Health Perspectives* 114 (2006): 1730–35.

17. Todd A. Jusko et al., "Blood Lead Concentrations <10 µ/dL and Child Intelligence at 6 Years of Age," *Environmental Health Perspectives* 116 (2008): 243–48.

18. Marie Lynn Miranda et al., "The Relationship between Early Childhood Blood Lead Levels and Performance on End-of-Grade Tests," *Environmental Health Perspectives* 115 (2007): 1242–47.

19. David C. Bellinger, "Neurological and Behavioral Consequences of Childhood Lead Exposure," *Public Library of Science Medicine* 5 (2008): 690–92; available online at *http://medicine.plosjournals.org/perlserv/?request=get-document&doi=10. 1371%2Fjournal.pmed.0050115.*

20. F. P. Perrera et al., "Prenatal Airborne Polycyclic Aromatic Hydrocarbon Exposure and Child IQ at Age 5 Years," *Pediatrics* 124 (2009): e195–e202.

21. Gayle C. Windham et al., "Autism Spectrum Disorders in Relation to Distribution of Hazardous Air Pollutants in the San Francisco Bay Area," *Environmental Health Perspectives* 114 (2006): 1438–44.

22. Sharon K. Sagiv et al., "Prenatal Organochlorine Exposure and Measures of Behavior in Infancy Using the Neonatal Behavioral Assessment Scale (NBAS)," *Environmental Health Perspectives* 116 (2008): 666–73.

23. Hannah S. Cho et al., "Potential Residential Exposure to Toxics Release Inventory Chemicals during Pregnancy and Childhood Brain Cancer," *Environmental Health Perspectives* 114 (2006): 1113–18.

24. Claire Infante-Rivard et al., "Maternal Exposure to Occupational Solvents and Childhood Leukemia," *Environmental Health Perspectives* 113 (2005): 787–92.

25. Kristina W. Whitworth et al., "Childhood Lymphohematopoietic Cancer Incidence and Hazardous Air Pollutants in Southeast Texas, 1995–2004," *Environmental Health Perspectives* 116 (2008): 1576–80.

26. Centers for Disease Control and Prevention, "Asthma — United States, 1982–1993," *Morbidity and Mortality Weekly Report* 43 (1995): 952–55.

27. American Lung Association, State of the Air (2007), 6; *www.lungusa.org/about-us/publications/.*

28. Jon Mark Hirshon et al., "Elevated Ambient Air Zinc Increases Pediatric Asthma Morbidity," *Environmental Health Perspectives* 116 (2008): 826–31.

29. Shao Lin et al., "Chronic Exposure to Ambient Ozone and Asthma Hospital Admissions among Children," *Environmental Health Perspectives* 116 (2008): 1725–30; Kelly Moore et al., "Ambient Ozone Concentrations Cause Increased Hospitalizations for Asthma in Children: An 18-year Study in Southern California," *Environmental Health Perspectives* 116 (2008): 1063–70; Rob McConnell et al., "Childhood Incident Asthma and Traffic-related Air Pollution at Home and School," *Environmental Health Perspectives* 118 (2010): 1021–27; Bert Brunekreef et al., "Self-reported Truck Traffic on the Street of Residence and Symptoms of Asthma and Allergic Disease: A Global Relationship in ISAAC Phase 3," *Environmental Health Perspectives* 117 (2009): 1791–98.

30. Janice J. Kim et al., "Residential Traffic and Children's Respiratory Health," *Environmental Health Perspectives* 116 (2008): 1274–79.

31. Irva Hertz-Picciotto et al., "Early Childhood Lower Respiratory Illness and Air Pollution," *Environmental Health Perspectives* 115 (2007): 1510–18.

32. Jennifer D. Parker et al., "Air Pollution and Childhood Respiratory Allergies in the United States," *Environmental Health Perspectives* 117 (2009): 140–47.

33. Audrey Smargiassi et al., "Risk of Asthmatic Episodes in Children Exposed to Sulfur Dioxide Stack Emissions from a Refinery Point Source in Montreal, Canada," *Environmental Health Perspectives* 117 (2009): 653–59.

34. Cande V. Ananth et al., "Rates of Preterm Delivery among Black Women and White Women in the United States over Two Decades: An Age-Period-Cohort Analysis," *American Journal of Epidemiology* 154 (2001): 657–65.

35. Sharon K. Sagiv et al., "A Time-Series Analysis of Air Pollution and Preterm Birth in Pennsylvania, 1997–2001," *Environmental Health Perspectives* 113 (2005): 602–6.

36. Michael Brauer et al., "A Cohort Study of Traffic-related Air Pollution Impacts on Birth Outcomes," *Environmental Health Perspectives* 116 (2008): 680–86; Michelle Wilhelm and Beate Ritz, "Local Variations in CO and Particulate Air Pollution and Adverse Birth Outcomes in Los Angeles County, California, USA," *Environmental Health Perspectives* 113 (2005): 1212–21; Muhammad T. Salaam et al., "Birth Outcomes and Prenatal Exposure to Ozone, Carbon Monoxide, and Particulate Matter: Results from the Children's Health Study," *Environmental Health Perspectives* 113 (2005): 1638–44.

37. Michelle L. Bell et al., "Ambient Air Pollution and Low Birth Weight in Connecticut and Massachusetts," *Environmental Health Perspectives* 115 (2007): 1118–24.

38. Craig A. Hansen et al., "The Effect of Ambient Air Pollution during Early Pregnancy on Fetal Ultrasound Measurements during Mid-Pregnancy," *Environmental Health Perspectives* 116 (2008): 362–69.

39. Bing-Fang Hwang and Jouni J. K. Jaakkola, "Ozone and Other Air Pollutants and the Risks of Oral Clefts," *Environmental Health Perspectives* 116 (2008): 1411–15.

40. Asa Bradman et al., "Organophosphate Urinary Metabolite Levels during Pregnancy and after Delivery in Women Living in an Agricultural Community," *Environmental Health Perspectives* 113 (2005): 1802–7.

41. Richard A. Fenske et al., "Biologic Monitoring to Characterize Organophosphorus Pesticide Exposure among Children and Workers: An Analysis of Recent Studies in Washington State," *Environmental Health Perspectives* 113 (2005): 1651–57.

42. Thomas A. Arcury et al., "Pesticide Urinary Metabolite Levels of Children in Eastern North Carolina Farmworker Households," *Environmental Health Perspectives* 115 (2007): 1254–60.

43. Donald T. Wigle et al., "A Systematic Review and Meta-analysis of Childhood Leukemia and Parental Occupational Pesticide Exposure," *Environmental Health Perspectives* 117 (2009): 1505–13.

44. Beth A. Mueller et al., "Fetal Deaths and Proximity to Hazardous Waste Sites in Washington State," *Environmental Health Perspectives* 115 (2007): 776–80.

45. Susan E. Carozza et al., "Risk of Childhood Cancers Associated with Residence in Agriculturally Intense Areas in the United States," *Environmental Health Perspectives* 116 (2008): 559–65.

46. Kristy J. Meyer et al., "Agricultural Pesticide Use and Hypospadias in Eastern Arkansas," *Environmental Health Perspectives* 114 (2006): 1589–95.

47. Ida N. Damgaard et al., "Persistent Pesticides in Human Breast Milk and Cryptorchidism," *Environmental Health Perspectives* 114 (2006): 1133–38.

48. Mariana F. Fernandez et al., "Human Exposure to Endocrine-Disrupting Chemicals and Prenatal Risk Factors for Cryptorchidism and Hypospadias: A Nested Case-Control Study," *Environmental Health Perspectives* 115 (2007): 8–14; Helle R. Andersen et al., "Impaired Reproductive Development in Sons of Women

Occupationally Exposed to Pesticides during Pregnancy," *Environmental Health Perspectives* 116 (2008): 566–72; Katharina M. Main et al., "Flame Retardants in Placenta and Breast Milk and Cryptorchidism in Newborn Boys," *Environmental Health Perspectives* 115 (2007): 1519–26.

49. Eric M. Roberts et al., "Maternal Residence Near Agricultural Pesticide Applications and Autism Spectrum Disorders among Children in the California Central Valley," *Environmental Health Perspectives* 115 (2007): 1482–89.

50. Marshalyn Yeargin-Allsopp et al., "Prevalence of Autism in a US Metropolitan Area," *Journal of the American Medical Association* 289 (2003): 49–55.

51. Noriaki Washino et al., "Correlations between Prenatal Exposure to Perfluorinated Chemicals and Reduced Fetal Growth," *Environmental Health Perspectives* 117 (2009): 660–67.

52. Anna Kärrman et al., "Exposure of Perfluorinated Chemicals through Lactation: Levels of Matched Human Milk and Serum and a Temporal Trend, 1996–2004, in Sweden," *Environmental Health Perspectives* 115 (2007): 226–30.

53. Houlihan et al., *BodyBurden,* 1–83.

54. Jeremie Rudant et al., "Household Exposure to Pesticides and Risk of Childhood Hematopoietic Malignancies: The ESCALE Study (SFCE)," *Environmental Health Perspectives* 115 (2007): 1787–93; Youn K. Shim et al., "Parental Exposure to Pesticides and Childhood Brain Cancer: U.S. Atlantic Coast Childhood Brain Cancer Study," *Environmental Health Perspectives* 117 (2009): 1002–6; Mary H. Ward et al., "Residential Exposure to Polychlorinated Biphenyls and Organochlorine Pesticides and Risk of Childhood Leukemia," *Environmental Health Perspectives* 117 (2009): 1007–13.

55. Ghislaine Scelo et al., "Household Exposure to Paint and Petroleum Solvents, Chromosomal Translocations, and the Risk of Childhood Leukemia," *Environmental Health Perspectives* 117 (2009): 133–39.

56. Luz Claudio, "Synthetic Turf Health Debate Takes Root," *Environmental Health Perspectives* 116 (2008): A117–22.

57. K. M. Main et al., "Human Breast Milk Contamination with Phthalates and Alterations of Endogenous Reproductive Hormones in Infants Three Months of Age," *Environmental Health Perspectives* 114 (2006): 270–76.

58. John D. Meeker et al., "Urinary Phthalate Metabolites in Relation to Preterm Birth in Mexico City," *Environmental Health Perspectives* 117 (2009): 1587–92.

59. Soo-Churl Cho et al., "Relationship between Environmental Phthalate Exposure and Intelligence of School-Age Children," *Environmental Health Perspectives* 118 (2010): 1027–32; Stephanie M. Engel et al., "Prenatal Phthalate Exposure Is Associated with Childhood Behavior and Executive Functioning," *Environmental Health Perspectives* 118 (2010): 565–71.

60. Environmental Working Group, 2009, *Pollution in People: Cord Blood in Minority Newborns, www.ewg.org/minoritycordblood/home.*

61. The Work Group for Safe Markets, "Baby's Toxic Bottle: Bisphenol, a Leaching from Popular Baby Bottles," *www.chej.org/documents/BabysToxicBottleFinal.pdf.* This work group is a cooperative of NGOs, including the Alliance for a Healthy Tomorrow; Boston Common Asset Management; Breast Cancer Fund; Center for Health, Environment, and Justice; Clean New York; Clean Water Action; Environ America; Environmental Defence (Canada); Environmental Health Fund;

Environmental Health Strategy Center; Healthy Legacy; Learning Disabilities Association of America; MOMS (Making Our Milk Safe); Oregon Environmental Council; and US PIRG.

62. Houlihan et al., *BodyBurden,* 31, 33.

63. Sonya Lunder et al., "Flame Retardants in Mother's Milk: Record Levels of Toxic Fire Retardants Found in American Mothers' Breast Milk," Environmental Working Group (2003): *www.ewg.org/reports/mothersmilk/.*

64. Nerissa Wu et al., "Human Exposure to PBDEs: Association of PBDE Body Burdens with Food Consumption and House Dust Concentrations," *Environmental Science and Technology* 41 (2007): 1584–89.

65. Lunder et al., "Flame Retardants in Mother's Milk," 16.

66. Julie B. Herbstman et al., "Prenatal Exposure to PBDEs and Neurodevelopment," *Environmental Health Perspectives* 118 (2010): 712–19.

67. Ibid., 27–31.

68. Ibid., 27–28.

69. National Environmental Justice Advisory Council, "Fish Consumption and Environmental Justice: A Report Developed from the National Environmental Justice Advisory Council Meeting of December 3–6, 2001."

70. E. Dewailly et al., "High Levels of PCBs in Breast Milk of Inuit Women from Arctic Quebec," *Bulletin of Environmental Contamination Toxicology* 43 (1989): 641–46; Paul W. Stewart et al., "The Relationship between Prenatal PCB Exposure and Intelligence (IQ) in 9-Year Old Children," *Environmental Health Perspectives* 116 (2008): 1416–22.

71. Olivier Deschênes et al., "Climate Change and Birth Weight," *American Economic Review: Papers and Proceedings* 99 (2009): 211–17.

72. Frank Ackerman, *Poisoned for Pennies: The Economics of Toxics and Precaution* (Washington, D.C.: Island Press, 2008); Frank Ackerman and Liza Heinzerling, *Priceless: On Knowing the Price of Everything and the Value of Nothing* (New York: New Press, 2004).

73. Ackerman, *Poisoned for Pennies,* 6–7.

74. Ibid., xiv.

Chapter 6: Theological Reflections on Ecology and the Environmental Crisis

1. Walter C. Lowdermilk, "The Eleventh Commandment" (Jerusalem, June 2, 1939), 1. Available at *http://watershed.org/news/spr_96/eleventh_comm.html.*

2. Ibid., 5.

3. Joseph Sittler, "A Theology for Earth," in *Evocations of Grace: The Writings of Joseph Sittler on Ecology, Theology, and Ethics,* ed. Steven Bouma-Prediger and Peter Bakken (Grand Rapids, Mich.: William B. Eerdmans, 2000), 20–31.

4. Sittler, "Ecological Commitment as Theological Responsibility," in *Evocations of Grace: The Writings of Joseph Sittler on Ecology, Theology, and Ethics,* ed. Steven Bouma-Prediger and Peter Bakken (Grand Rapids, Mich.: William B. Eerdmans, 2000), 76–82.

5. Ibid.

6. Carol J. Dempsey, O.P., "Creation, Evolution, Revelation, and Redemption: Connections and Intersections," in *Earth, Wind, and Fire: Biblical and Theological Perspectives on Creation*, ed. Carol J. Dempsey and Mary Margaret Pazdan (Collegeville, Minn.: Liturgical Press, 2004), 17.

7. For a more in-depth analysis of the relationship between biblical creation-Wisdom theology, revelation, and the ecological crisis, see Butkus, "Creation-in-Crisis: Biblical Creation Theology and the Disclosure of God," in *Theology and Sacred Scripture*, ed. Carol J. Dempsey and William P. Loewe (Maryknoll, N.Y.: Orbis Books, 2002), 35–52.

8. John F. Haught, "Revelation," *The New Dictionary of Theology*, ed. Joseph Komonchak et al. (Wilmington, Del.: Michael Glazier, 1987), 888.

9. Avery Dulles, *Models of Revelation* (Garden City, N.Y.: Doubleday, 1983; reprint, Maryknoll, N.Y.: Orbis Books, 1992), 100.

10. Ian Barbour, *Religion and Science: Historical and Contemporary Issues* (San Francisco: HarperCollins, 1997), 95, 103.

11. Haught, "Revelation," 898.

12. Rene Latourelle, S.J., *Theology of Revelation* (New York: Alba House, 1987), 332–40.

13. James Barr, *Biblical Faith and Natural Theology: The Gifford Lectures for 1991 Delivered in the University of Edinburgh* (Oxford: Clarendon Press, 1993), 151.

14. John F. Haught, *Christianity and Science: Toward a Theology of Nature* (Maryknoll, N.Y.: Orbis Books, 2007), 35.

15. Ibid., 37.

16. John F. Haught, *Mystery and Promise: A Theology of Revelation* (Collegeville, Minn.: Liturgical Press, 1993), 148.

17. Haught, *Christianity and Science*, 40–41.

18. Ibid., 35.

19. Sittler, "Ecological Commitment as Theological Responsibility," 79.

20. Sallie McFague, *The Body of God: An Ecological Theology* (Minneapolis: Fortress Press, 1993), 114.

21. Ibid.

22. John S. Kselman, "Grace, Old Testament," in the *Anchor Bible Dictionary*, ed. David Noel Freedman (New York: Bantam Doubleday, 1992), 1084–86.

23. Elizabeth Dreyer, *Manifestations of Grace* (Collegeville, Minn.: Liturgical Press, 1990), 47.

24. Ibid., 57.

25. Ibid.

26. Ontology, a component of philosophical theology concerned with metaphysics, seeks to understand the nature and relations of being, in particular human being.

27. Douglas John Hall, *Imaging God: Dominion as Stewardship* (Grand Rapids, Mich.: William B. Eerdmans, 1986), 119.

28. Ibid., 116.

29. Ibid., 120.

30. Hans-Georg Gadamer, *Truth and Method* (New York: Seabury Press, 1975), 273.

31. Thomas Berry, *The Sacred Universe: Earth, Spirituality, and Religion in the Twenty-first Century,* ed. Mary Evelyn Tucker (New York: Columbia University Press, 2009), 186.

32. Dreyer, *Manifestations of Grace,* 191.

33. Ibid., 162.

34. Stephen W. Hawking, *The Universe in a Nutshell* (New York: Bantam Books, 2001), 84.

35. Stephen W. Hawking, *A Brief History of Time* (New York: Bantam Books, 1988), 129.

36. Ibid., 126.

37. Ibid., 81.

38. John F. Haught, *Mystery and Promise,* 153–54.

39. Hawking, *The Universe in a Nutshell,* 87–88.

40. Joseph Silk, *A Short History of the Universe* (New York: Scientific American Library, 1994), 10.

41. John F. Haught, *Science and Religion: From Conflict to Conversation* (New York: Paulist Press, 1995), 125.

42. Hawking, *A Brief History of Time,* 128.

43. Hawking, *The Universe in a Nutshell,* 86.

44. Ibid., 87.

45. John D. Barrow and Frank J. Tipler, *The Anthropic Cosmological Principle* (Oxford: Oxford University Press, 1988), 5.

46. Ibid., 21.

47. Hawking, *A Brief History of Time,* 129.

48. Haught, *Science and Religion,* 126.

49. Ibid.

50. Haught, *Mystery and Promise,* 154.

51. Thomas Berry, *The Christian Future and the Fate of the Earth* (Maryknoll, N.Y.: Orbis Books, 2009), 89.

52. Ibid.

53. Ibid., 88.

54. Dreyer, *Manifestations of Grace,* 172.

55. Ibid., 199.

56. Willis Jenkins, *Ecologies of Grace: Environmental Ethics and Christian Theology* (New York: Oxford University Press, 2008).

57. Ibid., 7.

58. Ibid.

59. Ibid., 78.

60. Ibid. 81.

61. See the U.S. Catholic Bishops' pastoral letter *Renewing the Earth* (1991) and the Columbia River pastoral letter, *The Columbia River Watershed: Caring for Creation and the Common Good* (2001). Also for secular uses of stewardship, see the by-laws on stewardship of the Nature Conservancy and the Pew Charitable Trust Ocean Commission Report on ocean stewardship.

62. Edward Moore, "Likeness to God as Far as Possible: Deification Doctrine in Lamblichus and Three Eastern Christian Fathers," *Theandros,* An Online Journal of Orthodox Christian Theology and Philosophy 3, no. 1 (Fall 2005): available at *www.theandros.com/iamblichus.html.*

63. Jenkins, *Ecologies of Grace,* 97.

64. Ibid.

65. Ibid.

66. James Nash, *Loving Nature: Ecological Integrity and Christian Responsibility* (Nashville: Abingdon Press, 1991), 118.

67. Berry, *The Christian Future and the Fate of the Earth*, 30.

68. Ibid., 119.

Chapter 7: The Ecology of God

1. Pierre Teilhard de Chardin, *The Phenomenon of Man* (Harper and Row, 1961), 220.

2. Denis Edwards, *Jesus the Wisdom of God: An Ecological Theology* (Maryknoll, N.Y.: Orbis Books, 1995), 143.

3. Ibid.

4. Ibid.

5. The terms "apocryphal" and "deutero-canonical" refer to whether books related to the Bible are authoritative or nonauthoritative. The Greek term *apocrypha* means "hidden" or "hidden things." Thus the Books of Wisdom and Sirach are noncanonical (nonauthoritative) in the Protestant version of the Bible. The term "deutero-canonical" means "secondary canon," which means that Wisdom and Sirach are part of the official canon in the Roman Catholic and Greek Orthodox versions of the Bible.

6. Walter Brueggemann, "The Loss and Recovery of Creation in Old Testament Theology," *Theology Today* 53, no. 2 (July 1996): 177–90.

7. Terence E. Fretheim, *God and the World in the Old Testament: A Relational Theology of Creation* (Nashville: Abingdon Press, 2005), 219.

8. Ibid., 206–7.

9. Ibid., 213.

10. "The Land Ethic" is the last chapter of *A Sand County Almanac,* which was not published and did not become popular until after Leopold's death. See Aldo Leopold, *A Sand County Almanac with Essays in Conservation from Round River* (Oxford: Oxford University Press, 1966), 237–64.

11. Fretheim, *God and the World in the New Testament*, 209.

12. James Crenshaw, "In Search of Divine Presence," *Review and Expositor* 74 (1977): 365.

13. Leo Purdue, *Wisdom and Creation: The Theology of Wisdom Literature* (Nashville: Abingdon Press, 1994), 327.

14. Fretheim, *God and the World*, 217.

15. Ibid., 19–20.

16. Ibid., 270.

17. Ibid., 273.

18. Ibid., 194.

19. Ibid., 195

20. Ibid., 23.

21. Ibid.

22. Thomas Hosinski, *Stubborn Fact and Creative Advance: An Introduction to the Metaphysics of Alfred North Whitehead* (Lanham, Md.: Rowman and Littlefield, 1993), 127, 176.

23. Ibid., 177.

24. Ibid., 187.

25. Ibid., 236.

26. Jay B. McDaniel, "A Process Approach to Ecology," in *Handbook of Process Theology*, ed. Jay McDaniel and Donna Bowman (St. Louis: Chalice Press, 2006), 232.

27. Jay B. McDaniel, *With Roots and Wings: Christianity in an Age of Ecology and Dialogue* (Maryknoll, N.Y.: Orbis Books, 1995), 97 (emphasis added).

28. Ibid.

29. McDaniel, "A Process Approach to Ecology," 237.

30. Ibid.

31. Alfred North Whitehead, *Process and Reality: An Essay in Cosmology* (New York: Free Press, 1978), 351.

32. Terence E. Fretheim, *The Suffering of God: An Old Testament Perspective* (Philadelphia: Fortress Press, 1984), 127–48.

33. McDaniel, "A Process Approach to Ecology," 237.

34. Ibid., 237–38.

35. Ibid., 239.

36. Ibid., 241.

37. Ibid., 236.

38. Ibid.

39. Hosinski, *Stubborn Fact and Creative Advance*, 244.

40. Sallie McFague, *The Body of God: An Ecological Theology* (Minneapolis: Fortress Press, 1993), 14.

41. Ibid., 17–18.

42. Ibid., 19.

43. Ibid.

44. Ibid., 46.

45. Ibid., 96–97.

46. Ibid., 143–44.

47. Ibid., 145.

48. Ibid.

49. Ibid.

50. Ibid., 150.

51. Ibid.

52. Ibid., 160.

53. Ibid., 162.

54. Ibid., 164.

55. Ibid., 180.

56. Ibid., 181.

57. Denis Edwards, *Ecology at the Heart of Faith* (Maryknoll, N.Y.: Orbis Books, 2007), 76.

58. Ibid., 31.

59. Ibid., 37.

60. Ibid., 40.

61. Ibid., 41.

62. Ibid., 42.

63. Ibid., 45–46.

64. Edwards, *Jesus the Wisdom of God*, 108.

65. Ibid., 109.

66. Neoplatonism refers to the philosophical system of Plotinus (204–70 C.E.) who, building on the philosophy of Plato, proposed that all reality emanates from one ultimate source and that this ultimate One can be directly encountered through mystical insight. Because it elevated the value of spirit over matter, it is theologically deficient for a contemporary ecotheology.

67. Edwards, *Jesus the Wisdom of God,* 109.

68. Ibid., 109–10.

69. Ibid., 113.

70. Ibid., 114.

71. Ibid., 115.

72. Ibid., 116.

73. Ibid.

74. Ibid., 117.

75. Ibid., 119.

76. Ibid., 122.

77. Ibid.

78. Ibid., 125.

79. Ibid., 126.

80. Readers should bear in mind that most contemporary Pauline scholars do not think that the Letter to the Colossians was originally Paul's but most likely Deutero-Pauline, that is, authored by someone after Paul's death who knew the Pauline tradition and theology.

81. Edwards, *Jesus the Wisdom of God,* 82.

82. Ibid., 86.

83. McFague, *The Body of God,* 198.

84. Carol J. Dempsey, "Hope amidst Crisis: A Prophetic Vision of Cosmic Redemption," in *All Creation Is Groaning: An Interdisciplinary Vision for Life in a Sacred Universe,* ed. Carol J. Dempsey and Russell A. Butkus (Collegeville, Minn.: Liturgical Press, 1999), 299.

85. Edwards, *Jesus the Wisdom of God,* 45.

86. The Gospel of John is not mentioned here because of its unique literary-theological style; there are no parables in the Gospel of John. Jesus is often portrayed speaking in long reflective discourses and does not use parables in the short pithy style of teaching that we find in the synoptic gospels of Mark, Matthew, and Luke.

87. Edwards, *Jesus the Wisdom of God,* 48.

88. Tatha Wiley, "Creation Restored: God's Basileia, the Social Economy and the Human Good," in *Earth, Wind, and Fire: Biblical and Theological Perspectives on Creation,* ed. Carol J. Dempsey and Mary Margaret Pazdan (Collegeville, Minn.: Liturgical Press, 2004), 79.

89. Ibid.

90. Fretheim, *God and the World,* 273.

91. Ibid., 269–75.

92. Ibid., 275.

93. McFague, *Body of God,* 201.

94. Ibid.

95. Edwards, *Jesus the Wisdom of God,* 45.

96. Ibid., 153–71.

97. Ibid., 163.

Chapter 8: Sustainability for a Small Planet

1. The truncated list of documents included in this chapter necessarily ignores some very significant events and government publications, but a complete treatment of this topic would constitute a book in itself. For those with an interest in a more comprehensive historical vision of this topic, additional sources are readily available, including: D. H. Meadows et al., *Limits to Growth* (New York: Universe Books, 1972); G. O. Barney, ed., "Global 2000: The Report to the President — Entering the 21st Century" (Washington, D.C.: U.S. Government Printing Office, 1980); UNEP, *In Defense of the Earth: The Basic Texts on Environment* (Nairobi, Kenya: UNEP, 1981).

2. Society for Ecological Restoration International, see online at *www.ser.org/content/ecological_restoration_primer.asp*.

3. *World Commission on Environment and Development: Our Common Future* (New York: Oxford University Press, 1987); *www.un-documents.net/wced-ocf.htm*, section entitled "The Global Challenge."

4. Theodore Roosevelt, *A Book Lover's Holidays in the Open* (New York: Charles Scribner's Sons, 1916).

5. John F. Kennedy Presidential Library and Museum, "Remarks of Robert F. Kennedy at the University of Kansas, March 18, 1968," John F. Kennedy Presidential Library and Museum, *www.jfklibrary.org/Historical+Resources/Archives/Reference+Desk/Speeches/RFK/RFKSpeech68Mar18UKansas.htm*.

6. Edward Abbey, *One Life at a Time, Please* (New York: Henry Holt, 1978).

7. Ibid., point 25.

8. Ibid., points 16–28.

9. Russell Butkus and Steven Kolmes, "Got Wild Salmon? A Scientific and Ethical Analysis of Salmon Recovery in the Pacific Northwest and California," in *Salmon 2100: The Future of Wild Pacific Salmon*, ed. Robert T. Lackey, Denise H. Lach, and Sally L. Duncan (Bethesda, Md.: American Fisheries Society, 2006.

10. *Our Common Future*; *www.un-documents.net/wced-ocf.htm*, section entitled "The Global Challenge," points 40–73.

11. Ibid., points 75–90, 93–100.

12. Separate technical reports and synthesis documents are available online at Millennium Ecosystem Assessment, *www.millenniumassessment.org/en/index.aspx*.

13. Millennium Ecosystem Assessment, *Ecosystems and Human Well-being: Synthesis* (Washington, D.C.: Island Press, 2005), 1–2.

14. Paul Hawken, *Blessed Unrest* (New York: Viking Penguin, 2007), 342.

15. David Runnalls, "Our Common Inaction, Meeting the Call for Institutional Change," *Environment* 50 (2008): 18–28.

16. Ibid., 22–23.

17. Ibid., 24–25.

18. Ibid., 25.

19. Ibid., 25–26.

20. Elinor Ostrom, "The Challenge of Common-Pool Resources," *Environment* 50 (2008): 8–20.

21. Princeton University, "Carbon Mitigation Initiative," *http://cmi.princeton.edu/*.

22. World Trade Organization, "Sustainable Development," Environment: Issues, *www.wto.org/english/tratop_e/envir_e/sust_dev_e.htm*.

23. Ken Conca, "The WTO and the Undermining of Global Environmental Governance," *Review of International Political Economy* 7 (2000): 484–94.

24. The session was entitled "Information Session on Product Carbon Footprint and Labelling Schemes," and the PowerPoint presentations given at the session can be downloaded at *www.wto.org/english/tratop_e/envir_e/events_feb10_e/event_17feb10_e.htm*.

25. Steven A. Kolmes, "Food, Land Use, and Biofuels," *Science* eLetter, 2008, available at *www.sciencemag.org/cgi/eletters/319/5867/1238#top*.

26. Christopher L. Weber and H. Scott Matthews, "Food-miles and the Relative Climate Impacts of Food Choices in the United States," *Environmental Science and Technology* 42 (2008): 3508–13.

27. Caroline Saunders, "Carbon Footprints, Life Cycle Analysis, Food Miles: Global Trade Trends and Market Issues," *Political Science* 60 (2008): 73–88.

28. Tyler Colman and Pablo Paster, "Red, White, and 'Green': The Cost of Greenhouse Gas Emissions in the Global Wine Trade," *Journal of Wine Research* 20 (2009): 15–26.

29. An especially clear example is given by Interface, Inc., the world's largest manufacturer of soft-surfaced modular flooring, at their sustainability website *www.interfaceglobal.com/Sustainability.aspx*.

30. Gerald T. Gardner and Paul C. Stern, *The Short List: The Most Effective Actions U.S. Households Can Take to Curb Climate Change*, Environment 50 (2008): 12–25.

31. UN-Water Thematic Initiatives, "Coping with Water Scarcity," *www.unwater.org/downloads/waterscarcity.pdf*.

32. *www.foodandwaterwatch.org/*.

33. Maude Barlow, *Blue Covenant: The Global Water Crisis and the Coming Battle for the Right to Water* (Toronto: McClelland & Stewart, 1980).

34. For some examples and case studies of the Natural Step Process see online *www.naturalstep.org/it/usa/case-studies*.

35. Ibid.

36. Steven A. Kolmes and Russell A. Butkus, "Sustainability, Catholic Institutions of Higher Learning, and the Natural Step," *Journal of Catholic Higher Education* 28 (2009): 83–97.

37. Frederick Steiner, *Human Ecology: Following Nature's Lead* (Washington, D.C.: Island Press, 2002).

38. William McDonough and Michael Braungart, *Cradle to Cradle* (New York: North Point Press, 2002).

39. Stuart H. M. Butchart et al., "Global Biodiversity: Indicators of Recent Decline," *Science, www.sciencemag.org/cgi/content/abstract/science.1187512v1?sa_campaign=Email/pap/29–April-2010/10.1126/science.1187512*.

40. J. H. Fossøa, P. B. Mortensen, and D. M. Furevik, "The Deep-Water Coral Lophelia pertusa in Norwegian Waters: Distribution and Fishery Impacts," *Hydrobiologia* 471 (2002): 1–12.

41. J. B. Jones, "Environmental Impact of Trawling on the Seabed: A Review," *New Zealand Journal of Marine and Freshwater Research* 26 (1992): 59–67; Matthew Gianni, "High Seas Bottom Trawl Fisheries and Their Impacts on the Biodiversity of Vulnerable Deep-Sea Ecosystems: Options for International Action" (Gland, Switzerland: IUCN, available at *http://cmsdata.iucn.org/downloads/hs_bottomtrawling_execsumm.pdf*.

42. Rolf Willman and Kieran Kelleher, "Economic Trends in Global Marine Fisheries," in the *Handbook of Marine Fisheries Conservation and Management,* ed. R. Quentin Grafton et al. (New York: Oxford University Press, 2010), 20–42.

43. Callum M. Roberts et al., "Effects of Marine Reserves on Adjacent Fisheries," *Science* 294 (2001): 1920–23; Garry R. Russ and Angel C. Alcala, "Marine Reserves: Long-term Protection Is Required for Full Recovery of Predatory Fish Populations," *Oecologia* 138 (2004): 622–27.

44. Charles H. Peterson et al., "Long-Term Ecosystem Response to the Exxon Valdez Oil Spill," *Science* 302 (2003): 2082–86.

45. European Commission Environment, "Registration, Evaluation, Authorisation, and Restriction of Chemical Substances," see *http://ec.europa.eu/environment/chemicals/reach/reach_intro.htm.*

46. The National Academies, "What You Need to Know about Energy," online at *http://needtoknow.nas.edu/energy/.*

47. Brian Nattrass and Mary Altomare, *The Natural Step for Business* (Gabriola Island, B.C.: New Society Publishers, 1999); Annika Carlsson-Kanayama et al., "Participative Backcasting: A Tool for Involving Stakeholders in Local Sustainability Planning," *Futures* 40 (2008): 34–46.

48. Kolmes and Butkus, "Sustainability, Catholic Institutions of Higher Learning, and the Natural Step."

49. Steiner, *Human Ecology,* 13–24.

50. Paul Hawken, *Blessed Unrest* (New York: Viking Penguin, 2007).

51. Hawkin allowed the talk to be freely posted on websites and used in publications worldwide. A recent check using the Google search engine for the commonly used title of the talk "You are brilliant and the earth is hiring" produced roughly 951,000 hits. It is available at the University of Portland website, as the original venue of the talk, at *http://college.up.edu/envscience/default.aspx?cid=8042&pid=3084.*

Glossary

1,1,1–trichloroethane: a small heavily chlorinated synthetic organic compound, with chemical formula $C_2H_3Cl_3$. Prior to the Montreal Protocol it was a heavily used industrial solvent, but it depletes the stratospheric ozone layer and is generally being phased out. 1,1,1–trichloroethane can cause birth defects and other health problems.

1,3 butadiene: a simple synthetic organic compound with two carbon-carbon double bonds with the chemical formula C_4H_6. It is used in the synthesis of synthetic rubber, nylon, and in other industrial chemical reactions. 1,3 butadiene causes central nervous system damage and is suspected of being carcinogenic and of causing birth defects.

abiotic: pertaining to the nonliving component of the world, such as stones and the atmosphere.

acidification: increasing acidity, as with the increasing acidity of the world's oceans as excess CO_2 dissolves in sea water and forms carbonic acid.

acre-foot: the volume of water required to cover a surface area of one acre with one foot of water, this is the measurement commonly used in the Unites States for large-scale water measures in irrigation. It amounts to about 326,000 gallons of water, which is a generous supply for a typical American family of four for two years.

alkanes: a class of synthetic organic compounds composed only of carbon and hydrogen linked together by single covalent bonds. Among alkanes every carbon has four other atoms joined to it, each either a carbon or a hydrogen. Some alkanes have ring structures and are therefore cycloalkanes. Exposure to some alkanes (e.g., octane, chloroform) is hazardous to human health.

androcentrism: placing male human beings or the male point of view at the center of your perspective.

anthropic principle: the concept that the processes of cosmogenesis that produced the universe from the Big Bang onward were specifically tailored to produce intelligent life. This includes in different versions the Weak Anthropic Principle (WAP) and the Strong Anthropic Principle (SAP).

Anthropocene: the new geological epoch dominated by human economic activities such as industry and agriculture that are having far-reaching global impacts.

anthropocentric: placing human beings as the most central and significant entities in the world or universe.

aquifer: an underground layer of permeable rock containing water that can be pumped up for human uses, aquifer water is generally "fossil water" that accumulates only very slowly over time but which can be depleted rapidly.

autotrophic: an organism that produces complex organic molecules (carbohydrates, fats, protein) out of nonliving materials. Generally this involves photosynthesis (see

221

entry). Although some chemosynthetic organisms that do not need sunlight exist, these are primarily among bacteria and related forms.

axiological: related to the study of values in ethical analysis.

benzene: see mononuclear aromatic hydrocarbons.

biogeochemical cycle: the cycle through which an element such as carbon or nitrogen moves through the various living and nonliving compartments of the Earth, such as the air, the oceans, plants, animals, ocean-bottom sediments, the soil, etc. The element in question is transformed from being present in one type of molecule to other types as the cycle progresses.

biomass: material in the living compartment of the ecosystem, including the bodies of plants and animals and their wastes.

biotic: pertaining to the living component of the world, e.g., plants and animals.

bisphenol-A (BPA): an organic chemical used to make polycarbonate plastic, epoxy resins, and other materials. BPA has estrogenic properties, which have numerous implications for human development and health. Some countries have banned BPA from baby bottles; in the U.S. major retailers have begun to avoid selling baby bottles containing BPA, but it remains present in virtually all canned food linings at this time.

brominated flame retardants (PBDEs): see polybrominated diphenyl ethers.

Brundtland Commission: formally named the World Commission on Environment and Development, it was convened in 1983 by the United Nations to report on the relationship between environmental concerns and economic development. It is generally referred to as the Brundtland Commission after the person who chaired it, Gro Harlem Brundtland, a very influential woman who was trained as a physician, became prime minister of Norway, and eventually a major figure on the world stage for issues related to the public health and the environment. The strikingly prescient *Brundtland Commission Report*, entitled *Our Common Future*, was published by Oxford University Press in 1987 and remains available on the Internet.

calcareous: made up in whole or part of calcium carbonate, especially prevalent in oceanic animals with shells like snails and clams.

Carbon Mitigation Initiative (CMI): a joint venture of the Princeton University Environmental Institute, Ford Motor Company, and British Petroleum (BP). CMI maintains a website at *http://cmi.princeton.edu/* where it proposes a series of steps that might combine to prevent atmospheric CO_2 levels from reaching levels with the direst consequences.

cellulosic ethanol: ethanol produced by fermentation of the cellulose and/or lignin in plant cell walls. Corn stalks are often looked at as a raw material for this process, but other sources such as switch grass may prove to be more useful. Various processes to produce ethanol from wood have been used, especially in the First and Second World Wars, when access to petroleum was difficult and limited for many countries. Newer techniques based on enzymatic or microbial breakdown of the plant material rather than powerful acids are being developed as more efficient and less environmentally damaging alternatives. This type of ethanol production may become important in the future if the price of petroleum follows the anticipated dramatically upwards course over time.

chlorinated solvents: a large group of synthetic organic compounds that includes chlorine and are toxic to varying degrees. They can be absorbed by skin contact, inhalation, or through groundwater or food contamination.

chlorofluorocarbons (CFCs): first patented by Frigidaire in 1928 and rapidly employed by many firms, used to develop modern air conditioners and refrigerators, as a propellant in spray cans, and in the production of Styrofoam. Banned in stages throughout the 1970s and 1980s, CFCs proved to be highly destructive of the Earth's protective ozone layer.

Christology/Christological: the subset of systematic theology that is a theological analysis of Jesus Christ historically and traditionally understood as fully human and fully divine.

circular reasoning: see tautology.

clean coal: techniques under development intended to make it possible to burn coal with greatly reduced emissions of CO_2 and other pollutants. Processes being investigated include coal gasification, capturing CO_2 from the gases being vented and sequestering it underground or under water, liquification of captured CO_2, and other possibilities. A demonstration plant run by the German government exists in Spremberg, Germany, but the final fate of the liquefied CO_2 has not been determined, and the plant could not operate commercially in a competitive fashion at the present level of technology. There are many questions about the time frame and cost of developing clean coal technology; at present it seems to exist mainly as a public relations effort of the coal industry.

coccolithophores: microscopic planktonic organisms that float in the ocean and possess calcium carbonate outer scales or plates that are called coccoliths. They are an important part of the oceanic food web and as a group make a major contribution to the photosynthesis that takes place in the ocean.

constructive feedback loop (CFL): a process of social and/or environmental restoration and regeneration that is self-accelerating, with its rate of improvement increasing over time.

cosmogenesis: the origin, development, and evolution of the universe.

cosmology/cosmological: the scientific study of the origins, composition, and future of the universe and ultimately humanity's place in it.

DDE: a breakdown product of DDT, highly persistent in the environment. See DDT.

DDT: dichlorodiphenyltrichloroethane, a synthetic organic pesticide linked with health consequences. The first widely used synthetic organic pesticide, DDT was banned in the U.S. in 1972, but is still persistent in the environment. DDT is and also widely used today elsewhere in the world.

deforestation: large-scale loss of forests caused by human activities (logging, clearing for agriculture, etc.) and now also by climate change.

deontological: placing adherence to rules, obligations, or duties as the central concern in ethical reasoning and action.

desertification: the spread of deserts caused by human activities, frequently overgrazing that destroys grasslands and now also by climate change.

destructive feedback loop (DFL): a process of social and/or environmental deterioration and change that is self-accelerating, with its rate of deterioration increasing over time.

dicofol: an organochlorine pesticide related in structure to DDT. See organochlorine pesticide.

dieldrin: a synthetic organic pesticide linked with health consequences, banned from agricultural use in the United States in 1974 and also banned in the United States for mothproofing and use on termite infestations after 1987. It is still in use in some other countries. Dieldrin is highly persistent in the environment.

dinoflagellates: a type of microscopic planktonic marine or freshwater organisms; many are photosynthetic while others are predators or parasites.

disciplinarity: thought within traditional boundaries of knowledge characterized by discipline-specific language and discourse, for example, theology and science; usually identified in institutions of higher learning as specific departments of knowledge such as the "department of political science."

Dobson units (DU): a measure of ozone concentration in the upper atmosphere.

Documentary Hypothesis: the view from biblical scholarship, derived from the use of historical-critical methodology, postulating that the first five books of the Bible were composed by four separate authors known as the Yahwist (J), Elohist (E), Deuteronomist (D), and Priestly (P) authors, and then edited together by a Redactor (R).

dualism: the term often used in philosophy and theology, with a long history and a variety of interpretations, indicating that reality is composed of two fundamentally distinct entities, for example, spirit/matter, soul/body, good/evil.

ecotheology: also known as ecological theology, it is the systematic reinterpretation of the major tenants of Christian faith (for example, sin, grace, revelation, God, Jesus Christ, ethics, etc.) through the lens of ecology and the environmental crisis.

effluents: wastes released into surface waters.

endosulfan: an organochlorine pesticide that has already been widely banned around the world because of its toxicity and environmental persistence. It is presently being phased out in the United States, but it is still in use in India, where it is highly controversial and state governments as well as citizens groups are striving for a ban. In the best known example, physical and developmental effects of aerial spraying on the cashew plantations of Kerala are estimated to have cost many hundreds of lives and much diminished the quality of numerous others.

eschatology/eschatological: coming from the Greek word *eschaton*, meaning "end time," traditionally a subset of Christian theology that studies the "last things," often referring to death, resurrection, heaven, hell, and the future vision and hope of a new heaven and new Earth.

estuarine: related to the region where a river flows into the ocean, and therefore salt water and fresh water come together and mix.

eutrophication: excessive algal and plant growth that chokes bodies of fresh water due to excessive nitrogen and phosphorus levels, generally caused by fertilizer runoff or waste from concentrated animal feed operations. Eutrophication produces oxygen depletion and fish kills.

geothermal power: power extracted from the heat beneath the surface of the Earth.

heavy metals: a group of elements with toxic effects on humans. The composition of the group is treated differently by different authors, but it generally includes toxic pollutants such as lead, cadmium, mercury, hexavalent chromium, and arsenic. Some authors include radioactive elements, e.g., plutonium, uranium, and thorium.

hermeneutics/hermeneutical: the process of interpretation, particularly that oriented toward ancient texts such as the Bible.

heterotrophic: refers to an organism that requires organic carbon-based molecules to live; these can be herbivores, predators, parasites, or decomposers. In any of these cases they must consume other living or previously living organisms.

HIPPO: an acronym for the causes of environmental decline, namely, Habitat Loss, Invasive Species, Pollution, Population Growth, and Overharvesting/Overconsumption.

hominids: humans and evolutionarily related forms, including the great apes and early human precursor species (e.g., *Homo heidelbergensis*).

hydrogen fuel cell: An electrochemical device that takes a fuel source (generally gasoline, methane gas, or hydrogen) and uses it to produce an electric current. Conceptually a fuel cell is something like a battery into which fuel is placed in order to continue electricity production indefinitely. Various designs of fuel cells exist, many of which involve a semipermeable membrane that can separate protons from electrons. Commercially viable fuel cells have been in use in stationary applications for years in roles such as emergency backup power supplies. The issues surrounding the widespread application of hydrogen fuel cells are that, lacking a source of hydrogen gas to use as a fuel, a fossil fuel must be used to generate the hydrogen. This process produces substantial amounts of CO_2 (although less than the amount from an internal combustion engine producing the same amount of power).

hydrogen sulfide: a gas with chemical formula H_2S that smells of "rotten eggs" and is very toxic. Precipitation of iron sulfides are believed to have reduced H_2S levels in the early Earth atmosphere.

immanence/immanent: referring to the notion of divine reality and presence being within, or embodied in the physical universe.

incarnational: related to the idea of immanence; usually used to refer to Jesus Christ as the human embodiment of God.

interdisciplinarity: thought that brings together ideas or concepts from more than one traditional discipline in a way that integrates them and allows them to interact.

IPCC: Intergovernmental Panel on Climate Change, a scientific group that is the leading body for the assessment of climate change. It was established by the United Nations Environmental Programme (UNEP) and the World Meteorological Organization (WMO).

iron sulfides: see hydrogen sulfide.

Keeling Curve: the graph named for Charles David Keeling, a pioneer atmospheric scientist, it represents atmospheric carbon dioxide concentrations from 1958 to the present day.

keystone species: a species that has a great effect on the biological community in which it resides by directly or indirectly interacting with many other species of organisms. Loss of a keystone species, because of these multiple connections, can cause an entire biological community to become unstable and collapse.

kingdom/reign of God: the eschatological symbol of future salvation at the center of Jesus' historical proclamation and ministry.

liberation theology: the method of contextual theology originating in Latin America that uses the praxiological method with the aim of promoting faithful ethical engagement and social justice for the poor.

lymphoblastic childhood leukemia: a childhood cancer of the white blood cells that causes damage and eventually death by spreading rapidly dividing cells throughout the body, and by crowding out normal cells in the bone marrow. Survival was very unlikely a few decades ago, but new treatments allow many cases of lymphoblastic childhood leukemia to be cured.

metapurpose: the overall purpose or ultimate goal of Christian engagement in the world.

mononuclear aromatic hydrocarbons: synthetic organic compounds that generally are in ring form and alternate single and double bonds between the carbons, in this case with only one ring structure. The simplest mononuclear aromatic hydrocarbon is benzene, with a six-carbon ring. Many mononuclear aromatic hydrocarbons have significant adverse human health effects.

mountaintop removal: a technique of surface coal mining in which the tops of mountains that have coal seams in them are removed with explosives and heavy equipment. After the coal is mined, some of the removed material is piled back on top of the mountain to restore something supposed to be like its original contour, and the rest is dumped into adjacent valleys. Mountaintop removal has devastating environmental consequences for the area where mining has taken place, permanently removing forests and destroying stream systems. Adverse human health effects from polluted water and airborne dusts and toxic materials associated with the large-scale use of explosives have been reported.

multidisciplinarity: thought that examines issues through the lenses of more than one traditional discipline but does not proceed to the integration of knowledge.

NAFTA (North American Free Trade Agreement): an agreement signed in 1992 by the United States, Canada, and Mexico, setting trade rules. Some features of NAFTA, such as chapter 11, which allows corporations to sue foreign governments, inhibit more stringent environmental regulations. Consequences such as local pollution impacts in rapidly industrialized areas unprepared to deal with toxic contaminants have been heavily criticized.

Natural Step: an international organization and strategic process that describes a system of analysis and implementation to help organizations and people move toward a sustainable future.

natural evil: refers to natural events or, in scientific language, natural perturbations that cause human suffering such as earthquakes, hurricanes, tornados, volcanic eruptions, etc. It is a subset of the theological problem of evil also known in theology as theodicy.

neutron: a subatomic particle with no electrical charge. Almost all atomic nuclei contain neutrons. See also quark.

nitrification: a process by which ammonia is converted into nitrite (NO_2^-), followed by conversion of nitrite into nitrate (NO_3^-). These progressive oxidation reactions (combination of the original ammonia with oxygen) are carried out by bacteria and related forms and result in the nitrate molecules that are most readily taken up by plant roots to enter the biological world.

nitrogen fixation: a process by which N_2 in the atmosphere (nitrogen gas) is converted into ammonia. N_2 is essentially unavailable to living organisms except a few nitrogen fixers. Once ammonia is produced, the nitrogen enters a state where it is available for biosynthesis and exchange in the biological world. Nitrogen fixation is carried out by bacteria and related forms that are sometimes in the soil or water and sometimes in root nodules of leguminous plants such as beans.

nondeterioration: the principle that environmental characteristics must be held at least steady at their present level, because even a slow deterioration each year will eventually produce significant loss of environmental function.

normative: referring to how things ought to be, how they should be valued. Normative statements or beliefs are about what is right and what is wrong.

nuclear fission: nuclear reactions in which very large radioactive atoms disintegrate into smaller atoms and release energy in the process. This is the technology employed in contemporary nuclear power plants.

nuclear fusion: nuclear reactions in which hydrogen atoms combine to form helium at extremely high temperatures and release energy in the process. This is the process that takes place in the sun, and a technology that some scientists hope might someday be employed in future nuclear power plants.

ocean thermal energy conversion (OTEC): energy extracted by taking advantage of the temperature differential between warm tropical surface sea waters and cold water deep in the ocean.

ontology: the subdiscipline of theology and philosophy that studies and interprets the nature of being and existence.

organochlorine: a synthetic organic compound containing at least one chlorine atom as part of its structure; see "organic solvents," dieldrin, DDT, DDE, polychlorinated biphenyls (PCBs), chlorofluorocarbons (CFCs), 1,1,1–trichloroethane, organochlorine pesticide, dicofol, endosulfan, etc. Many organochlorines have great environmental persistence and toxic effects based in part on their tendency to accumulate in fatty tissues and undergo biological magnification as one organism consumes another and absorbs the materials from the fat as it is digested.

organochlorine pesticide: an organochlorine compound designed to kill insects; these include dieldrin, DDT, DDE, dicofol, and many others. Organochlorine pesticides tend to be toxic and highly persistent in the environment, although this varies from compound to compound. Some newer ones (e.g., dicofol) have much shorter periods of environmental persistence. See also organochlorine.

organohalogenated compounds: synthetic organic compounds with one of the various halogen atoms (either chlorine, fluorine, bromine, or iodine) linked to one or more carbons. These include chlorofluorocarbons (CFCs) and various organochlorine compounds, as well as many others.

original grace: the ecotheological view that God's free gift of God's supporting and abiding presence in the universe was there from the origin of the universe.

orthopraxis: literally meaning "right action," associated with faithful Christian living, emphasizing ethical obligations and social action.

ozone: tri-atomic oxygen, O_3. Ozone in the lower atmosphere is a pollutant generally derived from auto exhaust acted on by strong sunlight; exposure to it has varied and significant human health consequences. In the stratosphere, high above the Earth, a layer of naturally forming ozone acts as a radiation shield by blocking a significant amount of the ionizing radiation that would otherwise adversely impact life on the planet's surface.

ozone layer: a layer of O_3 high in the Earth's atmosphere, which prevents much harmful UV radiation from reaching the Earth's surface.

panentheism: the philosophical and theological idea that God is in the world and the world is in God, but that God is simultaneously distinct from the world.

pantheism: the philosophical and theological idea that God is identical with the world or universe.

particulate pollution: tiny particles of solid material released into the air by natural processes (volcanoes, fires) and by burning fossil fuels. Particulate pollution particle size is designated by a PM value, with PM_{10} describing particles in the size range of 10 microns in diameter, $PM_{2.5}$ describing particles on the order of 2.5 microns in diameter, and PM_1 describing particles on the order of 1 micron in diameter. (A micron is a millionth of a meter, and a meter is approximately a yard.) Inhaling particulate pollution can permanently damage lungs, and cause cardiovascular disease, asthma, and detrimental developmental effects. In general, smaller particles lodge deeper in the structure of the lungs and cause the most damage.

PCBs: polychlorinated biphenyls, a class of synthetic organic compounds linked to health consequences. They were used for coolants, electrical insulation, in carbon paper, and a myriad of other industrial uses. Banned in the United States in 1979, PCBs are highly persistent in the environment and are still a significant pollutant.

Perfluorinated compounds (PFCs): a family of compounds that are components of nonstick coatings, fabric and leather waterproofing, food packaging, etc. These have human health impacts.

PFOA: perfluorooctanoate, also known as perfluorooctanic acid, a component or unintentional byproduct in the production of nonstick surfaces and water-proofing agents for clothing and food containers. PFOA is carcinogenic and a developmental toxin.

photosynthesis: the production of energy-rich carbohydrate molecules by plants, using sunlight, CO_2, and water as raw materials. This is the route by which virtually all the energy that runs the ecosystem enters both terrestrial and aquatic biological communities.

photovoltaic energy: energy produced by converting sunlight directly into electrical power in a photovoltaic cell.

phthalates: a group of synthetic organic chemicals used as plasticizers to increase the flexibility or durability of plastics, heavily used to soften polyvinyl chloride (PVC). Phthalates have significant health effects on humans, including endocrine disruption and a link to autism. Phthalates are still in use, but efforts to phase them out have taken place in various countries. The European Union and United States have taken steps to ban certain phthalates from children's toys.

planktonic: floating in the water column and carried by currents, as with many unicellular algae, small invertebrates, and jellyfish.

$PM_{10}/PM_5/PM_{2.5}$: see particulate pollution.

pneumatology/pneumatological: referring to the theological emphasis on the Holy Spirit or the Spirit of God.

polybrominated diphenyl ethers (PBDEs): organobromine compounds used as flame retardants. Significant human health consequences of PBDE exposure, especially in developmental stages, are known. The EU has banned PBDE flame retardants, but they remain in use in the United States despite evidence that they have detrimental impacts on people exposed to them and that they can be replaced. See also organohalogenated compounds.

polycyclic aromatic hydrocarbons (PAHs): synthetic organic compounds that generally are in ring form and alternate single and double bonds between the carbons, in this case with multiple rings in their structure. The simplest polycyclic aromatic hydrocarbon is naphthalene, with two fused six-carbon rings. Many polycyclic aromatic hydrocarbons have significant adverse human health effects.

postnormal science: a method of inquiry appropriate in situations where policy decisions with significant implications must be made in the face of uncertain and highly complex knowledge. Postnormal science calls for an extended peer community to be involved in decision making, in order to bring local and historical knowledge to bear on a situation and to build a consensus for action.

ppb: parts per billion. One part per billion is one molecule of the compound being discussed among one billion molecules of other materials. Some pollutants can have very serious health and environmental effects at the ppb level.

ppm: parts per million. One part per million is one molecule of the compound being discussed among one million molecules of other materials. Many pollutants can have very serious health and environmental effects at the ppm level.

praxis/praxiological: the process of embodying or expressing ideas in action, particularly in ethical commitment and social transformation.

prescind: to separate off, to give individual consideration and attention.

pressure retarded osmosis: a method of producing electrical power using the salinity differential that is present in an estuary where a river flows into the ocean; then a pressure chamber takes advantage of the tendency of water to flow from areas of high salinity to low salinity. The salt water and fresh water differ in salt concentrations, and by using selectively permeable membranes this can be exploited to produce usable power. To date this is in an experimental stage of development.

primordial singularity: the event that began the universe. This has been referred to at times as the Big Bang.

processive: of or related to the experience of process, functioning in both theology and science.

proton: a subatomic particle with a charge of +1. There are one or more protons in every atomic nucleus. See also quark.

pteropods: free-swimming oceanic snails. These include the shelled sea butterflies and the shell-less sea angels. These can be an abundant and important part of the marine food web.

quark: elementary particles that combine to form hadrons; hadrons include protons and neutrons, the subatomic particles that make up atomic nuclei.

reign of God: see kingdom of God.

respiration: the process by which living organisms convert nutrients into energy to support the lives and activities of their cell(s).

revelation: God's self-disclosure in human experience, for example, in the Bible, Jesus Christ, creation, etc.

reverse electrodialysis: a method of producing electrical power using the salinity differential that is present in an estuary where a river flows into the ocean. The salt water and fresh water differ in salt concentrations, and by using selectively permeable membranes this can be exploited to produce usable power. To date this is in an experimental stage of development.

riparian: related to the banks of a river.

sacramentality: the belief that creation — the physical universe — is imbued with the hidden presence of God. Technically defined as a world that discloses God's presence by visible and tangible signs.

salinity gradients: differences in salt concentration as between the fresh water in a river and the salt water in the ocean that may be able to be used to produce electrical power via either reverse electrodialysis or pressure retarded osmosis (see entries).

salinized: made increasingly salty. For farmland this occurs when irrigation takes place in a hot climate and water evaporates leaving the minerals dissolved in it behind; the minerals accumulate in increasing concentrations in the soil.

stabilization triangle: an idea used by the Carbon Mitigation Initiative to describe how CO_2 emissions might be reduced in a stepwise fashion to avoid disastrous consequences. See Carbon Mitigation Initiative.

successional stages/types: the changes in an ecological community as it recovers from a disturbance or as previously unoccupied habitat becomes occupied by increasingly complicated assemblages of plants and animals (e.g., after the retreat of a glacier).

sulfur dioxide: a chemical with the formula SO_2, produced by natural processes such as volcanic eruptions and by burning fossil fuels. Some coal is especially high in SO_2 emission when burned. In the atmosphere SO_2 undergoes chemical reactions that produce acid rain. Methods for removing the sulfur from coal prior to burning it exist and can greatly reduce SO_2 emissions.

supercritical/ultrasupercritical coal power plants: a new generation of coal-fired power plants that operate at exceptionally high temperatures and pressures and that are significantly more efficient at producing electrical power from coal than earlier types of coal-fired power plants. The downside to supercritical/ultrasupercritical coal power plants is that they require much more water to operate than do conventional coal-fired power plants, and this can stress limited freshwater resources that themselves are becoming a major environmental issue.

supernova: a stellar explosion that emits vast amounts of energy and is associated with the ejection of much of the mass of the exploding star. A supernova can briefly outshine the rest of the galaxy in which it is located.

sustainability: the vision or goal that ecological, social, and economic aspects of human activity must maintain balance with the capacity of the natural world to regenerate resources in order to provide an undiminished future to coming generations.

synergistic effects: situations where one entity (such as a chemical or process) increases the effect of another entity (e.g., a second chemical or process). Synergistic effects produce combined influences greater than the summed influences of the two individual entities involved.

synfuel: a liquid fuel made out of coal, oil shale, or natural gas, as a replacement for gasoline. Synfuel production is technologically feasible and limited only by the relative cost of synfuel and of gasoline.

synthetic organic compounds: molecules designed and created in laboratories and factories, based on carbon compounds. Examples are many pesticides, herbicides, industrial chemicals, and pharmaceuticals.

taxa (sing. **taxon**): named units of plants or animals recognized as separate entities by biologists.

theism: the traditional view in Christianity of one God, usually emphasizing the distinction between God and creation.

thermodynamics: the study of energy and work, including heat and mechanical work.

toluene: a mononuclear aromatic hydrocarbon in which a methyl group, CH_3, has replaced one hydrogen atom. It has been heavily used as an industrial solvent and in paint, ink, adhesives, and other materials. It has neurotoxic, developmental, and other health effects. "Huffing" or "sniffing" paint or glue produces high levels of toluene exposure.

toxics release inventory sites (TRI): sites federally licensed to release toxins at specified maximum levels; may be large- or small-scale commercial facilities.

toxins: poisonous substances produced by living organisms. Sometimes industrial chemicals or pollutants produced by humans are referred to as "toxicants" instead. We use the term "toxins" for human-produced materials as well, to reflect the fact that we are in fact living members of the ecosystem and that these materials are produced and released by us into the system in which we live, breathe, and have our being.

transcendence/transcendent: the idea in theology that God is separate, distinct, or above creation.

transdisciplinarity: thought that transcends the normal traditional disciplines and develops overarching or synthetic worldviews and concepts.

trophic level: the place a plant or animal occupies in a food chain, going from plants to herbivores to carnivores.

VSP: viable salmonid population, short for viable salmonid populations and the recovery of evolutionarily significant units, an approach designed by NOAA-Fisheries for salmon recovery planning that is largely based on fish population levels and reproduction rates.

World Business Council for Sustainable Development (WBCSD): an organization that represents more than two hundred CEOs from some of the world's largest companies attempting to move our economy toward sustainability.

World Trade Organization (WTO): an international organization that began in 1995 as a replacement for the General Agreement on Tariffs and Trade, which had been in place since 1948. The WTO is supposed to provide a framework for negotiating trade agreements and resolving trade disputes. The WTO has been very controversial, in part because it has great power as an unelected entity. At times it can overrule national governments. It is also controversial in part because it is a major part of the economic globalization that has produced considerable job loss in some countries and rapid resource extraction in others. The WTO is viewed negatively by an unusual coalition of libertarian, labor, and environmental groups, and WTO meetings have led to violence in the past.

Index